# Game
# Programming
# Patterns

Robert Nystrom

gb genever benning

This book was lovingly typeset by the author in Sina Nova, Source Sans
Pro, and Source Code Pro. Layout is organized around three 1.9 inch
columns with a 0.3 inch gutter. Text follows a 3.6 pt baseline grid.

ISBN: 978-0-9905829-0-8

*To Megan, for faith and time,
the two essential ingredients.*

# Contents

# Acknowledgements

I've heard only other authors know what's involved in writing a book, but there is another tribe who know the precise weight of that burden—those with the misfortune of being in a relationship with a writer. I wrote this in a space of time painstakingly carved from the dense rock of life for me by my wife Megan. Washing dishes and giving the kids baths may not be "writing", but without her doing those, this book wouldn't be here.

I started this project while a programmer at Electronic Arts. I don't think the company knew quite what to make of it, and I'm grateful to Michael Malone, Olivier Nallet, and Richard Wifall for supporting it and providing detailed, insightful feedback on the first few chapters.

Halfway through writing, I decided to forgo a traditional publisher. I knew that meant losing the guidance an editor brings, but I had email from dozens of readers telling me where they wanted the book to go. I'd lose proofreaders, but I had over 250 bug reports to help improve the prose. I'd give up the incentive of a writing schedule, but with readers patting my back when I finished each chapter, I had plenty of motivation.

What I didn't lose was a good copy editor. Lauren Briese showed up just when I needed her and did a wonderful job.

They call this "self publishing", but "crowd publishing" is closer to the mark. Writing can be lonely work, but I was never alone. Even when I put the book on a shelf for two years, the encouragement continued. Without the dozens of people who didn't let me forget that they were waiting for more chapters, I never would have picked it back up and finished.

Special thanks go to Colm Sloan who pored over every single chapter in the book *twice* and gave me mountains of fantastic feedback, all out of the goodness of his own heart. I owe you a beer or twenty.

To everyone who emailed or commented, upvoted or favorited, tweeted or retweeted, anyone who reached out to me, or told a friend about the book, or sent me a bug report: my heart is filled with gratitude for you. Completing this book was one of my biggest goals in life, and you made it happen. Thank you!

— *Bob Nystrom, September 6th, 2014*

# Introduction

# I.

*Chapter 1: Architecture, Performance, and Games*

In fifth grade, my friends and I were given access to a little unused classroom housing a couple of very beat-up TRS-80s. Hoping to inspire us, a teacher found a printout of some simple BASIC programs for us to tinker with.

The audio cassette drives on the computers were broken, so any time we wanted to run some code, we'd have to carefully type it in from scratch. This led us to prefer programs that were only a few lines long:

```
10 PRINT "BOBBY IS RADICAL!!!"
20 GOTO 10
```

Maybe if the computer prints it enough times, it will magically become true.

Even so, the process was fraught with peril. We didn't know *how* to program, so a tiny syntax error was impenetrable to us. If the program didn't work, which was often, we started over from the beginning.

At the back of the stack of pages was a real monster: a program that took up several dense pages of code. It took a while before we worked up the courage to even try it, but it was irresistible—the title above the listing was "Tunnels and Trolls". We had no idea what it did, but it sounded like a game, and what could be cooler than a computer game that you programmed yourself?

We never did get it running, and after a year, we moved out of that classroom. (Much later when I actually knew a bit of BASIC, I realized that it was just a character generator for the table-top game and not a game in itself.) But the die was cast—from there on out, I wanted to be a game programmer.

Many of my summers were also spent catching snakes and turtles in the swamps of southern Louisiana. If it wasn't so blisteringly hot outside, there's a good chance this would be a herpetology book instead of a programming one.

When I was in my teens, my family got a Macintosh with QuickBASIC and later THINK C. I spent almost all of my summer vacations hacking together games. Learning on my own was slow and painful. I'd get something up and running easily—maybe a map screen or a little puzzle—but as the program grew, it got harder and harder.

At first, the challenge was just getting something working. Then, it became figuring out how to write programs bigger than what would fit in my head. Instead of just reading about "How to Program in C++", I started trying to find books about how to *organize* programs.

Fast-forward several years, and a friend hands me a book: *Design Patterns: Elements of Reusable Object-Oriented Software*. Finally! The book I'd been looking for since I was a teenager. I read it cover to cover in one sitting. I still struggled with my own programs, but it was such a relief to see that other people struggled too and came up with solutions. I felt like I finally had a couple of *tools* to use instead of just my bare hands.

This was the first time we'd met, and five minutes after being introduced, I sat down on his couch and spent the next few hours completely ignoring him and reading. I'd like to think my social skills have improved at least a little since then.

In 2001, I landed my dream job: software engineer at Electronic Arts. I couldn't wait to get a look at some real games and see how the pros put them together. What was the architecture like for an enormous game like Madden Football? How did the different systems interact? How did they get a single codebase to run on multiple platforms?

Cracking open the source code was a humbling and surprising experience. There was brilliant code in graphics, AI, animation, and visual effects. We had people who knew how to squeeze every last cycle out of a CPU and put it to good use. Stuff I didn't even know was *possible*, these people did before lunch.

But the *architecture* this brilliant code hung from was often an afterthought. They were so focused on *features* that organization went overlooked. Coupling was rife between modules. New features were often bolted onto the codebase wherever they could be made to fit. To my disillusioned eyes, it looked like many programmers, if they ever cracked open *Design Patterns* at all, never got past Singleton (p. 73).

Of course, it wasn't really that bad. I'd imagined game programmers sitting in some ivory tower covered in whiteboards, calmly discussing architectural minutiae for weeks on end. The reality was that the code I was looking at was written by people working to meet intense deadlines. They did the best they could, and, as I gradually realized, their best was often very good. The more time I spent working on game code, the more bits of brilliance I found hiding under the surface.

Unfortunately, "hiding" was often a good description. There were gems buried in the code, but many people walked right over them. I watched coworkers struggle to reinvent good solutions when examples of exactly what they needed were nestled in the same codebase they were standing on.

That problem is what this book aims to solve. I dug up and polished the best patterns I've found in games, and presented them here so that we can spend our time inventing new things instead of *re*-inventing them.

## What's in Store

There are already dozens of game programming books out there. Why write another? Most game programming books I've seen fall into one of two categories:

- **Domain-specific books.** These narrowly-focused books give you a deep dive on some specific aspect of game development. They'll teach you about 3D graphics, real-time rendering, physics simulation, artificial intelligence, or audio. These are the areas that many game programmers specialize in as their careers progress.

- **Whole-engine books.** In contrast, these try to span all of the different parts of an entire game engine. They are oriented towards building a complete engine suited to some specific genre of game, usually a 3D first-person shooter.

I like both of these kinds of books, but I think they leave some gaps. Books specific to a domain rarely tell you how that chunk of code interacts with the rest of the game. You may be a wizard at physics and rendering, but do you know how to tie them together gracefully?

The second category covers that, but I often find whole-engine books to be too monolithic and too genre-specific. Especially with the rise of mobile and casual gaming, we're in a period where lots of different genres of games are being created. We aren't all just cloning Quake anymore. Books that walk you through a single engine aren't helpful when *your* game doesn't fit that mold.

Another example of this *à la carte* style is the widely beloved *Game Programming Gems* series.

Instead, what I'm trying to do here is more *à la carte*. Each of the chapters in this book is an independent idea that you can apply to your code. This way, you can mix and match them in a way that works best for the game *you* want to make.

## How it Relates to Design Patterns

Any programming book with "Patterns" in its name clearly bears a relationship to the classic *Design Patterns: Elements of Reusable Object-Oriented Software* by Erich Gamma, Richard Helm, Ralph Johnson, and John Vlissides (ominously called the "Gang of Four").

*Design Patterns* itself was in turn inspired by a previous book. The idea of crafting a language of patterns to describe open-ended solutions to problems comes from *A Pattern Language*, by Christopher Alexander (along with Sarah Ishikawa and Murray Silverstein).

Their book was about architecture (like *real* architecture with buildings and walls and stuff), but they hoped others would use the same structure to describe solutions in other fields. *Design Patterns* is the Gang of Four's attempt to do that for software.

By calling this book "Game Programming Patterns", I'm not trying to imply that the Gang of Four's book is inapplicable to games. On the contrary: the Design Patterns Revisited section of this book covers many of the patterns from *Design Patterns*, but with an emphasis on how they can be applied to game programming.

Conversely, I think this book is applicable to non-game software too. I could just as well have called this book *More Design Patterns*, but I think games make for more engaging examples. Do you really want to read yet another book about employee records and bank accounts?

That being said, while the patterns introduced here are useful in other software, I think they're particularly well-suited to engineering challenges commonly encountered in games:

- Time and sequencing are often a core part of a game's architecture. Things must happen in the right order and at the right time.

- Development cycles are highly compressed, and a number of programmers need to be able to rapidly build and iterate on a rich set of different behavior without stepping on each other's toes or leaving footprints all over the codebase.

- After all of this behavior is defined, it starts interacting. Monsters bite the hero, potions are mixed together, and bombs blast enemies and friends alike. Those interactions must happen without the codebase turning into an intertwined hairball.

- And, finally, performance is critical in games. Game developers are in a constant race to see who can squeeze the most out of their platform. Tricks for shaving off cycles can mean the difference between an A-rated game and millions of sales or dropped frames and angry reviewers.

# How to Read the Book

*Game Programming Patterns* is divided into three broad sections. The first introduces and frames the book. It's the chapter you're reading now along with the next one.

The second section, "Design Patterns Revisited" (p. 19), goes through a handful of patterns from the Gang of Four book. With each chapter, I give my spin on a pattern and how I think it relates to game programming.

The last section is the real meat of the book. It presents thirteen design patterns that I've found useful. They're grouped into four categories: "Sequencing Patterns" (p. 105), "Behavioral Patterns" (p. 153), "Decoupling Patterns" (p. 211), and "Optimization Patterns" (p. 267). Each of these patterns is described using a consistent structure so that you can use this book as a reference and quickly find what you need:

- The **Intent** section provides a snapshot description of the pattern in terms of the problem it intends to solve. This is first so that you can hunt through the book quickly to find a pattern that will help you with your current struggle.

- The **Motivation** section describes an example problem that we will be applying the pattern to. Unlike concrete algorithms, a pattern is usually formless unless applied to some specific problem. Teaching a pattern without an example is like teaching baking without mentioning dough. This section provides the dough that the later sections will bake.

- The **Pattern** section distills the essence of the pattern out of the previous example. If you want a dry textbook description of the pattern, this is it. It's also a good refresher if you're familiar with a pattern already and want to make sure you don't forget an ingredient.

- So far, the pattern has only been explained in terms of a single example. But how do you know if the pattern will be good for *your* problem? The **When to Use It** section provides some guidelines on when the pattern is useful and when it's best avoided. The **Keep in Mind** section points out consequences and risks when using the pattern.

- If, like me, you need concrete examples to really *get* something, then **Sample Code** is your section. It walks step by step through a full implementation of the pattern so you can see exactly how it works.

- Patterns differ from single algorithms because they are open-ended. Each time you use a pattern, you'll likely implement it differently. The next section, **Design Decisions**, explores that space and shows you different options to consider when applying a pattern.

- To wrap it up, there's a short **See Also** section that shows how this pattern relates to others and points you to real-world open source code that uses it.

## About the Sample Code

Code samples in this book are in C++, but that isn't to imply that these patterns are only useful in that language or that C++ is a better language for them than others. Almost any language will work fine, though some patterns do tend to presume your language has objects and classes.

I chose C++ for a couple of reasons. First, it's the most popular language for commercially shipped games. It is the *lingua franca* of the industry. Moreso, the C syntax that C++ is based on is also the basis for Java, C#, JavaScript, and many other languages. Even if you don't know C++, the odds are good you can understand the code samples here with a little bit of effort.

The goal of this book is *not* to teach you C++. The samples are kept as simple as possible and don't represent good C++ style or usage. Read the code samples for the idea being expressed, not the code expressing it.

In particular, the code is not written in "modern"—C++11 or newer—style. It does not use the standard library and rarely uses templates. This makes for "bad" C++ code, but I hope that by keeping it stripped down, it will be more approachable to people coming from C, Objective-C, Java, and other languages.

To avoid wasting space on code you've already seen or that isn't relevant to the pattern, code will sometimes be omitted in examples. When this occurs, an ellipsis will be placed in the sample to show where the missing code goes.

Consider a function that will do some work and then return a value. The pattern being explained is only concerned with the return value, and not the work being done. In that case, the sample code will look like:

```
bool update()
{
  // Do work...
  return isDone();
}
```

## Where to Go From Here

Patterns are a constantly changing and expanding part of software development. This book continues the process started by the Gang of Four of documenting and sharing the software patterns they saw, and that process will continue after the ink dries on these pages.

You are a core part of that process. As you develop your own patterns and refine (or refute!) the patterns in this book, you contribute to the software community. If you have suggestions, corrections, or other feedback about what's in here, please get in touch!

# Architecture, Performance, and Games

# 1

Before we plunge headfirst into a pile of patterns, I thought it might help to give you some context about how I think about software architecture and how it applies to games. It may help you understand the rest of this book better. If nothing else, when you get dragged into an argument about how terrible (or awesome) design patterns and software architecture are, it will give you some ammo to use.

## What is Software Architecture?

If you read this book cover to cover, you won't come away knowing the linear algebra behind 3D graphics or the calculus behind game physics. It won't show you how to alpha-beta prune your AI's search tree or simulate a room's reverberation in your audio playback.

Instead, this book is about the code *between* all of that. It's less about writing code than it is about *organizing* it. Every program has *some* organization, even if it's just "jam the whole thing into `main()` and see what happens", so I think it's more interesting to talk about what makes for *good* organization. How do we tell a good architecture from a bad one?

Note that I didn't presume which side you're taking in that fight. Like any arms dealer, I have wares for sale to all combatants.

Wow, this paragraph would make a terrible ad for the book.

I've been mulling over this question for about five years. Of course, like you, I have an intuition about good design. We've all suffered through codebases so bad, the best you could hope to do for them is take them out back and put them out of their misery.

Let's admit it, most of us are *responsible* for a few of those.

A lucky few have had the opposite experience, a chance to work with beautifully designed code. The kind of codebase that feels like a perfectly appointed luxury hotel festooned with concierges waiting eagerly on your every whim. What's the difference between the two?

## What is *good* software architecture?

For me, good design means that when I make a change, it's as if the entire program was crafted in anticipation of it. I can solve a task with just a few choice function calls that slot in perfectly, leaving not the slightest ripple on the placid surface of the code.

That sounds pretty, but it's not exactly actionable. "Just write your code so that changes don't disturb its placid surface." Right.

Let me break that down a bit. The first key piece is that *architecture is about change*. Someone has to be modifying the codebase. If no one is touching the code—whether because it's perfect and complete or so wretched no one will sully their text editor with it—its design is irrelevant. The measure of a design is how easily it accommodates changes. With no changes, it's a runner who never leaves the starting line.

## How do you make a change?

Before you can change the code to add a new feature, to fix a bug, or for whatever reason caused you to fire up your editor, you have to understand what the existing code is doing. You don't have to know the whole program, of course, but you need to load all of the relevant pieces of it into your primate brain.

It's weird to think that this is literally an OCR process.

We tend to gloss over this step, but it's often the most time-consuming part of programming. If you think paging some data from disk into RAM is slow, try paging it into a simian cerebrum over a pair of optical nerves.

Once you've got all the right context into your wetware, you think for a bit and figure out your solution. There can be a lot of back and forth here, but often this is relatively straightforward. Once you understand the problem and the parts of the code it touches, the actual coding is sometimes trivial.

You beat your meaty fingers on the keyboard for a while until the right colored lights blink on screen and you're done, right? Not just yet!

Before you write tests and send it off for code review, you often have some cleanup to do.

You jammed a bit more code into your game, but you don't want the next person to come along to trip over the wrinkles you left throughout the source. Unless the change is minor, there's usually a bit of reorganization to do to make your new code integrate seamlessly with the rest of the program. If you do it right, the next person to come along won't be able to tell when any line of code was written.

In short, the flow chart for programming is something like:

Did I say "tests"? Oh, yes, I did. It's hard to write unit tests for some game code, but a large fraction of the codebase is perfectly testable.

I won't get on a soapbox here, but I'll ask you to consider doing more automated testing if you aren't already. Don't you have better things to do than manually validate stuff over and over again?

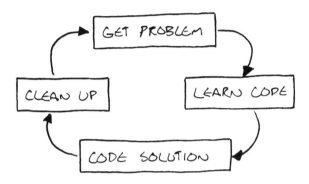

Figure 1.1 – Your workday in a nutshell

The fact that there is no escape from that loop is a little alarming now that I think about it.

## How can decoupling help?

While it isn't obvious, I think much of software architecture is about that learning phase. Loading code into neurons is so painfully slow that it pays to find strategies to reduce the volume of it. This book has an entire section on *decoupling* patterns, and a large chunk of *Design Patterns* is about the same idea.

You can define "decoupling" a bunch of ways, but I think if two pieces of code are coupled, it means you can't understand one without understanding the other. If you *de*-couple them, you can reason about either side independently. That's great because if only one of those pieces is relevant to your problem, you just need to load *it* into your monkey brain and not the other half too.

To me, this is a key goal of software architecture: **minimize the amount of knowledge you need to have in-cranium before you can make progress.**

The later stages come into play too, of course. Another definition of decoupling is that a *change* to one piece of code doesn't necessitate a change to another. We obviously need to change *something*, but the less coupling we have, the less that change ripples throughout the rest of the game.

## At What Cost?

This sounds great, right? Decouple everything and you'll be able to code like the wind. Each change will mean touching only one or two select methods, and you can dance across the surface of the codebase leaving nary a shadow.

This feeling is exactly why people get excited about abstraction, modularity, design patterns, and software architecture. A well-architected program really is a joyful experience to work in, and everyone loves being more productive. Good architecture makes a *huge* difference in productivity. It's hard to overstate how profound an effect it can have.

But, like all things in life, it doesn't come free. Good architecture takes real effort and discipline. Every time you make a change or implement a feature, you have to work hard to integrate it gracefully into the rest of the program. You have to take great care to both organize the code well and *keep* it organized throughout the thousands of little changes that make up a development cycle.

The second half of this—maintaining your design—deserves special attention. I've seen many programs start out beautifully and then die a death of a thousand cuts as programmers add "just one tiny little hack" over and over again.

Like gardening, it's not enough to put in new plants. You must also weed and prune.

You have to think about which parts of the program should be decoupled and introduce abstractions at those points. Likewise, you have to determine where extensibility should be engineered in so future changes are easier to make.

People get really excited about this. They envision future developers (or just their future self) stepping into the codebase and finding it open-ended, powerful, and just beckoning to be extended. They imagine The One Game Engine To Rule Them All.

But this is where it starts to get tricky. Whenever you add a layer of abstraction or a place where extensibility is supported, you're *speculating* that you will need that flexibility later. You're adding code and complexity to your game that takes time to develop, debug, and maintain.

That effort pays off if you guess right and end up touching that code later. But predicting the future is *hard*, and when that modularity doesn't end up being helpful, it quickly becomes actively harmful. After all, it is more code you have to deal with.

Some folks coined the term "YAGNI"—You aren't gonna need it—as a mantra to use to fight this urge to speculate about what your future self may want.

When people get overzealous about this, you get a codebase whose architecture has spiraled out of control. You've got interfaces and abstractions everywhere. Plug-in systems, abstract base classes, virtual methods galore, and all sorts of extension points.

It takes you forever to trace through all of that scaffolding to find some real code that does something. When you need to make a change, sure, there's probably an interface there to help, but good luck finding it. In theory, all of this decoupling means you have less code to understand before you can extend it, but the layers of abstraction themselves end up filling your mental scratch disk.

Codebases like this are what turn people *against* software architecture, and design patterns in particular. It's easy to get so wrapped up in the code itself that you lose sight of the fact that you're trying to ship a *game*. The siren song of extensibility sucks in countless developers who spend years working on an "engine" without ever figuring out what it's an engine *for*.

## Performance and Speed

There's another critique of software architecture and abstraction that you hear sometimes, especially in game development: that it hurts your game's performance. Many patterns that make your code more flexible rely on virtual dispatch, interfaces, pointers, messages, and other mechanisms that all have at least some runtime cost.

There's a reason for this. A lot of software architecture is about making your program more flexible. It's about making it take less effort to change it. That means encoding fewer assumptions in the program. You use interfaces so that your code works with *any* class that implements it instead of just the one that does today. You use observers (p. 43) and messaging (p. 233) to let two parts of the game talk to each other so that tomorrow, it can easily be three or four.

But performance is all about assumptions. The practice of optimization thrives on concrete limitations. Can we safely assume we'll never have more than 256 enemies? Great, we can pack an ID into a single byte. Will we only call a method on one concrete type here? Good, we can statically dispatch or inline it. Are all of the entities going to be the same class? Great, we can make a nice contiguous array (p. 269) of them.

This doesn't mean flexibility is bad, though! It lets us change our game quickly, and *development* speed is absolutely vital for getting to a fun experience. No one, not even Will Wright, can come up with a balanced game design on paper. It demands iteration and experimentation.

The faster you can try out ideas and see how they feel, the more you can try and the more likely you are to find something great. Even after you've

One interesting counter-example is templates in C++. Template metaprogramming can sometimes give you the abstraction of interfaces without any penalty at runtime.

There's a spectrum of flexibility here. When you write code to call a concrete method in some class, you're fixing that class at *author* time—you've hard-coded which class you call into. When you go through a virtual method or interface, the class that gets called isn't known until *runtime*. That's much more flexible but implies some runtime overhead.

Template metaprogramming is somewhere between the two. There, you make the decision of which class to call at *compile time* when the template is instantiated.

found the right mechanics, you need plenty of time for tuning. A tiny imbalance can wreck the fun of a game.

There's no easy answer here. Making your program more flexible so you can prototype faster will have some performance cost. Likewise, optimizing your code will make it less flexible.

My experience, though, is that it's easier to make a fun game fast than it is to make a fast game fun. One compromise is to keep the code flexible until the design settles down and then tear out some of the abstraction later to improve your performance.

## The Good in Bad Code

That brings me to the next point which is that there's a time and place for different styles of coding. Much of this book is about making maintainable, clean code, so my allegiance is pretty clearly to doing things the "right" way, but there's value in slapdash code too.

Writing well-architected code takes careful thought, and that translates to time. Moreso, *maintaining* a good architecture over the life of a project takes a lot of effort. You have to treat your codebase like a good camper does their campsite: always try to leave it a little better than you found it.

This is good when you're going to be living in and working on that code for a long time. But, like I mentioned earlier, game design requires a lot of experimentation and exploration. Especially early on, it's common to write code that you *know* you'll throw away.

If you just want to find out if some gameplay idea plays right at all, architecting it beautifully means burning more time before you actually get it on screen and get some feedback. If it ends up not working, that time spent making the code elegant goes to waste when you delete it.

Prototyping—slapping together code that's just barely functional enough to answer a design question—is a perfectly legitimate programming practice. There is a very large caveat, though. If you write throwaway code, you *must* ensure you're able to throw it away. I've seen bad managers play this game time and time again:

*Boss:*  "Hey, we've got this idea that we want to try out. Just a prototype, so don't feel you need to do it right. How quickly can you slap something together?"

*Dev:*  "Well, if I cut lots of corners, don't test it, don't document it, and it has tons of bugs, I can give you some temp code in a few days."

*Boss:*  "Great!"

*A few days pass...*

*Boss:*  "Hey, that prototype is great. Can you just spend a few hours cleaning it up a bit now and we'll call it the real thing?"

You need to make sure the people using the throwaway code understand that even though it kind of looks like it works, it *cannot* be maintained and *must* be rewritten. If there's a *chance* you'll end up having to keep it around, you may have to defensively write it well.

One trick to ensuring your prototype code isn't obliged to become real code is to write it in a language different from the one your game uses. That way, you have to rewrite it before it can end up in your actual game.

## Striking a Balance

We have a few forces in play:

- We want nice architecture so the code is easier to understand over the lifetime of the project.

- We want fast runtime performance.

- We want to get today's features done quickly.

I think it's interesting that these are all about some kind of speed: our long-term development speed, the game's execution speed, and our short-term development speed.

These goals are at least partially in opposition. Good architecture improves productivity over the long term, but maintaining it means every change requires a little more effort to keep things clean.

The implementation that's quickest to write is rarely the quickest to *run*. Instead, optimization takes significant engineering time. Once it's done, it tends to calcify the codebase: highly optimized code is inflexible and very difficult to change.

There's always pressure to get today's work done today and worry about everything else tomorrow. But if we cram in features as quickly as we can, our codebase will become a mess of hacks, bugs, and inconsistencies that saps our future productivity.

There's no simple answer here, just trade-offs. From the email I get, this disheartens a lot of people. Especially for novices who just want to make a game, it's intimidating to hear, "There is no right answer, just different flavors of wrong."

But, to me, this is exciting! Look at any field that people dedicate careers to mastering, and in the center you will always find a set of intertwined constraints. After all, if there was an easy answer, everyone would just do that. A field you can master in a week is ultimately boring. You don't hear of someone's distinguished career in ditch digging.

To me, this has much in common with games themselves. A game like chess can never be mastered because all of the pieces are so perfectly balanced against one another. This means you can spend your life exploring the vast space of viable strategies. A poorly designed game collapses to the one winning tactic played over and over until you get bored and quit.

## Simplicity

Lately, I feel like if there is any method that eases these constraints, it's *simplicity*. In my code today, I try very hard to write the cleanest, most direct solution to the problem. The kind of code where after you read it, you understand exactly what it does and can't imagine any other possible solution.

I aim to get the data structures and algorithms right (in about that order) and then go from there. I find if I can keep things simple, there's less code overall. That means less code to load into my head in order to change it. It often runs fast because there's simply not as much overhead and not much code to execute. (This certainly isn't always the case though. You can pack a lot of looping and recursion in a tiny amount of code.)

However, note that I'm not saying simple code takes less time to *write*. You'd think it would since you end up with less total code, but a good solution isn't an accretion of code, it's a *distillation* of it.

We're rarely presented with an elegant problem. Instead, it's a pile of use cases. You want the X to do Y when Z, but W when A, and so on. In other words, a long list of different example behaviors. The solution that takes the least mental effort is to just code up those use cases one at a time. If you look at novice programmers, that's what they often do: they churn out reams of conditional logic for each case that popped into their head.

But there's nothing elegant in that, and code in that style tends to fall over when presented with input even slightly different than the examples the coder considered. When we think of elegant solutions, what we often

Maybe you do; I didn't research that analogy. For all I know, there could be avid ditch digging hobbyists, ditch digging conventions, and a whole subculture around it. Who am I to judge?

Blaise Pascal famously ended a letter with, "I would have written a shorter letter, but I did not have the time."

Another choice quote comes from Antoine de Saint-Exupery: "Perfection is achieved, not when there is nothing more to add, but when there is nothing left to take away."

Closer to home, I'll note that every time I revise a chapter in this book, it gets shorter. Some chapters are tightened by 20% by the time they're done.

have in mind is a *general* one: a small bit of logic that still correctly covers a large space of use cases.

Finding that is a bit like pattern matching or solving a puzzle. It takes effort to see through the scattering of example use cases to find the hidden order underlying them all. It's a great feeling when you pull it off.

## Get On With It, Already

Almost everyone skips the introductory chapters, so I congratulate you on making it this far. I don't have much in return for your patience, but I'll offer up a few bits of advice that I hope may be useful to you:

- Abstraction and decoupling make evolving your program faster and easier, but don't waste time doing them unless you're confident the code in question needs that flexibility.

- Think about and design for performance throughout your development cycle, but put off the low-level, nitty-gritty optimizations that lock assumptions into your code until as late as possible.

  Trust me, two months before shipping is *not* when you want to start worrying about that nagging little "game only runs at 1 FPS" problem.

- Move quickly to explore your game's design space, but don't go so fast that you leave a mess behind you. You'll have to live with it, after all.

- If you are going to ditch code, don't waste time making it pretty. Rock stars trash hotel rooms because they know they're going to check out the next day.

- But, most of all, **if you want to make something fun, have fun making it.**

# Design Patterns Revisited

# II.

*Design Patterns: Elements of Reusable Object-Oriented Software* is nearly twenty years old by my watch. Unless you're looking over my shoulder, there's a good chance *Design Patterns* will be old enough to drink by the time you read this. For an industry as quickly moving as software, that's practically ancient. The enduring popularity of the book says something about how timeless design is compared to many frameworks and methodologies.

While I think *Design Patterns* is still relevant, we've learned a lot in the past couple of decades. In this section, we'll walk through a handful of the original patterns the Gang of Four documented. For each pattern, I hope to have something useful or interesting to say.

I think some patterns are overused (Singleton (p. 73)), while others are underappreciated (Command (p. 21)). A couple are here because I want to explore their relevance to games (Flyweight (p. 33) and Observer (p. 43)). Finally, sometimes I just think it's fun to see how patterns are enmeshed in the larger field of programming (Prototype (p. 59) and State (p. 87)).

# Command

# 2

*"Encapsulate a request as an object, thereby letting users parameterize clients with different requests, queue or log requests, and support undoable operations."*

Command is one of my favorite patterns. Most large programs I write, games or otherwise, end up using it somewhere. When I've used it in the right place, it's neatly untangled some really gnarly code. For such a swell pattern, the Gang of Four has a predictably abstruse description. Look at it up there.

I think we can all agree that that's a terrible sentence. First of all, it mangles whatever metaphor it's trying to establish. Outside of the weird world of software where words can mean anything, a "client" is a *person*—someone you do business with. Last I checked, human beings can't be "parameterized".

Then, the rest of that sentence is just a list of stuff you could maybe possibly use the pattern for. Not very illuminating unless your use case happens to be in that list. *My* pithy tagline for the Command pattern is:

**A command is a reified method call.**

Of course, "pithy" often means "impenetrably terse", so this may not be much of an improvement. Let me unpack that a bit. "Reify", in case you've

"Reify" comes from the Latin "res", for "thing", with the English suffix "–fy". So it basically means "thingify", which, honestly, would be a more fun word to use.

never heard it, means "make real". Another term for reifying is making something "first-class".

Both terms mean taking some *concept* and turning it into a piece of *data*—an object—that you can stick in a variable, pass to a function, etc. So by saying the Command pattern is a "reified method call", what I mean is that it's a method call wrapped in an object.

That sounds a lot like a "callback", "first-class function", "function pointer", "closure", or "partially applied function" depending on which language you're coming from, and indeed those are all in the same ballpark. The Gang of Four later says: "Commands are an object-oriented replacement for callbacks."

That would be a better slugline for the pattern than the one they chose. But all of this is abstract and nebulous. I like to start chapters with something concrete, and I blew that. To make up for it, from here on out it's all examples where commands are a brilliant fit.

## Configuring Input

Somewhere in every game is a chunk of code that reads in raw user input — button presses, keyboard events, mouse clicks, whatever. It takes each input and translates it to a meaningful action in the game:

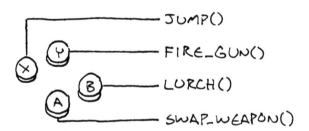

*Figure 2.1 – Buttons mapped to game actions*

A dead simple implementation looks like:

```
void InputHandler::handleInput()
{
  if (isPressed(BUTTON_X)) jump();
  else if (isPressed(BUTTON_Y)) fireGun();
  else if (isPressed(BUTTON_A)) swapWeapon();
  else if (isPressed(BUTTON_B)) lurchIneffectively();
}
```

Pro tip: Don't press B very often.

This function typically gets called once per frame by the game loop (p. 123), and I'm sure you can figure out what it does. This code works if we're willing to hard-wire user inputs to game actions, but many games let the user *configure* how their buttons are mapped.

To support that, we need to turn those direct calls to `jump()` and `fireGun()` into something that we can swap out. "Swapping out" sounds a lot like assigning a variable, so we need an *object* that we can use to represent a game action. Enter: the Command pattern.

We define a base class that represents a triggerable game command:

```
class Command
{
public:
  virtual ~Command() {}
  virtual void execute() = 0;
};
```

When you have an interface with a single method that doesn't return anything, there's a good chance it's the Command pattern.

Then we create subclasses for each of the different game actions:

```
class JumpCommand : public Command
{
public:
  virtual void execute() { jump(); }
};

class FireCommand : public Command
{
public:
  virtual void execute() { fireGun(); }
};

// You get the idea...
```

In our input handler, we store a pointer to a command for each button:

```
class InputHandler
{
public:
  void handleInput();

  // Methods to bind commands...

private:
  Command* buttonX_;
  Command* buttonY_;
  Command* buttonA_;
  Command* buttonB_;
};
```

Now the input handling just delegates to those:

```
void InputHandler::handleInput()
{
  if (isPressed(BUTTON_X)) buttonX_->execute();
  else if (isPressed(BUTTON_Y)) buttonY_->execute();
  else if (isPressed(BUTTON_A)) buttonA_->execute();
  else if (isPressed(BUTTON_B)) buttonB_->execute();
}
```

Notice how we don't check for NULL here? This assumes each button will have *some* command wired up to it.

If we want to support buttons that do nothing without having to explicitly check for NULL, we can define a command class whose `execute()` method does nothing. Then, instead of setting a button handler to NULL, we point it to that object. This is a pattern called "Null Object."

Where each input used to directly call a function, now there's a layer of indirection.

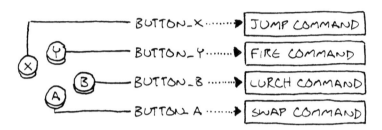

*Figure 2.2 – Buttons mapped to assignable commands*

This is the Command pattern in a nutshell. If you can see the merit of it already, consider the rest of this chapter a bonus.

## Directions for Actors

The command classes we just defined work for the previous example, but they're pretty limited. The problem is that they assume there are these top-level `jump()`, `fireGun()`, etc. functions that implicitly know how to find the player's avatar and make him dance like the puppet he is.

That assumed coupling limits the usefulness of those commands. The *only* thing the `JumpCommand` can make jump is the player. Let's loosen that restriction. Instead of calling functions that find the commanded object themselves, we'll *pass in* the object that we want to order around:

```
class Command
{
public:
  virtual ~Command() {}
  virtual void execute(GameActor& actor) = 0;
};
```

Here, `GameActor` is our "game object" class that represents a character in the game world. We pass it in to `execute()` so that the derived command can invoke methods on an actor of our choice, like so:

```
class JumpCommand : public Command
{
public:
  virtual void execute(GameActor& actor)
  {
    actor.jump();
  }
};
```

Now, we can use this one class to make any character in the game hop
around. We're just missing a piece between the input handler and the
command that takes the command and invokes it on the right object.
First, we change handleInput() so that it *returns* commands:

```
Command* InputHandler::handleInput()
{
  if (isPressed(BUTTON_X)) return buttonX_;
  if (isPressed(BUTTON_Y)) return buttonY_;
  if (isPressed(BUTTON_A)) return buttonA_;
  if (isPressed(BUTTON_B)) return buttonB_;

  // Nothing pressed, so do nothing.
  return NULL;
}
```

It can't execute the command immediately since it doesn't know what
actor to pass in. Here's where we take advantage of the fact that the
command is a reified call—we can *delay* when the call is executed.

Then, we need some code that takes that command and runs it on the
actor representing the player. Something like:

```
Command* command = inputHandler.handleInput();
if (command)
{
  command->execute(actor);
}
```

Assuming actor is a reference to the player's character, this correctly
drives him based on the user's input, so we're back to the same behavior
we had in the first example. But adding a layer of indirection between the
command and the actor that performs it has given us a neat little ability:
*we can let the player control any actor in the game now by changing the actor
we execute the commands on.*

In practice, that's not a common feature, but there is a similar use case
that *does* pop up frequently. So far, we've only considered the player-driven
character, but what about all of the other actors in the world? Those are
driven by the game's AI. We can use this same command pattern as the

interface between the AI engine and the actors; the AI code simply emits **Command** objects.

The decoupling here between the AI that selects commands and the actor code that performs them gives us a lot of flexibility. We can use different AI modules for different actors. Or we can mix and match AI for different kinds of behavior. Want a more aggressive opponent? Just plug-in a more aggressive AI to generate commands for it. In fact, we can even bolt AI onto the *player's* character, which can be useful for things like demo mode where the game needs to run on auto-pilot.

By making the commands that control an actor first-class objects, we've removed the tight coupling of a direct method call. Instead, think of it as a queue or stream of commands:

*Figure 2.3 – A poorly drawn analogy*

For lots more on what queueing can do for you, see Event Queue (p. 233).

Why did I feel the need to draw a picture of a "stream" for you? And why does it look like a tube?

Some code (the input handler or AI) produces commands and places them in the stream. Other code (the dispatcher or actor itself) consumes commands and invokes them. By sticking that queue in the middle, we've decoupled the producer on one end from the consumer on the other.

## Undo and Redo

The final example is the most well-known use of this pattern. If a command object can *do* things, it's a small step for it to be able to *undo* them. Undo is used in some strategy games where you can roll back moves that you didn't like. It's *de rigueur* in tools that people use to *create* games. The surest way to make your game designers hate you is giving them a level editor that can't undo their fat-fingered mistakes.

If we take those commands and make them *serializable*, we can send the stream of them over the network. We can take the player's input, push it over the network to another machine, and then replay it. That's one important piece of making a networked multi-player game.

Without the Command pattern, implementing undo is surprisingly hard. With it, it's a piece of cake. Let's say we're making a single-player, turn-based game and we want to let users undo moves so they can focus more on strategy and less on guesswork.

I may be speaking from experience here.

We're conveniently already using commands to abstract input handling, so every move the player makes is already encapsulated in them. For example, moving a unit may look like:

```
class MoveUnitCommand : public Command
{
public:
  MoveUnitCommand(Unit* unit, int x, int y)
  : unit_(unit),
    x_(x),
    y_(y)
  {}

  virtual void execute()
  {
    unit_->moveTo(x_, y_);
  }

private:
  Unit* unit_;
  int x_;
  int y_;
};
```

Note this is a little different from our previous commands. In the last example, we wanted to *abstract* the command from the actor that it modified. In this case, we specifically want to *bind* it to the unit being moved. An instance of this command isn't a general "move something" operation that you could use in a bunch of contexts; it's a specific concrete move in the game's sequence of turns.

This highlights a variation in how the Command pattern gets implemented. In some cases, like our first couple of examples, a command is a reusable object that represents a *thing that can be done*. Our earlier input handler held on to a single command object and called its execute() method anytime the right button was pressed.

Here, the commands are more specific. They represent a thing that can be done at a specific point in time. This means that the input handling code will be *creating* an instance of this every time the player chooses a move. Something like:

Of course, in a non-garbage-collected language like C++, this means the code executing commands will also be responsible for freeing their memory.

```
Command* handleInput()
{
  Unit* unit = getSelectedUnit();

  if (isPressed(BUTTON_UP)) {
    // Move the unit up one.
    int destY = unit->y() - 1;
    return new MoveUnitCommand(
        unit, unit->x(), destY);
  }

  if (isPressed(BUTTON_DOWN)) {
    // Move the unit down one.
    int destY = unit->y() + 1;
    return new MoveUnitCommand(
        unit, unit->x(), destY);
  }

  // Other moves...

  return NULL;
}
```

The fact that commands are one-use-only will come to our advantage in a second. To make commands undoable, we define another operation each command class needs to implement:

```
class Command
{
public:
  virtual ~Command() {}
  virtual void execute() = 0;
  virtual void undo() = 0;
};
```

An undo() method reverses the game state changed by the corresponding execute() method. Here's our previous move command with undo support:

```
class MoveUnitCommand : public Command
{
public:
  MoveUnitCommand(Unit* unit, int x, int y)
  : unit_(unit), x_(x), y_(y)
    xBefore_(0), yBefore_(0),
  {}

  virtual void execute()
  {
    // Remember the unit's position before the move
    // so we can restore it.
    xBefore_ = unit_->x();
    yBefore_ = unit_->y();
    unit_->moveTo(x_, y_);
  }

  virtual void undo()
  {
    unit_->moveTo(xBefore_, yBefore_);
  }

private:
  Unit* unit_;
  int x_, y_;
  int xBefore_, yBefore_;
};
```

Note that we added some more state to the class. When a unit moves, it forgets where it used to be. If we want to be able to undo that move, we have to remember the unit's previous position ourselves, which is what xBefore_ and yBefore_ do.

To let the player undo a move, we keep around the last command they executed. When they bang on Control-Z, we call that command's undo() method. (If they've already undone, then it becomes "redo" and we execute the command again.)

Supporting multiple levels of undo isn't much harder. Instead of remembering the last command, we keep a list of commands and a reference to the "current" one. When the player executes a command, we append it to the list and point "current" at it.

> This seems like a place for the Memento pattern, but I haven't found it to work well. Since commands tend to modify only a small part of an object's state, snapshotting the rest of its data is a waste of memory. It's cheaper to manually store only the bits you change.
>
> *Persistent data structures* are another option. With these, every modification to an object returns a new one, leaving the original unchanged. Through clever implementation, these new objects share data with the previous ones, so it's much cheaper than cloning the entire object.
>
> Using a persistent data structure, each command stores a reference to the object before the command was performed, and undo just means switching back to the old object.

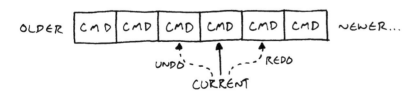

*Figure 2.4 – Traversing the undo stack*

When the player chooses "Undo", we undo the current command and move the current pointer back. When they choose "Redo", we advance the pointer and then execute that command. If they choose a new command after undoing some, everything in the list after the current command is discarded.

The first time I implemented this in a level editor, I felt like a genius. I was astonished at how straightforward it was and how well it worked. It takes discipline to make sure every data modification goes through a command, but once you do that, the rest is easy.

## Classy and Dysfunctional?

Earlier, I said commands are similar to first-class functions or closures, but every example I showed here used class definitions. If you're familiar with functional programming, you're probably wondering where the functions are.

I wrote the examples this way because C++ has pretty limited support for first-class functions. Function pointers are stateless, functors are weird and still require defining a class, and the lambdas in C++11 are tricky to work with because of manual memory management.

That's *not* to say you shouldn't use functions for the Command pattern in other languages. If you have the luxury of a language with real closures, by all means, use them! In some ways, the Command pattern is a way of emulating closures in languages that don't have them.

For example, if we were building a game in JavaScript, we could create a move unit command just like this:

```
function makeMoveUnitCommand(unit, x, y) {
  // This function here is the command object:
  return function() {
    unit.moveTo(x, y);
  }
}
```

We could add support for undo as well using a pair of closures:

Redo may not be common in games, but re-*play* is. A naïve implementation would record the entire game state at each frame so it can be replayed, but that would use too much memory.

Instead, many games record the set of commands every entity performed each frame. To replay the game, the engine just runs the normal game simulation, executing the pre-recorded commands.

I say *some* ways here because building actual classes or structures for commands is still useful even in languages that have closures. If your command has multiple operations (like undoable commands), mapping that to a single function is awkward.

Defining an actual class with fields also helps readers easily tell what data the command contains. Closures are a wonderfully terse way of automatically wrapping up some state, but they can be so automatic that it's hard to see what state they're actually holding.

```
function makeMoveUnitCommand(unit, x, y) {
  var xBefore, yBefore;
  return {
    execute: function() {
      xBefore = unit.x();
      yBefore = unit.y();
      unit.moveTo(x, y);
    },
    undo: function() {
      unit.moveTo(xBefore, yBefore);
    }
  };
}
```

If you're comfortable with a functional style, this way of doing things is natural. If you aren't, I hope this chapter helped you along the way a bit. For me, the usefulness of the Command pattern really shows how effective the functional paradigm is for many problems.

## See Also

- You may end up with a lot of different command classes. In order to make it easier to implement those, it's often helpful to define a concrete base class with a bunch of convenient high-level methods that the derived commands can compose to define their behavior. That turns the command's main `execute()` method into the Subclass Sandbox pattern (p. 181).

- In our examples, we explicitly chose which actor would handle a command. In some cases, especially where your object model is hierarchical, it may not be so cut-and-dried. An object may respond to a command, or it may decide to pawn it off on some subordinate object. If you do that, you've got yourself the Chain of Responsibility pattern.

- Some commands are stateless chunks of pure behavior like the `JumpCommand` in the first example. In cases like that, having more than one instance of that class wastes memory since all instances are equivalent. The Flyweight pattern (p. 33) addresses that.

You could make it a singleton (p. 73) too, but friends don't let friends create singletons.

# Flyweight

# 3

*"Use sharing to support large numbers of fine-grained objects efficiently."*

The fog lifts, revealing a majestic old growth forest. Ancient hemlocks, countless in number, tower over you forming a cathedral of greenery. The stained glass canopy of leaves fragments the sunlight into golden shafts of mist. Between giant trunks, you can make out the massive forest receding into the distance.

This is the kind of otherworldly setting we dream of as game developers, and scenes like these are often enabled by a pattern whose name couldn't possibly be more modest: the humble Flyweight.

## Forest for the Trees

I can describe a sprawling woodland with just a few sentences, but actually *implementing* it in a realtime game is another story. When you've got an entire forest of individual trees filling the screen, all that a graphics programmer sees is the millions of polygons they'll have to somehow shovel onto the GPU every sixtieth of a second.

We're talking thousands of trees, each with detailed geometry containing thousands of polygons. Even if you have enough *memory* to describe that forest, in order to render it, that data has to make its way over the bus from the CPU to the GPU.

Each tree has a bunch of bits associated with it:

- A mesh of polygons that define the shape of the trunk, branches, and greenery.

- Textures for the bark and leaves.

- Its location and orientation in the forest.

- Tuning parameters like size and tint so that each tree looks different.

If you were to sketch it out in code, you'd have something like this:

```
class Tree
{
private:
  Mesh mesh_;
  Texture bark_;
  Texture leaves_;
  Vector position_;
  double height_;
  double thickness_;
  Color barkTint_;
  Color leafTint_;
};
```

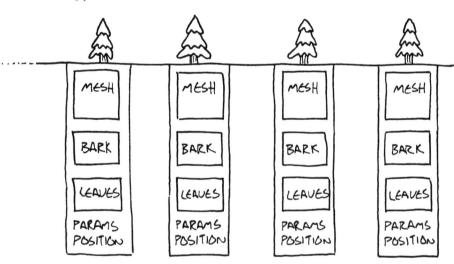

*Figure 3.1 – Note that the stuff in the small boxes is the same for each tree*

That's a lot of data, and the mesh and textures are particularly large. An entire forest of these objects is too much to throw at the GPU in one frame. Fortunately, there's a time-honored trick to handling this.

The key observation is that even though there may be thousands of trees in the forest, they mostly look similar. They will likely all use the same mesh and textures. That means most of the fields in these objects are the *same* between all of those instances.

<aside>
You'd have to be crazy or a billionaire to budget for the artists to individually model each tree in an entire forest.
</aside>

We can model that explicitly by splitting the object in half. First, we pull out the data that all trees have in common and move it into a separate class:

```
class TreeModel
{
private:
  Mesh mesh_;
  Texture bark_;
  Texture leaves_;
};
```

The game only needs a single one of these, since there's no reason to have the same meshes and textures in memory a thousand times. Then, each *instance* of a tree in the world has a *reference* to that shared `TreeModel`. What remains in `Tree` is the state that is instance-specific:

<aside>
This looks a lot like the Type Object pattern (p. 193). Both involve delegating part of an object's state to some other object shared between a number of instances. However, the intent behind the patterns differs.

With a type object, the goal is to minimize the number of classes you have to define by lifting "types" into your own object model. Any memory sharing you get from that is a bonus. The Flyweight pattern is purely about efficiency.
</aside>

```
class Tree
{
private:
  TreeModel* model_;

  Vector position_;
  double height_;
  double thickness_;
  Color barkTint_;
  Color leafTint_;
};
```

You can visualize it like this:

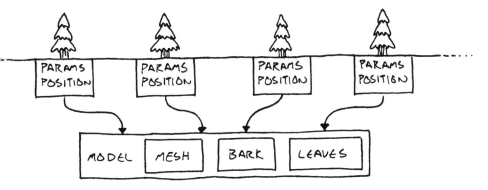

*Figure 3.2 – Four tree instances sharing a model*

This is all well and good for storing stuff in main memory, but that doesn't help rendering. Before the forest gets on screen, it has to work its way over to the GPU. We need to express this resource sharing in a way that the graphics card understands.

## A Thousand Instances

To minimize the amount of data we have to push to the GPU, we want to be able to send the shared data—the `TreeModel`—just *once*. Then, separately, we push over every tree instance's unique data—its position, color, and scale. Finally, we tell the GPU, "Use that one model to render each of these instances."

Fortunately, today's graphics APIs and cards support exactly that. The details are fiddly and out of the scope of this book, but both Direct3D and OpenGL can do something called *instanced rendering*.

In both APIs, you provide two streams of data. The first is the blob of common data that will be rendered multiple times—the mesh and textures in our arboreal example. The second is the list of instances and their parameters that will be used to vary that first chunk of data each time it's drawn. With a single draw call, an entire forest grows.

## The Flyweight Pattern

Now that we've got one concrete example under our belts, I can walk you through the general pattern. Flyweight, like its name implies, comes into play when you have objects that need to be more lightweight, generally because you have too many of them.

With instanced rendering, it's not so much that they take up too much memory as it is they take too much *time* to push each separate tree over the bus to the GPU, but the basic idea is the same.

The pattern solves that by separating out an object's data into two kinds. The first kind of data is the stuff that's not specific to a single *instance* of that object and can be shared across all of them. The Gang of Four calls this the *intrinsic* state, but I like to think of it as the "context-free" stuff. In the example here, this is the geometry and textures for the tree.

The rest of the data is the *extrinsic* state, the stuff that is unique to that instance. In this case, that is each tree's position, scale, and color. Just like in the chunk of sample code up there, this pattern saves memory by sharing one copy of the intrinsic state across every place where an object appears.

The fact that this API is implemented directly by the graphics card means the Flyweight pattern may be the only Gang of Four design pattern to have actual hardware support.

From what we've seen so far, this seems like basic resource sharing, hardly worth being called a pattern. That's partially because in this example here, we could come up with a clear separate *identity* for the shared state: the `TreeModel`.

I find this pattern to be less obvious (and thus more clever) when used in cases where there isn't a really well-defined identity for the shared object. In those cases, it feels more like an object is magically in multiple places at the same time. Let me show you another example.

## A Place To Put Down Roots

The ground these trees are growing on needs to be represented in our game too. There can be patches of grass, dirt, hills, lakes, rivers, and whatever other terrain you can dream up. We'll make the ground *tile-based*: the surface of the world is a huge grid of tiny tiles. Each tile is covered in one kind of terrain.

Each terrain type has a number of properties that affect gameplay:

- A movement cost that determines how quickly players can move through it.

- A flag for whether it's a watery terrain that can be crossed by boats.

- A texture used to render it.

Because we game programmers are paranoid about efficiency, there's no way we'd store all of that state in each tile in the world. Instead, a common approach is to use an enum for terrain types:

> After all, we already learned our lesson with those trees.

```
enum Terrain
{
  TERRAIN_GRASS,
  TERRAIN_HILL,
  TERRAIN_RIVER
  // Other terrains...
};
```

Then the world maintains a huge grid of those:

```
class World
{
private:
  Terrain tiles_[WIDTH][HEIGHT];
};
```

To actually get the useful data about a tile, we do something like:

> Here I'm using a nested array to store the 2D grid. That's efficient in C/C++ because it will pack all of the elements together. In Java or other memory-managed languages, doing that will actually give you an array of rows where each element is a *reference* to the array of columns, which may not be as memory-friendly as you'd like.
>
> In either case, real code would be better served by hiding this implementation detail behind a nice 2D grid data structure. I'm doing this here just to keep it simple.

```
int World::getMovementCost(int x, int y)
{
  switch (tiles_[x][y])
  {
    case TERRAIN_GRASS: return 1;
    case TERRAIN_HILL:  return 3;
    case TERRAIN_RIVER: return 2;
      // Other terrains...
  }
}

bool World::isWater(int x, int y)
{
  switch (tiles_[x][y])
  {
    case TERRAIN_GRASS: return false;
    case TERRAIN_HILL:  return false;
    case TERRAIN_RIVER: return true;
      // Other terrains...
  }
}
```

You get the idea. This works, but I find it ugly. I think of movement cost and wetness as *data* about a terrain, but here that's embedded in code. Worse, the data for a single terrain type is smeared across a bunch of methods. It would be really nice to keep all of that encapsulated together. After all, that's what objects are designed for.

It would be great if we could have an actual terrain *class*, like:

```
class Terrain
{
public:
  Terrain(int moveCost, bool isWater,
          Texture texture)
  : moveCost_(moveCost),
    isWater_(isWater),
    texture_(texture)
  {}

  int getMoveCost() const { return moveCost_; }
  bool isWater() const { return isWater_; }
  const Texture& getTexture() const
  {
    return texture_;
  }

private:
  int moveCost_;
  bool isWater_;
  Texture texture_;
};
```

You'll notice that all of the methods here are const. That's no coincidence. Since the same object is used in multiple contexts, if you were to modify it, the changes would appear in multiple places simultaneously.

That's probably not what you want. Sharing objects to save memory should be an optimization that doesn't affect the visible behavior of the app. Because of this, Flyweight objects are almost always immutable.

But we don't want to pay the cost of having an instance of that for each tile in the world. If you look at that class, you'll notice that there's actually *nothing* in there that's specific to *where* that tile is. In flyweight terms, *all* of a terrain's state is "intrinsic" or "context-free".

Given that, there's no reason to have more than one of each terrain type. Every grass tile on the ground is identical to every other one. Instead of having the world be a grid of enums or Terrain objects, it will be a grid of *pointers* to `Terrain` objects:

```
class World
{
private:
  Terrain* tiles_[WIDTH][HEIGHT];
  // Other stuff...
};
```

Each tile that uses the same terrain will point to the same terrain instance.

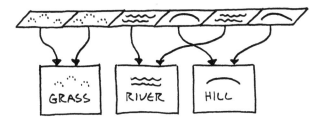

*Figure 3.3 – A row of tiles reusing terrain objects*

Since the terrain instances are used in multiple places, their lifetimes would be a little more complex to manage if you were to dynamically allocate them. Instead, we'll just store them directly in the world:

```
class World
{
public:
  World()
  : grassTerrain_(1, false, GRASS_TEXTURE),
    hillTerrain_(3, false, HILL_TEXTURE),
    riverTerrain_(2, true, RIVER_TEXTURE)
  {}

private:
  Terrain grassTerrain_;
  Terrain hillTerrain_;
  Terrain riverTerrain_;
  // Other stuff...
};
```

Then we can use those to paint the ground like this:

```cpp
void World::generateTerrain()
{
  // Fill the ground with grass.
  for (int x = 0; x < WIDTH; x++)
  {
    for (int y = 0; y < HEIGHT; y++)
    {
      // Sprinkle some hills.
      if (random(10) == 0)
      {
        tiles_[x][y] = &hillTerrain_;
      }
      else
      {
        tiles_[x][y] = &grassTerrain_;
      }
    }
  }

  // Lay a river.
  int x = random(WIDTH);
  for (int y = 0; y < HEIGHT; y++) {
    tiles_[x][y] = &riverTerrain_;
  }
}
```

I'll admit this isn't the world's greatest procedural terrain generation algorithm.

Now instead of methods on World for accessing the terrain properties, we can expose the Terrain object directly:

```cpp
const Terrain& World::getTile(int x, int y) const
{
  return *tiles_[x][y];
}
```

This way, World is no longer coupled to all sorts of details of terrains. If you want some property of the tile, you can get it right from that object:

```cpp
int cost = world.getTile(2, 3).getMovementCost();
```

We're back to the pleasant API of working with real objects, and we did this with almost no overhead—a pointer is often no larger than an enum.

## What About Performance?

I say "almost" here because the performance bean counters will rightfully want to know how this compares to using an enum. Referencing the terrain by pointer implies an indirect lookup. To get to some terrain data like the movement cost, you first have to follow the pointer in the grid to find the terrain object and then find the movement cost there. Chasing a pointer like this can cause a cache miss, which can slow things down.

For lots more on pointer chasing and cache misses, see the chapter on Data Locality (p. 269).

As always, the golden rule of optimization is *profile first*. Modern computer hardware is too complex for performance to be a game of pure reason anymore. In my tests for this chapter, there was no penalty for using a flyweight over an enum. Flyweights were actually noticeably faster. But that's entirely dependent on how other stuff is laid out in memory.

What I *am* confident of is that using flyweight objects shouldn't be dismissed out of hand. They give you the advantages of an object-oriented style without the expense of tons of objects. If you find yourself creating an enum and doing lots of switches on it, consider this pattern instead. If you're worried about performance, at least profile first before changing your code to a less maintainable style.

## See Also

- In the tile example, we just eagerly created an instance for each terrain type and stored it in `World`. That made it easy to find and reuse the shared instances. In many cases, though, you won't want to create *all* of the flyweights up front.

  If you can't predict which ones you actually need, it's better to create them on demand. To get the advantage of sharing, when you request one, you first see if you've already created an identical one. If so, you just return that instance.

  This usually means that you have to encapsulate construction behind some interface that can first look for an existing object. Hiding a constructor like this is an example of the Factory Method pattern.

- In order to return a previously created flyweight, you'll have to keep track of the pool of ones that you've already instantiated. As the name implies, that means that an object pool (p. 305) might be a helpful place to store them.

- When you're using the State pattern (p. 87), you often have "state" objects that don't have any fields specific to the machine that the state is being used in. The state's identity and methods are enough to be useful. In that case, you can apply this pattern and reuse that same state instance in multiple state machines at the same time without any problems.

# Observer

# 4

*"Define a one-to-many dependency between objects so that when one object changes state, all its dependents are notified and updated automatically."*

You can't throw a rock at a computer without hitting an application built using the Model-View-Controller architecture, and underlying that is the Observer pattern. Observer is so pervasive that Java put it in its core library (`java.util.Observer`) and C# baked it right into the *language* (the `event` keyword).

Observer is one of the most widely used and widely known of the original Gang of Four patterns, but the game development world can be strangely cloistered at times, so maybe this is all news to you. In case you haven't left the abbey in a while, let me walk you through a motivating example.

Like so many things in software, MVC was invented by Smalltalkers in the seventies. Lispers probably claim they came up with it in the sixties but didn't bother writing it down.

## Achievement Unlocked

Say we're adding an achievements system to our game. It will feature dozens of different badges players can earn for completing specific milestones like "Kill 100 Monkey Demons", "Fall off a Bridge", or "Complete a Level Wielding Only a Dead Weasel".

*Figure 4.1 – Unintended double meaning*

This is tricky to implement cleanly since we have such a wide range of achievements that are unlocked by all sorts of different behaviors. If we aren't careful, tendrils of our achievement system will twine their way through every dark corner of our codebase. Sure, "Fall off a Bridge" is somehow tied to the physics engine, but do we really want to see a call to `unlockFallOffBridge()` right in the middle of the linear algebra in our collision resolution algorithm?

This is a rhetorical question. No self-respecting physics programmer would ever let us sully their beautiful mathematics with something as pedestrian as *gameplay*.

What we'd like, as always, is to have all the code concerned with one facet of the game nicely lumped in one place. The challenge is that achievements are triggered by a bunch of different aspects of gameplay. How can that work without coupling the achievement code to all of them?

That's what the observer pattern is for. It lets one piece of code announce that something interesting happened *without actually caring who receives the notification.*

For example, we've got some physics code that handles gravity and tracks which bodies are relaxing on nice flat surfaces and which are plummeting toward sure demise. To implement the "Fall off a Bridge" badge, we could just jam the achievement code right in there, but that's a mess. Instead, we can just do:

```
void Physics::updateEntity(Entity& entity)
{
  bool wasOnSurface = entity.isOnSurface();
  entity.accelerate(GRAVITY);
  entity.update();
  if (wasOnSurface && !entity.isOnSurface())
  {
    notify(entity, EVENT_START_FALL);
  }
}
```

All it does is say, "Uh, I don't know if anyone cares, but this thing just fell. Do with that as you will."

The physics engine does have to decide what notifications to send, so it isn't entirely decoupled. But in architecture, we're most often trying to make systems *better*, not *perfect*.

The achievement system registers itself so that whenever the physics code sends a notification, the achievement receives it. It can then check to see if the falling body is our less-than-graceful hero, and if his perch prior to this new, unpleasant encounter with classical mechanics was a bridge. If so, it unlocks the proper achievement with associated fireworks and fanfare, and it does all of this with no involvement from the physics code.

Of course, if we *permanently* remove achievements and nothing else ever listens to the physics engine's notifications, we may as well remove the notification code too. But during the game's evolution, it's nice to have this flexibility.

In fact, we can change the set of achievements or tear out the entire achievement system without touching a line of the physics engine. It will still send out its notifications, oblivious to the fact that nothing is receiving them anymore.

# How it Works

If you don't already know how to implement the pattern, you could probably guess from the previous description, but to keep things easy on you, I'll walk through it quickly.

## The observer

We'll start with the nosy class that wants to know when another object does something interesting. These inquisitive objects are defined by this interface:

```
class Observer
{
public:
  virtual ~Observer() {}
  virtual void onNotify(const Entity& entity,
                        Event event) = 0;
};
```

Any concrete class that implements this becomes an observer. In our example, that's the achievement system, so we'd have something like so:

```
class Achievements : public Observer
{
public:
  virtual void onNotify(const Entity& entity,
                        Event event)
  {
    switch (event)
    {
    case EVENT_ENTITY_FELL:
      if (entity.isHero() && heroIsOnBridge_)
      {
        unlock(ACHIEVEMENT_FELL_OFF_BRIDGE);
      }
      break;

      // Handle other events...
      // Update heroIsOnBridge_...
    }
  }

private:
  void unlock(Achievement achievement)
  {
    // Unlock if not already unlocked...
  }

  bool heroIsOnBridge_;
};
```

The parameters to onNotify() are up to you. That's why this is the Observer *pattern* and not the Observer "ready-made code you can paste into your game". Typical parameters are the object that sent the notification and a generic "data" parameter you stuff other details into.

If you're coding in a language with generics or templates, you'll probably use them here, but it's also fine to tailor them to your specific use case. Here, I'm just hardcoding it to take a game entity and an enum that describes what happened.

## The subject

The notification method is invoked by the object being observed. In Gang of Four parlance, that object is called the "subject". It has two jobs. First, it holds the list of observers that are waiting oh-so-patiently for a missive from it:

```
class Subject
{
private:
  Observer* observers_[MAX_OBSERVERS];
  int numObservers_;
};
```

The important bit is that the subject exposes a *public* API for modifying that list:

```
class Subject
{
public:
  void addObserver(Observer* observer)
  {
    // Add to array...
  }

  void removeObserver(Observer* observer)
  {
    // Remove from array...
  }

  // Other stuff...
};
```

That allows outside code to control who receives notifications. The subject communicates with the observers, but it isn't *coupled* to them. In our example, no line of physics code will mention achievements. Yet, it can still talk to the achievements system. That's the clever part about this pattern.

It's also important that the subject has a *list* of observers instead of a single one. It makes sure that observers aren't implicitly coupled to *each other*. For example, say the audio engine also observes the fall event so that it can play an appropriate sound. If the subject only supported one observer, when the audio engine registered itself, that would *un*-register the achievements system.

That means those two systems would interfere with each other—and in a particularly nasty way, since the second would disable the first. Supporting a list of observers ensures that each observer is treated independently from the others. As far as they know, each is the only thing in the world with eyes on the subject.

The other job of the subject is sending notifications:

```
class Subject
{
protected:
  void notify(const Entity& entity, Event event)
  {
    for (int i = 0; i < numObservers_; i++)
    {
      observers_[i]->onNotify(entity, event);
    }
  }

  // Other stuff...
};
```

Note that this code assumes observers don't modify the list in their onNotify() methods. A more robust implementation would either prevent or gracefully handle concurrent modification like that.

## Observable physics

Now, we just need to hook all of this into the physics engine so that it can send notifications and the achievement system can wire itself up to receive them. We'll stay close to the original *Design Patterns* recipe and inherit Subject:

```
class Physics : public Subject
{
public:
  void updateEntity(Entity& entity);
};
```

This lets us make notify() in Subject protected. That way the derived physics engine class can call it to send notifications, but code outside it cannot. Meanwhile, addObserver() and removeObserver() are public, so anything that can get to the physics system can observe it.

Now, when the physics engine does something noteworthy, it calls notify() like in the motivating example before. That walks the observer list and gives them all the heads up.

In real code, I would avoid using inheritance here. Instead, I'd make Physics *have* an instance of Subject. Instead of observing the physics engine itself, the subject would be a separate "falling event" object. Observers could register themselves using something like:

```
physics.entityFell()
  .addObserver(this);
```

To me, this is the difference between "observer" systems and "event" systems. With the former, you observe *the thing that did something interesting*. With the latter, you observe an object that represents *the interesting thing that happened*.

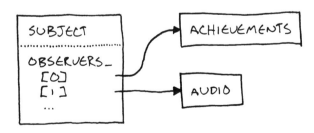

*Figure 4.2 – A subject and its list of observer references*

Pretty simple, right? Just one class that maintains a list of pointers to instances of some interface. It's hard to believe that something so straightforward is the communication backbone of countless programs and app frameworks.

But the Observer pattern isn't without its detractors. When I've asked other game programmers what they think about this pattern, they bring up a few complaints. Let's see what we can do to address them, if anything.

## "It's Too Slow"

I hear this a lot, often from programmers who don't actually know the details of the pattern. They have a default assumption that anything that smells like a "design pattern" must involve piles of classes and indirection and other creative ways of squandering CPU cycles.

The Observer pattern gets a particularly bad rap here because it's been known to hang around with some shady characters named "events", "messages", and even "data binding". Some of those systems *can* be slow (often deliberately, and for good reason). They involve things like queuing or doing dynamic allocation for each notification.

But, now that you've seen how the pattern is actually implemented, you know that isn't the case. Sending a notification is simply walking a list and calling some virtual methods. Granted, it's a *bit* slower than a statically dispatched call, but that cost is negligible in all but the most performance-critical code.

I find this pattern fits best outside of hot code paths anyway, so you can usually afford the dynamic dispatch. Aside from that, there's virtually no overhead. We aren't allocating objects for messages. There's no queueing. It's just an indirection over a synchronous method call.

### It's too *fast?*

In fact, you have to be careful because the Observer pattern *is* synchronous. The subject invokes its observers directly, which means it doesn't resume its own work until all of the observers have returned from their notification methods. A slow observer can block a subject.

This sounds scary, but in practice, it's not the end of the world. It's just something you have to be aware of. UI programmers—who've been doing event-based programming like this for ages—have a time-worn motto for this: "stay off the UI thread".

This is why I think documenting patterns is important. When we get fuzzy about terminology, we lose the ability to communicate clearly and succinctly. You say, "Observer", and someone hears "Events" or "Messaging" because either no one bothered to write down the difference or they didn't happen to read it.

That's what I'm trying to do with this book. To cover my bases, I've got a chapter on events and messages too: Event Queue (p. 233).

If you're responding to an event synchronously, you need to finish and return control as quickly as possible so that the UI doesn't lock up. When you have slow work to do, push it onto another thread or a work queue.

You do have to be careful mixing observers with threading and explicit locks, though. If an observer tries to grab a lock that the subject has, you can deadlock the game. In a highly threaded engine, you may be better off with asynchronous communication using an Event Queue (p. 233).

## "It Does Too Much Dynamic Allocation"

Whole tribes of the programmer clan—including many game developers—have moved onto garbage collected languages, and dynamic allocation isn't the boogie man that it used to be. But for performance-critical software like games, memory allocation still matters, even in managed languages. Dynamic allocation takes time, as does reclaiming memory, even if it happens automatically.

In the example code before, I used a fixed array because I'm trying to keep things dead simple. In real implementations, the observer list is almost always a dynamically allocated collection that grows and shrinks as observers are added and removed. That memory churn spooks some people.

Of course, the first thing to notice is that it only allocates memory when observers are being wired up. *Sending* a notification requires no memory allocation whatsoever—it's just a method call. If you hook up your observers at the start of the game and don't mess with them much, the amount of allocation is minimal.

If it's still a problem, though, I'll walk through a way to implement adding and removing observers without any dynamic allocation at all.

Many game developers are less worried about allocation and more worried about *fragmentation*. When your game needs to run continuously for days without crashing in order to get certified, an increasingly fragmented heap can prevent you from shipping.

The Object Pool chapter (p. 305) goes into more detail about this and a common technique for avoiding it.

### Linked observers

In the code we've seen so far, `Subject` owns a list of pointers to each `Observer` watching it. The `Observer` class itself has no reference to this list. It's just a pure virtual interface. Interfaces are preferred over concrete, stateful classes, so that's generally a good thing.

But if we *are* willing to put a bit of state in `Observer`, we can solve our allocation problem by threading the subject's list *through the observers themselves*. Instead of the subject having a separate collection of pointers, the observer objects become nodes in a linked list:

*Figure 4.3 – The subject points to a linked list of observers*

To implement this, first we'll get rid of the array in `Subject` and replace it with a pointer to the head of the list of observers:

```
class Subject
{
  Subject()
  : head_(NULL)
  {}

  // Methods...
private:
  Observer* head_;
};
```

Then we'll extend `Observer` with a pointer to the next observer in the list:

```
class Observer
{
  friend class Subject;

public:
  Observer()
  : next_(NULL)
  {}

  // Other stuff...
private:
  Observer* next_;
};
```

We're also making `Subject` a friend class here. The subject owns the API for adding and removing observers, but the list it will be managing is now inside the `Observer` class itself. The simplest way to give it the ability to poke at that list is by making it a friend.

Registering a new observer is just wiring it into the list. We'll take the easy option and insert it at the front:

```
void Subject::addObserver(Observer* observer)
{
  observer->next_ = head_;
  head_ = observer;
}
```

The other option is to add it to the end of the linked list. Doing that adds a bit more complexity. `Subject` has to either walk the list to find the end or keep a separate `tail_` pointer that always points to the last node.

Adding it to the front of the list is simpler, but does have one side effect. When we walk the list to send a notification to every observer, the most *recently* registered observer gets notified *first*. So if you register observers A, B, and C, in that order, they will receive notifications in C, B, A order.

In theory, this doesn't matter one way or the other. It's a tenet of good observer discipline that two observers observing the same subject should have no ordering dependencies relative to each other. If the ordering *does* matter, it means those two observers have some subtle coupling that could end up biting you.

Let's get removal working:

```
void Subject::removeObserver(Observer* observer)
{
  if (head_ == observer)
  {
    head_ = observer->next_;
    observer->next_ = NULL;
    return;
  }

  Observer* current = head_;
  while (current != NULL)
  {
    if (current->next_ == observer)
    {
      current->next_ = observer->next_;
      observer->next_ = NULL;
      return;
    }

    current = current->next_;
  }
}
```

Removing a node from a linked list usually requires a bit of ugly special case handling for removing the very first node, like you see here. There's a more elegant solution using a pointer to a pointer.

I didn't do that here because it confuses at least half the people I show it to. It's a worthwhile exercise for you to do, though: It helps you really think in terms of pointers.

Because we have a singly linked list, we have to walk it to find the observer we're removing. We'd have to do the same thing if we were using a regular array for that matter. If we use a *doubly* linked list, where each observer has a pointer to both the observer after it and before it, we can remove an observer in constant time. If this were real code, I'd do that.

The only thing left to do is send a notification. That's as simple as walking the list:

```
void Subject::notify(const Entity& entity,
                      Event event)
{
  Observer* observer = head_;
  while (observer != NULL)
  {
    observer->onNotify(entity, event);
    observer = observer->next_;
  }
}
```

Here, we walk the entire list and notify every single observer in it. This ensures that all of the observers get equal priority and are independent of each other.

We could tweak this such that when an observer is notified, it can return a flag indicating whether the subject should keep walking the list or stop. If you do that, you're pretty close to having the Chain of Responsibility pattern.

Not too bad, right? A subject can have as many observers as it wants, without a single whiff of dynamic memory. Registering and unregistering is as fast as it was with a simple array. We have sacrificed one small feature, though.

Since we are using the observer object itself as a list node, that implies it can only be part of one subject's observer list. In other words, an observer can only observe a single subject at a time. In a more traditional implementation where each subject has its own independent list, an observer can be in more than one of them simultaneously.

You may be able to live with that limitation. I find it more common for a *subject* to have multiple *observers* than vice versa. If it *is* a problem for you, there is another more complex solution you can use that still doesn't require dynamic allocation. It's too long to cram into this chapter, but I'll sketch it out and let you fill in the blanks…

### A pool of list nodes

Like before, each subject will have a linked list of observers. However, those list nodes won't be the observer objects themselves. Instead, they'll be separate little "list node" objects that contain a pointer to the observer and then a pointer to the next node in the list.

Linked lists come in two flavors. In the one you learned in school, you have a node object that contains the data. In our previous linked observer example, that was flipped around: the *data* (in this case the observer) contained the *node* (i.e. the next_ pointer).

The latter style is called an "intrusive" linked list because using an object in a list intrudes into the definition of that object itself. That makes intrusive lists less flexible but, as we've seen, also more efficient. They're popular in places like the Linux kernel where that trade-off makes sense.

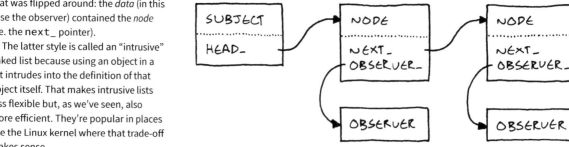

Figure 4.4 – A subject and a linked list of nodes pointing to observers

Since multiple nodes can all point to the same observer, that means an observer can be in more than one subject's list at the same time. We're back to being able to observe multiple subjects simultaneously.

The way you avoid dynamic allocation is simple: since all of those nodes are the same size and type, you pre-allocate an object pool (p. 305) of them. That gives you a fixed-size pile of list nodes to work with, and you can use and reuse them as you need without having to hit an actual memory allocator.

# Remaining Problems

I think we've banished the three boogie men used to scare people off this pattern. As we've seen, it's simple, fast, and can be made to play nice with memory management. But does that mean you should use observers all the time?

Now, that's a different question. Like all design patterns, the Observer pattern isn't a cure-all. Even when implemented correctly and efficiently, it may not be the right solution. The reason design patterns get a bad rap is because people apply good patterns to the wrong problem and end up making things worse.

Two challenges remain, one technical and one at something more like the maintainability level. We'll do the technical one first because those are always easiest.

### Destroying subjects and observers

The sample code we walked through is solid, but it side-steps an important issue: what happens when you delete a subject or an observer? If you carelessly call `delete` on some observer, a subject may still have a pointer to it. That's now a dangling pointer into deallocated memory. When that subject tries to send a notification, well... let's just say you're not going to have a good time.

Destroying the subject is easier since in most implementations, the observer doesn't have any references to it. But even then, sending the subject's bits to the memory manager's recycle bin may cause some problems. Those observers may still be expecting to receive notifications in the future, and they don't know that that will never happen now. They aren't observers at all, really, they just think they are.

You can deal with this in a couple of different ways. The simplest is to do what I did and just punt on it. It's an observer's job to unregister itself from any subjects when it gets deleted. More often than not, the observer

Not to point fingers, but I'll note that *Design Patterns* doesn't mention this issue at all.

As is often the case, the hard part isn't doing it, it's *remembering* to do it.

*does* know which subjects it's observing, so it's usually just a matter of adding a `removeObserver()` call to its destructor.

If you don't want to leave observers hanging when a subject gives up the ghost, that's easy to fix. Just have the subject send one final "dying breath" notification right before it gets destroyed. That way, any observer can receive that and take whatever action it thinks is appropriate.

Mourn, send flowers, compose elegy, etc.

People—even those of us who've spent enough time in the company of machines to have some of their precise nature rub off on us—are reliably terrible at being reliable. That's why we invented computers: they don't make the mistakes we so often do.

A safer answer is to make observers automatically unregister themselves from every subject when they get destroyed. If you implement the logic for that once in your base observer class, everyone using it doesn't have to remember to do it themselves. This does add some complexity, though. It means each *observer* will need a list of the *subjects* it's observing. You end up with pointers going in both directions.

### Don't worry, I've got a GC

All you cool kids with your hip modern languages with garbage collectors are feeling pretty smug right now. Think you don't have to worry about this because you never explicitly delete anything? Think again!

Imagine this: you've got some UI screen that shows a bunch of stats about the player's character like their health and stuff. When the player brings up the screen, you instantiate a new object for it. When they close it, you just forget about the object and let the GC clean it up.

Every time the character takes a punch to the face (or elsewhere, I suppose), it sends a notification. The UI screen observes that and updates the little health bar. Great. Now what happens when the player dismisses the screen, but you don't unregister the observer?

The UI isn't visible anymore, but it won't get garbage collected since the character's observer list still has a reference to it. Every time the screen is loaded, we add a new instance of it to that increasingly long list.

The entire time the player is playing the game, running around, and getting in fights, the character is sending notifications that get received by *all* of those screens. They aren't on screen, but they receive notifications and waste CPU cycles updating invisible UI elements. If they do other things like play sounds, you'll get noticeably wrong behavior.

An even surer sign of its significance: it has a Wikipedia article.

This is such a common issue in notification systems that it has a name: the *lapsed listener problem*. Since subjects retain references to their listeners, you can end up with zombie UI objects lingering in memory. The lesson here is to be disciplined about unregistration.

## What's going on?

The other, deeper issue with the Observer pattern is a direct consequence of its intended purpose. We use it because it helps us loosen the coupling between two pieces of code. It lets a subject indirectly communicate with some observer without being statically bound to it.

This is a real win when you're trying to reason about the subject's behavior, and any hangers-on would be an annoying distraction. If you're poking at the physics engine, you really don't want your editor—or your mind—cluttered up with a bunch of stuff about achievements.

On the other hand, if your program isn't working and the bug spans some chain of observers, reasoning about that communication flow is much more difficult. With an explicit coupling, it's as easy as looking up the method being called. This is child's play for your average IDE since the coupling is static.

But if that coupling happens through an observer list, the only way to tell who will get notified is by seeing which observers happen to be in that list *at runtime*. Instead of being able to *statically* reason about the communication structure of the program, you have to reason about its *imperative, dynamic* behavior.

My guideline for how to cope with this is pretty simple. If you often need to think about *both* sides of some communication in order to understand a part of the program, don't use the Observer pattern to express that linkage. Prefer something more explicit.

When you're hacking on some big program, you tend to have lumps of it that you work on all together. We have lots of terminology for this like "separation of concerns" and "coherence and cohesion" and "modularity", but it boils down to "this stuff goes together and doesn't go with this other stuff".

The observer pattern is a great way to let those mostly unrelated lumps talk to each other without them merging into one big lump. It's less useful *within* a single lump of code dedicated to one feature or aspect.

That's why it fits our example well: achievements and physics are almost entirely unrelated domains, likely implemented by different people. We want the bare minimum of communication between them so that working on either one doesn't require much knowledge of the other.

# Observers Today

*Design Patterns* came out in 1994. Back then, object-oriented programming was *the* hot paradigm. Every programmer on Earth wanted to "Learn OOP in 30 Days," and middle managers paid them based on the number of classes they created. Engineers judged their mettle by the depth of their inheritance hierarchies.

The Observer pattern got popular during that zeitgeist, so it's no surprise that it's class-heavy. But mainstream coders now are more comfortable with functional programming. Having to implement an entire interface just to receive a notification doesn't fit today's aesthetic.

It feels heavyweight and rigid. It *is* heavyweight and rigid. For example, you can't have a single class that uses different notification methods for different subjects.

A more modern approach is for an "observer" to be only a reference to a method or function. In languages with first-class functions, and especially ones with closures, this is a much more common way to do observers.

For example, C# has "events" baked into the language. With those, the observer you register is a "delegate", which is that language's term for a reference to a method. In JavaScript's event system, observers *can* be objects supporting a special `EventListener` protocol, but they can also just be functions. The latter is almost always what people use.

If I were designing an observer system today, I'd make it function-based instead of class-based. Even in C++, I would tend toward a system that let you register member function pointers as observers instead of instances of some `Observer` interface.

That same year, Ace of Base had not one but *three* hit singles, so that may tell you something about our taste and discernment back then.

This is why the subject usually passes itself to the observer. Since an observer only has a single `onNotify()` method, if it's observing multiple subjects, it needs to be able to tell which one called it.

These days, practically *every* language has closures. C++ overcame the challenge of closures in a language without garbage collection, and even Java finally got its act together and introduced them in JDK 8.

# Observers Tomorrow

Event systems and other observer-like patterns are incredibly common these days. They're a well-worn path. But if you write a few large apps using them, you start to notice something. A lot of the code in your observers ends up looking the same. It's usually something like:

1. Get notified that some state has changed.

2. Imperatively modify some chunk of UI to reflect the new state.

It's all, "Oh, the hero health is 7 now? Let me set the width of the health bar to 70 pixels." After a while, that gets pretty tedious. Computer science academics and software engineers have been trying to eliminate that tedium for a *long* time. Their attempts have gone under a number of different names: "dataflow programming", "functional reactive programming", etc.

While there have been some successes, usually in limited domains like audio processing or chip design, the Holy Grail still hasn't been found. In the meantime, a less ambitious approach has started gaining traction. Many recent application frameworks now use "data binding".

Unlike more radical models, data binding doesn't try to entirely eliminate imperative code and doesn't try to architect your entire application around a giant declarative dataflow graph. What it does do is automate the busywork where you're tweaking a UI element or calculated property to reflect a change to some value.

Like other declarative systems, data binding is probably a bit too slow and complex to fit inside the core of a game engine. But I would be surprised if I didn't see it start making inroads into less critical areas of the game like UI.

In the meantime, the good old Observer pattern will still be here waiting for us. Sure, it's not as exciting as some hot technique that manages to cram both "functional" and "reactive" in its name, but it's dead simple and it works. To me, those are often the two most important criteria for a solution.

# Prototype

# 5

*"Specify the kinds of objects to create using a prototypical instance, and create new objects by copying this prototype."*

The first time I heard the word "prototype" was in *Design Patterns*. Today, it seems like everyone is saying it, but it turns out they aren't talking about the design pattern. We'll cover that here, but I'll also show you other, more interesting places where the term "prototype" and the concepts behind it have popped up. But first, let's revisit the original pattern.

## The Prototype Design Pattern

Pretend we're making a game in the style of Gauntlet. We've got creatures and fiends swarming around the hero, vying for their share of his flesh. These unsavory dinner companions enter the arena by way of "spawners", and there is a different spawner for each kind of enemy.

For the sake of this example, let's say we have different classes for each kind of monster in the game—`Ghost`, `Demon`, `Sorcerer`, etc., like:

I don't say "original" lightly here. *Design Patterns* cites Ivan Sutherland's legendary Sketchpad project in *1963* as one of the first examples of this pattern in the wild. While everyone else was listening to Dylan and the Beatles, Sutherland was busy just, you know, inventing the basic concepts of CAD, interactive graphics, and object-oriented programming.

```
class Monster
{
  // Stuff...
};

class Ghost : public Monster {};
class Demon : public Monster {};
class Sorcerer : public Monster {};
```

A spawner constructs instances of one particular monster type. To support every monster in the game, we *could* brute-force it by having a spawner class for each monster class, leading to a parallel class hierarchy:

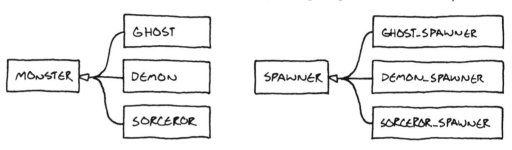

*Figure 5.1 – Parallel class hierarchies*

Implementing it would look like this:

```
class Spawner
{
public:
  virtual ~Spawner() {}
  virtual Monster* spawnMonster() = 0;
};

class GhostSpawner : public Spawner
{
public:
  virtual Monster* spawnMonster()
  {
    return new Ghost();
  }
};

class DemonSpawner : public Spawner
{
public:
  virtual Monster* spawnMonster()
  {
    return new Demon();
  }
};

// You get the idea...
```

Unless you get paid by the line of code, this is obviously not a fun way to hack this together. Lots of classes, lots of boilerplate, lots of redundancy, lots of duplication, lots of repeating myself...

The Prototype pattern offers a solution. The key idea is that *an object can spawn other objects similar to itself*. If you have one ghost, you can make more ghosts from it. If you have a demon, you can make other demons. Any monster can be treated as a *prototypal* monster used to generate other versions of itself.

To implement this, we give our base class, Monster, an abstract clone() method:

```
class Monster
{
public:
  virtual ~Monster() {}
  virtual Monster* clone() = 0;

  // Other stuff...
};
```

Each monster subclass provides an implementation that returns a new object identical in class and state to itself. For example:

```
class Ghost : public Monster {
public:
  Ghost(int health, int speed)
  : health_(health),
    speed_(speed)
  {}

  virtual Monster* clone()
  {
    return new Ghost(health_, speed_);
  }

private:
  int health_;
  int speed_;
};
```

Once all our monsters support that, we no longer need a spawner class for each monster class. Instead, we define a single one:

```
class Spawner
{
public:
  Spawner(Monster* prototype)
  : prototype_(prototype)
  {}

  Monster* spawnMonster()
  {
    return prototype_->clone();
  }

private:
  Monster* prototype_;
};
```

It internally holds a monster, a hidden one whose sole purpose is to be used by the spawner as a template to stamp out more monsters like it, sort of like a queen bee who never leaves the hive.

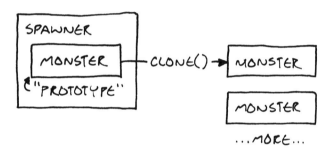

*Figure 5.2 - A spawner containing a prototype*

To create a ghost spawner, we create a prototypal ghost instance and then create a spawner holding that prototype:

```
Monster* ghostPrototype = new Ghost(15, 3);
Spawner* ghostSpawner = new Spawner(ghostPrototype);
```

One neat part about this pattern is that it doesn't just clone the *class* of the prototype, it clones its *state* too. This means we could make a spawner for fast ghosts, weak ghosts, or slow ghosts just by creating an appropriate prototype ghost.

I find something both elegant and yet surprising about this pattern. I can't imagine coming up with it myself, but I can't imagine *not* knowing about it now that I do.

## How well does it work?

Well, we don't have to create a separate spawner class for each monster, so that's good. But we *do* have to implement `clone()` in each monster class. That's just about as much code as the spawners.

There are also some nasty semantic ratholes when you sit down to try to write a correct `clone()`. Does it do a deep clone or shallow one? In other words, if a demon is holding a pitchfork, does cloning the demon clone the pitchfork too?

Also, not only does this not look like it's saving us much code in this contrived problem, there's the fact that it's a *contrived problem*. We had to take as a given that we have separate classes for each monster. These days, that's definitely *not* the way most game engines roll.

Most of us learned the hard way that big class hierarchies like this are a pain to manage, which is why we instead use patterns like Component (p. 213) and Type Object (p. 193) to model different kinds of entities without enshrining each in its own class.

## Spawn functions

Even if we do have different classes for each monster, there are other ways to decorticate this *Felis catus*. Instead of making separate spawner *classes* for each monster, we could make spawn *functions*, like so:

```
Monster* spawnGhost()
{
  return new Ghost();
}
```

This is less boilerplate than rolling a whole class for constructing a monster of some type. Then the one spawner class can simply store a function pointer:

```
typedef Monster* (*SpawnCallback)();

class Spawner
{
public:
  Spawner(SpawnCallback spawn)
  : spawn_(spawn)
{}

  Monster* spawnMonster() { return spawn_(); }

private:
  SpawnCallback spawn_;
};
```

To create a spawner for ghosts, you do:

```
Spawner* ghostSpawner = new Spawner(spawnGhost);
```

## Templates

I'm not sure if C++ programmers learned to love them or if templates just scared some people completely away from C++. Either way, everyone I see using C++ today uses templates too.

The Spawner class here is so that code that doesn't care what kind of monster a spawner creates can just use it and work with pointers to Monster.

If we only had the SpawnerFor<T> class, there would be no single supertype the instantiations of that template all shared, so any code that worked with spawners of any monster type would itself need to take a template parameter.

By now, most C++ developers are familiar with templates. Our spawner class needs to construct instances of some type, but we don't want to hard code some specific monster class. The natural solution then is to make it a *type parameter*, which templates let us do:

```
class Spawner
{
public:
  virtual ~Spawner() {}
  virtual Monster* spawnMonster() = 0;
};

template <class T>
class SpawnerFor : public Spawner
{
public:
  virtual Monster* spawnMonster() { return new T(); }
};
```

Using it looks like:

```
Spawner* ghostSpawner = new SpawnerFor<Ghost>();
```

## First-class types

In some ways, the Type Object pattern (p. 193) is another workaround for the lack of first-class types. That pattern can still be useful even in languages with them, though, because it lets *you* define what a "type" is. You may want different semantics than what the language's built-in classes provide.

The previous two solutions address the need to have a class, Spawner, which is parameterized by a type. In C++, types aren't generally first-class, so that requires some gymnastics. If you're using a dynamically-typed language like JavaScript, Python, or Ruby where classes *are* regular objects you can pass around, you can solve this much more directly.

When you make a spawner, just pass in the class of monster that it should construct—the actual runtime object that represents the monster's class. Easy as pie.

With all of these options, I honestly can't say I've found a case where I felt the Prototype *design pattern* was the best answer. Maybe your experience will be different, but for now let's put that away and talk about something else: prototypes as a *language paradigm*.

# The Prototype Language Paradigm

Many people think "object-oriented programming" is synonymous with "classes". Definitions of OOP tend to feel like credos of opposing religious denominations, but a fairly non-contentious take on it is that *OOP lets you define "objects" which bundle data and code together.* Compared to structured languages like C and functional languages like Scheme, the defining characteristic of OOP is that it tightly binds state and behavior together.

You may think classes are the one and only way to do that, but a handful of guys including Dave Ungar and Randall Smith beg to differ. They created a language in the '80s called Self. While as OOP as can be, it has no classes.

## Self

In a pure sense, Self is *more* object-oriented than a class-based language. We think of OOP as marrying state and behavior, but languages with classes actually have a line of separation between them.

Consider the semantics of your favorite class-based language. To access some state on an object, you look in the memory of the instance itself. State is *contained* in the instance.

To invoke a method, though, you look up the instance's class, and then you look up the method *there*. Behavior is contained in the *class*. There's always that level of indirection to get to a method, which means fields and methods are different.

For example, to invoke a virtual method in C++, you look in the instance for the pointer to its vtable, then look up the method there.

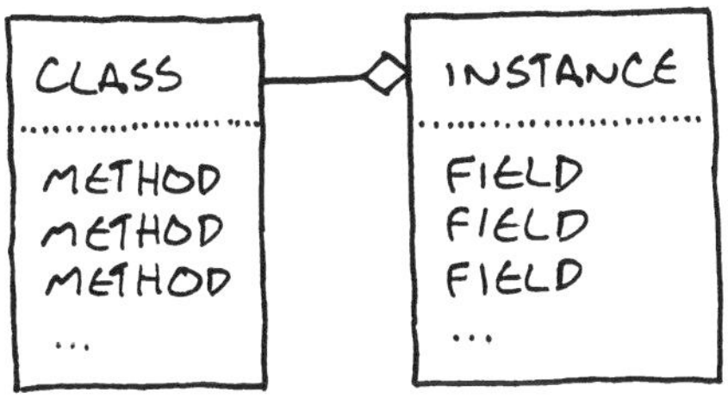

*Figure 5.3 – Methods stored in the class, fields in the instance*

Self eliminates that distinction. To look up *anything*, you just look on the object. An instance can contain both state and behavior. You can have a single object that has a method completely unique to it.

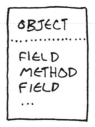

*Figure 5.4 – No man is an island, but this object is*

If that was all Self did, it would be hard to use. Inheritance in class-based languages, despite its faults, gives you a useful mechanism for reusing polymorphic code and avoiding duplication. To accomplish something similar without classes, Self has *delegation*.

To find a field or call a method on some object, we first look in the object itself. If it has it, we're done. If it doesn't, we look at the object's *parent*. This is just a reference to some other object. When we fail to find a property on the first object, we try its parent, and its parent, and so on. In other words, failed lookups are *delegated* to an object's parent.

I'm simplifying here. Self actually supports multiple parents. Parents are just specially marked fields, which means you can do things like inherit parents or change them at runtime, leading to what's called *dynamic inheritance*.

*Figure 5.5 – An object delegates to its parent*

Parent objects let us reuse behavior (and state!) across multiple objects, so we've covered part of the utility of classes. The other key thing classes do is give us a way to create instances. When you need a new thingamabob, you can just do `new Thingamabob()`, or whatever your preferred language's syntax is. A class is a factory for instances of itself.

Without classes, how do we make new things? In particular, how do we make a bunch of new things that all have stuff in common? Just like the design pattern, the way you do this in Self is by *cloning*.

In Self, it's as if *every* object supports the Prototype design pattern automatically. Any object can be cloned. To make a bunch of similar objects, you:

1. Beat one object into the shape you want. You can just clone the base `Object` built into the system and then stuff fields and methods into it.

2. Clone it to make as many... uh... clones as you want.

This gives us the elegance of the Prototype design pattern without the tedium of having to implement `clone()` ourselves; it's built into the system. This is such a beautiful, clever, minimal system that as soon as I learned about it, I started creating a prototype-based language to get more experience with it.

I realize building a language from scratch is not the most efficient way to learn, but what can I say? I'm a bit peculiar. If you're curious, the language is called Finch.

### How did it go?

I was super excited to play with a pure prototype-based language, but once I had mine up and running, I discovered an unpleasant fact: it just wasn't that fun to program in.

Sure, the language was simple to implement, but that was because it punted the complexity onto the user. As soon as I started trying to use it, I found myself missing the structure that classes give. I ended up trying to recapitulate it at the library level since the language didn't have it.

Maybe this is because my prior experience is in class-based languages, so my mind has been tainted by that paradigm. But my hunch is that most people just like well-defined "kinds of things".

In addition to the runaway success of class-based languages, look at how many games have explicit character classes and a precise roster of different sorts of enemies, items, and skills, each neatly labeled. You don't see many games where each monster is a unique snowflake, like "sort of halfway between a troll and a goblin with a bit of snake mixed in".

While prototypes are a really cool paradigm and one that I wish more people knew about, I'm glad that most of us aren't actually programming using them every day. The code I've seen that fully embraces prototypes has a weird mushiness to it that I find hard to wrap my head around.

I've since heard through the grapevine that many of the Self programmers came to the same conclusion. The project was far from a loss, though. Self was so dynamic that it needed all sorts of virtual machine innovations in order to run fast enough.

The ideas they invented for just-in-time compilation, garbage collection, and optimizing method dispatch are the exact same techniques—often implemented by the same people!—that now make many of the world's dynamically-typed languages fast enough to use for massively popular applications.

It's also telling how *little* code there actually is written in a prototypal style. I've looked.

### What about JavaScript?

OK, if prototype-based languages are so unfriendly, how do I explain JavaScript? Here's a language with prototypes used by millions of people every day. More computers run JavaScript than any other language on Earth.

Brendan Eich, the creator of JavaScript, took inspiration directly from Self, and many of JavaScript's semantics are prototype-based. Each object can have an arbitrary set of properties, both fields and "methods" (which

As a language designer, one appealing thing about prototypes is that they are simpler to implement than classes. Eich took full advantage of this: the first version of JavaScript was created in ten days.

are really just functions stored as fields). An object can also have another object, called its "prototype", that it delegates to if a field access fails.

But, despite that, I believe that JavaScript in practice has more in common with class-based languages than with prototypal ones. One hint that JavaScript has taken steps away from Self is that the core operation in a prototype-based language, *cloning*, is nowhere to be seen.

There is no method to clone an object in JavaScript. The closest it has is `Object.create()`, which lets you create a new object that delegates to an existing one. Even that wasn't added until ECMAScript 5, fourteen years after JavaScript came out. Instead of cloning, let me walk you through the typical way you define types and create objects in JavaScript. You start with a *constructor function*:

```
function Weapon(range, damage) {
  this.range = range;
  this.damage = damage;
}
```

This creates a new object and initializes its fields. You invoke it like:

```
var sword = new Weapon(10, 16);
```

The `new` here invokes the body of the `Weapon()` function with `this` bound to a new empty object. The body adds a bunch of fields to it, then the now-filled-in object is automatically returned.

The `new` also does one other thing for you. When it creates that blank object, it wires it up to delegate to a prototype object. You can get to that object directly using `Weapon.prototype`.

While state is added in the constructor body, to define *behavior*, you usually add methods to the prototype object. Something like this:

```
Weapon.prototype.attack = function(target) {
  if (distanceTo(target) > this.range) {
    console.log("Out of range!");
  } else {
    target.health -= this.damage;
  }
}
```

This adds an `attack` property to the weapon prototype whose value is a function. Since every object returned by `new Weapon()` delegates to `Weapon.prototype`, you can now call `sword.attack()` and it will call that function. It looks a bit like this:

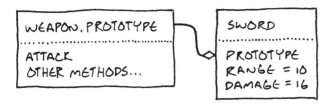

Figure 5.6 – A sword object and its weapon prototype

Let's review:

- The way you create objects is by a "new" operation that you invoke using an object that represents the type—the constructor function.

- State is stored on the instance itself.

- Behavior goes through a level of indirection—delegating to the prototype — and is stored on a separate object that represents the set of methods shared by all objects of a certain type.

Call me crazy, but that sounds a lot like my description of classes earlier. You *can* write prototype-style code in JavaScript (*sans* cloning), but the syntax and idioms of the language encourage a class-based approach.

Personally, I think that's a good thing. Like I said, I find doubling down on prototypes makes code harder to work with, so I like that JavaScript wraps the core semantics in something a little more classy.

## Prototypes for Data Modeling

OK, I keep talking about things I *don't* like prototypes for, which is making this chapter a real downer. I think of this book as more comedy than tragedy, so let's close this out with an area where I *do* think prototypes, or more specifically *delegation*, can be useful.

If you were to count all the bytes in a game that are code compared to the ones that are data, you'd see the fraction of data has been increasing steadily since the dawn of programming. Early games procedurally generated almost everything so they could fit on floppies and old game cartridges. In many games today, the code is just an "engine" that drives the game, which is defined entirely in data.

That's great, but pushing piles of content into data files doesn't magically solve the organizational challenges of a large project. If anything, it makes it harder. The reason we use programming languages is because they have tools for managing complexity.

Instead of copying and pasting a chunk of code in ten places, we move it into a function that we can call by name. Instead of copying a method in a bunch of classes, we can put it in a separate class that those classes inherit from or mix in.

When your game's data reaches a certain size, you really start wanting similar features. Data modeling is a deep subject that I can't hope to do justice here, but I do want to throw out one feature for you to consider in your own games: using prototypes and delegation for reusing data.

Let's say we're defining the data model for the shameless Gauntlet rip-off I mentioned earlier. The game designers need to specify the attributes for monsters and items in some kind of files.

One common approach is to use JSON. Data entities are basically *maps*, or *property bags*, or any of a dozen other terms because there's nothing programmers like more than inventing a new name for something that already has one.

One common approach is to use JSON. Data entities are basically *maps*, or *property bags*, or any of a dozen other terms because there's nothing programmers like more than inventing a new name for something that already has one.

So a goblin in the game might be defined something like this:

I mean completely original title in no way inspired by any previously existing top-down multi-player dungeon crawl arcade games. Please don't sue me.

We've re-invented them so many times that Steve Yegge calls them "The Universal Design Pattern".

```
{
  "name": "goblin grunt",
  "minHealth": 20,
  "maxHealth": 30,
  "resists": ["cold", "poison"],
  "weaknesses": ["fire", "light"]
}
```

This is pretty straightforward and even the most text-averse designer can handle that. So you throw in a couple of sibling branches on the Great Goblin Family Tree:

```
{
  "name": "goblin wizard",
  "minHealth": 20,
  "maxHealth": 30,
  "resists": ["cold", "poison"],
  "weaknesses": ["fire", "light"],
  "spells": ["fire ball", "lightning bolt"]
}

{
  "name": "goblin archer",
  "minHealth": 20,
  "maxHealth": 30,
  "resists": ["cold", "poison"],
  "weaknesses": ["fire", "light"],
  "attacks": ["short bow"]
}
```

Now, if this was code, our aesthetic sense would be tingling. There's a lot of duplication between these entities, and well-trained programmers *hate* that. It wastes space and takes more time to author. You have to read carefully to tell if the data even *is* the same. It's a maintenance headache. If we decide to make all of the goblins in the game stronger, we need to remember to update the health of all three of them. Bad bad bad.

If this was code, we'd create an abstraction for a "goblin" and reuse that across the three goblin types, but dumb JSON can't do that. So let's make it a bit smarter.

We'll declare that if an object has a `"prototype"` field, then that defines the name of another object that this one delegates to. Any properties that don't exist on the first object fall back to being looked up on the prototype.

With that, we can simplify the JSON for our goblin horde:

This makes the `"prototype"` a piece of *meta*data instead of data. Goblins have warty green skin and yellow teeth. They don't have prototypes. Prototypes are a property of the *data object representing the goblin*, and not the goblin itself.

```
{
  "name": "goblin grunt",
  "minHealth": 20,
  "maxHealth": 30,
  "resists": ["cold", "poison"],
  "weaknesses": ["fire", "light"]
}

{
  "name": "goblin wizard",
  "prototype": "goblin grunt",
  "spells": ["fire ball", "lightning bolt"]
}

{
  "name": "goblin archer",
  "prototype": "goblin grunt",
  "attacks": ["short bow"]
}
```

Since the archer and wizard have the grunt as their prototype, we don't have to repeat the health, resists, and weaknesses in each of them. The logic we've added to our data model is super simple—basic single delegation—but we've already gotten rid of a bunch of duplication.

One interesting thing to note here is that we didn't set up a fourth "base goblin" *abstract* prototype for the three concrete goblin types to delegate to. Instead, we just picked one of the goblins who was the simplest and delegated to it.

That feels natural in a prototype-based system where any object can be used as a clone to create new refined objects, and I think it's equally natural here too. It's a particularly good fit for data in games where you often have one-off special entities in the game world.

Think about bosses and unique items. These are often refinements of a more common object in the game, and prototypal delegation is a good fit for defining those. The magic Sword of Head-Detaching, which is really just a longsword with some bonuses, can be expressed as that directly:

```
{
  "name": "Sword of Head-Detaching",
  "prototype": "longsword",
  "damageBonus": "20"
}
```

A little extra power in your game engine's data modeling system can make it easier for designers to add lots of little variations to the armaments and beasties populating your game world, and that richness is exactly what delights players.

# Singleton                                    6

*"Ensure a class has one instance, and provide a global point of access to it."*

This chapter is an anomaly. Every other chapter in this book shows you how to use a design pattern. This chapter shows you how *not* to use one.

Despite noble intentions, the Singleton pattern described by the Gang of Four usually does more harm than good. They stress that the pattern should be used sparingly, but that message was often lost in translation to the game industry.

Like any pattern, using Singleton where it doesn't belong is about as helpful as treating a bullet wound with a splint. Since it's so overused, most of this chapter will be about *avoiding* singletons, but first, let's go over the pattern itself.

When much of the industry moved to object-oriented programming from C, one problem they ran into was "how do I get an instance?" They had some method they wanted to call but didn't have an instance of the object that provides that method in hand. Singletons (in other words, making it global) were an easy way out.

## The Singleton Pattern

Cast your eyes upward and you can see how *Design Patterns* summarizes Singleton. We'll split it at "and" and consider each half separately.

### Restricting a class to one instance

There are times when a class cannot perform correctly if there is more than one instance of it. The common case is when the class interacts with an external system that maintains its own global state.

Consider a class that wraps an underlying file system API. Because file operations can take a while to complete, our class performs operations asynchronously. This means multiple operations can be running concurrently, so they must be coordinated with each other. If we start one call to create a file and another one to delete that same file, our wrapper needs to be aware of both to make sure they don't interfere with each other.

To do this, a call into our wrapper needs to have access to every previous operation. If users could freely create instances of our class, one instance would have no way of knowing about operations that other instances started. Enter the singleton. It provides a way for a class to ensure at compile time that there is only a single instance of the class.

### Providing a global point of access

Several different systems in the game will use our file system wrapper: logging, content loading, game state saving, etc. If those systems can't create their own instances of our file system wrapper, how can they get ahold of one?

Singleton provides a solution to this too. In addition to creating the single instance, it also provides a globally available method to get it. This way, anyone anywhere can get their paws on our blessed instance. All together, the classic implementation looks like this:

```
class FileSystem
{
public:
  static FileSystem& instance()
  {
    // Lazy initialize.
    if (instance_ == NULL)
    {
      instance_ = new FileSystem();
    }
    return *instance_;
  }

private:
  FileSystem() {}

  static FileSystem* instance_;
};
```

The static `instance_` member holds an instance of the class, and the private constructor ensures that it is the *only* one. The public static `instance()` method grants access to the instance from anywhere in the codebase. It is also responsible for instantiating the singleton instance lazily the first time someone asks for it.

A modern take looks like this:

```cpp
class FileSystem
{
public:
  static FileSystem& instance()
  {
    static FileSystem *instance = new FileSystem();
    return *instance;
  }

private:
  FileSystem() {}
};
```

C++11 mandates that the initializer for a local static variable is only run once, even in the presence of concurrency. So, assuming you've got a modern C++ compiler, this code is thread-safe where the first example is not.

Of course, the thread-safety of your singleton class itself is an entirely different question! This just ensures that its *initialization* is.

## Why We Use It

It seems we have a winner. Our file system wrapper is available wherever we need it without the tedium of passing it around everywhere. The class itself cleverly ensures we won't make a mess of things by instantiating a couple of instances. It's got some other nice features too:

- **It doesn't create the instance if no one uses it.** Saving memory and CPU cycles is always good. Since the singleton is initialized only when it's first accessed, it won't be instantiated at all if the game never asks for it.

- **It's initialized at runtime.** A common alternative to Singleton is a class with static member variables. I like simple solutions, so I use static classes instead of singletons when possible, but there's one limitation static members have: automatic initialization. The compiler initializes statics before `main()` is called. This means they can't use information known only once the program is up and running (for example, configuration loaded from a file). It also means they can't reliably depend on each other —the compiler does not guarantee the order in which statics are initialized relative to each other.

Lazy initialization solves both of those problems. The singleton will be initialized as late as possible, so by that time any information it needs should be available. As long as they don't have circular dependencies, one singleton can even refer to another when initializing itself.

- **You can subclass the singleton.** This is a powerful but often overlooked capability. Let's say we need our file system wrapper to be cross-platform. To make this work, we want it to be an abstract interface for a file system with subclasses that implement the interface for each platform. Here is the base class:

```cpp
class FileSystem
{
public:
  virtual ~FileSystem() {}
  virtual char* read(char* path) = 0;
  virtual void write(char* path, char* text) = 0;
};
```

Then we define derived classes for a couple of platforms:

```cpp
class PS3FileSystem : public FileSystem
{
public:
  virtual char* read(char* path)
  {
    // Use Sony file IO API...
  }

  virtual void write(char* path, char* text)
  {
    // Use sony file IO API...
  }
};

class WiiFileSystem : public FileSystem
{
public:
  virtual char* read(char* path)
  {
    // Use Nintendo file IO API...
  }

  virtual void write(char* path, char* text)
  {
    // Use Nintendo file IO API...
  }
};
```

Next, we turn `FileSystem` into a singleton:

```
class FileSystem
{
public:
  static FileSystem& instance();

  virtual ~FileSystem() {}
  virtual char* read(char* path) = 0;
  virtual void write(char* path, char* text) = 0;

protected:
  FileSystem() {}
};
```

The clever part is how the instance is created:

```
FileSystem& FileSystem::instance()
{
#if PLATFORM == PLAYSTATION3
  static FileSystem *instance = new PS3FileSystem();
#elif PLATFORM == WII
  static FileSystem *instance = new WiiFileSystem();
#endif

  return *instance;
}
```

With a simple compiler switch, we bind our file system wrapper to the appropriate concrete type. Our entire codebase can access the file system using `FileSystem::instance()` without being coupled to any platform-specific code. That coupling is instead encapsulated within the implementation file for the `FileSystem` class itself.

This takes us about as far as most of us go when it comes to solving a problem like this. We've got a file system wrapper. It works reliably. It's available globally so every place that needs it can get to it. It's time to check in the code and celebrate with a tasty beverage.

## Why We Regret Using It

In the short term, the Singleton pattern is relatively benign. Like many design choices, we pay the cost in the long term. Once we've cast a few unnecessary singletons into cold hard code, here's the trouble we've bought ourselves:

## It's a global variable

When games were still written by a couple of guys in a garage, pushing the hardware was more important than ivory-tower software engineering principles. Old-school C and assembly coders used globals and statics without any trouble and shipped good games. As games got bigger and more complex, architecture and maintainability started to become the bottleneck. We struggled to ship games not because of hardware limitations, but because of *productivity* limitations.

So we moved to languages like C++ and started applying some of the hard-earned wisdom of our software engineer forebears. One lesson we learned is that global variables are bad for a variety of reasons:

- **They make it harder to reason about code.** Say we're tracking down a bug in a function someone else wrote. If that function doesn't touch any global state, we can wrap our heads around it just by understanding the body of the function and the arguments being passed to it.

  Now, imagine right in the middle of that function is a call to `SomeClass::getSomeGlobalData()`. To figure out what's going on, we have to hunt through the entire codebase to see what touches that global data. You don't really hate global state until you've had to `grep` a million lines of code at three in the morning trying to find the one errant call that's setting a static variable to the wrong value.

- **They encourage coupling.** The new coder on your team isn't familiar with your game's beautifully maintainable loosely coupled architecture, but he's just been given his first task: make boulders play sounds when they crash onto the ground. You and I know we don't want the physics code to be coupled to *audio* of all things, but he's just trying to get his task done. Unfortunately for us, the instance of our `AudioPlayer` is globally visible. So, one little `#include` later, and our new guy has compromised a carefully constructed architecture.

  Without a global instance of the audio player, even if he *did* `#include` the header, he still wouldn't be able to do anything with it. That difficulty sends a clear message to him that those two modules should not know about each other and that he needs to find another way to solve his problem. *By controlling access to instances, you control coupling.*

- **They aren't concurrency-friendly.** The days of games running on a simple single-core CPU are pretty much over. Code today must at the very least *work* in a multi-threaded way even if it doesn't take

Computer scientists call functions that don't access or modify global state "pure" functions. Pure functions are easier to reason about, easier for the compiler to optimize, and let you do neat things like memoization where you cache and reuse the results from previous calls to the function.

While there are challenges to using purity exclusively, the benefits are enticing enough that computer scientists have created languages like Haskell that *only* allow pure functions.

full advantage of concurrency. When we make something global, we've created a chunk of memory that every thread can see and poke at, whether or not they know what other threads are doing to it. That path leads to deadlocks, race conditions, and other hell-to-fix thread-synchronization bugs.

Issues like these are enough to scare us away from declaring a global variable, and thus the Singleton pattern too, but that still doesn't tell us how we *should* design the game. How do you architect a game without global state?

There are some extensive answers to that question (most of this book in many ways *is* an answer to just that), but they aren't apparent or easy to come by. In the meantime, we have to get games out the door. The Singleton pattern looks like a panacea. It's in a book on object-oriented design patterns, so it *must* be architecturally sound, right? And it lets us design software the way we have been doing for years.

Unfortunately, it's more placebo than cure. If you scan the list of problems that globals cause, you'll notice that the Singleton pattern doesn't solve any of them. That's because a singleton *is* global state—it's just encapsulated in a class.

## It solves two problems even when you just have one

The word "and" in the Gang of Four's description of Singleton is a bit strange. Is this pattern a solution to one problem or two? What if we have only one of those? Ensuring a single instance is useful, but who says we want to let *everyone* poke at it? Likewise, global access is convenient, but that's true even for a class that allows multiple instances.

The latter of those two problems, convenient access, is almost always why we turn to the Singleton pattern. Consider a logging class. Most modules in the game can benefit from being able to log diagnostic information. However, passing an instance of our Log class to every single function clutters the method signature and distracts from the intent of the code.

The obvious fix is to make our Log class a singleton. Every function can then go straight to the class itself to get an instance. But when we do that, we inadvertently acquire a strange little restriction. All of a sudden, we can no longer create more than one logger.

At first, this isn't a problem. We're writing only a single log file, so we only need one instance anyway. Then, deep in the development cycle, we run into trouble. Everyone on the team has been using the logger for their own diagnostics, and the log file has become a massive dumping ground.

Programmers have to wade through pages of text just to find the one entry they care about.

We'd like to fix this by partitioning the logging into multiple files. To do this, we'll have separate loggers for different game domains: online, UI, audio, gameplay. But we can't. Not only does our Log class no longer allow us to create multiple instances, that design limitation is entrenched in every single call site that uses it:

```
Log::instance().write("Some event.");
```

In order to make our Log class support multiple instantiation (like it originally did), we'll have to fix both the class itself and every line of code that mentions it. Our convenient access isn't so convenient anymore.

It could be even worse than this. Imagine your Log class is in a library being shared across several *games*. Now, to change the design, you'll have to coordinate the change across several groups of people, most of whom have neither the time nor the motivation to fix it.

## Lazy initialization takes control away from you

In the desktop PC world of virtual memory and soft performance requirements, lazy initialization is a smart trick. Games are a different animal. Initializing a system can take time: allocating memory, loading resources, etc. If initializing the audio system takes a few hundred milliseconds, we need to control when that's going to happen. If we let it lazy-initialize itself the first time a sound plays, that could be in the middle of an action-packed part of the game, causing visibly dropped frames and stuttering gameplay.

See Object Pool (p. 305) for a detailed explanation of memory fragmentation.

Likewise, games generally need to closely control how memory is laid out in the heap to avoid fragmentation. If our audio system allocates a chunk of heap when it initializes, we want to know *when* that initialization is going to happen, so that we can control *where* in the heap that memory will live.

Because of these two problems, most games I've seen don't rely on lazy initialization. Instead, they implement the Singleton pattern like this:

```
class FileSystem
{
public:
  static FileSystem& instance() { return instance_; }

private:
  FileSystem() {}

  static FileSystem instance_;
};
```

That solves the lazy initialization problem, but at the expense of discarding several singleton features that *do* make it better than a raw global variable.

With a static instance, we can no longer use polymorphism, and the class must be constructible at static initialization time. Nor can we free the memory that the instance is using when not needed.

Instead of creating a singleton, what we really have here is a simple static class. That isn't necessarily a bad thing, but if a static class is all you need, why not get rid of the `instance()` method entirely and use static functions instead? Calling `Foo::bar()` is simpler than `Foo::instance().bar()`, and also makes it clear that you really are dealing with static memory.

## What We Can Do Instead

If I've accomplished my goal so far, you'll think twice before you pull Singleton out of your toolbox the next time you have a problem. But you still have a problem that needs solving. What tool *should* you pull out? Depending on what you're trying to do, I have a few options for you to consider, but first...

### See if you need the class at all

Many of the singleton classes I see in games are "managers"—those nebulous classes that exist just to babysit other objects. I've seen codebases where it seems like *every* class has a manager: Monster, MonsterManager, Particle, ParticleManager, Sound, SoundManager, ManagerManager. Sometimes, for variety, they'll throw a "System" or "Engine" in there, but it's still the same idea.

While caretaker classes are sometimes useful, often they just reflect unfamiliarity with OOP. Consider these two contrived classes:

```
class Bullet
{
public:
  int getX() const { return x_; }
  int getY() const { return y_; }
  void setX(int x) { x_ = x; }
  void setY(int y) { y_ = y; }

private:
  int x_,
  int y_;
};
```

The usual argument for choosing singletons over static classes is that if you decide to change the static class into a non-static one later, you'll need to fix every call site. In theory, you don't have to do that with singletons because you could be passing the instance around and calling it like a normal instance method.

In practice, I've never seen it work that way. Everyone just does `Foo::instance().bar()` in one line. If we changed Foo to not be a singleton, we'd still have to touch every call site. Given that, I'd rather have a simpler class and a simpler syntax to call into it.

```
class BulletManager
{
public:
  Bullet* create(int x, int y)
  {
    Bullet* bullet = new Bullet();
    bullet->setX(x);
    bullet->setY(y);
    return bullet;
  }

  bool isOnScreen(Bullet& bullet)
  {
    return bullet.getX() >= 0 &&
           bullet.getY() >= 0 &&
           bullet.getX() < SCREEN_WIDTH &&
           bullet.getY() < SCREEN_HEIGHT;
  }

  void move(Bullet& bullet)
  {
    bullet.setX(bullet.getX() + 5);
  }
};
```

Maybe this example is a bit dumb, but I've seen plenty of code that reveals a design just like this after you scrape away the crusty details. If you look at this code, it's natural to think that BulletManager should be a singleton. After all, anything that has a Bullet will need the manager too, and how many instances of BulletManager do you need?

The answer here is *zero*, actually. Here's how we solve the "singleton" problem for our manager class:

```
class Bullet
{
public:
  Bullet(int x, int y)
  : x_(x), y_(y)
  {}

  bool isOnScreen()
  {
    return x_ >= 0 && x_ < SCREEN_WIDTH &&
           y_ >= 0 && y_ < SCREEN_HEIGHT;
  }

  void move() { x_ += 5; }

private:
  int x_, y_;
};
```

There we go. No manager, no problem. Poorly designed singletons are often "helpers" that add functionality to another class. If you can, just move all of that behavior into the class it helps. After all, OOP is about letting objects take care of themselves.

Outside of managers, though, there are other problems where we'd reach to Singleton for a solution. For each of those problems, there are some alternative solutions to consider.

## To limit a class to a single instance

This is one half of what the Singleton pattern gives you. As in our file system example, it can be critical to ensure there's only a single instance of a class. However, that doesn't necessarily mean we also want to provide *public*, *global* access to that instance. We may want to restrict access to certain areas of the code or even make it private to a single class. In those cases, providing a public global point of access weakens the architecture.

We want a way to ensure single instantiation *without* providing global access. There are a couple of ways to accomplish this. Here's one:

> For example, we may be wrapping our file system wrapper inside *another* layer of abstraction.

```
class FileSystem
{
public:
  FileSystem()
  {
    assert(!instantiated_);
    instantiated_ = true;
  }

  ~FileSystem() { instantiated_ = false; }

private:
  static bool instantiated_;
};

bool FileSystem::instantiated_ = false;
```

This class allows anyone to construct it, but it will assert and fail if you try to construct more than one instance. As long as the right code creates the instance first, then we've ensured no other code can either get at that instance or create their own. The class ensures the single instantiation requirement it cares about, but it doesn't dictate how the class should be used.

The downside with this implementation is that the check to prevent multiple instantiation is only done at *runtime*. The Singleton pattern, in contrast, guarantees a single instance at compile time by the very nature of the class's structure.

> An *assertion* function is a way of embedding a contract into your code. When assert() is called, it evaluates the expression passed to it. If it evaluates to true, then it does nothing and lets the game continue. If it evaluates to false, it immediately halts the game at that point. In a debug build, it will usually bring up the debugger or at least print out the file and line number where the assertion failed.
>
> An assert() means, "I assert that this should always be true. If it's not, that's a bug and I want to stop *now* so you can fix it." This lets you define contracts between regions of code. If a function asserts that one of its arguments is not NULL, that says, "The contract between me and the caller is that I will not be passed NULL."
>
> Assertions help us track down bugs as soon as the game does something unexpected, not later when that error finally manifests as something visibly wrong to the user. They are fences in your codebase, corralling bugs so that they can't escape from the code that created them.

## To provide convenient access to an instance

Convenient access is the main reason we reach for singletons. They make it easy to get our hands on an object we need to use in a lot of different places. That ease comes at a cost, though—it becomes equally easy to get our hands on the object in places where we *don't* want it being used.

The general rule is that we want variables to be as narrowly scoped as possible while still getting the job done. The smaller the scope an object has, the fewer places we need to keep in our head while we're working with it. Before we take the shotgun approach of a singleton object with *global* scope, let's consider other ways our codebase can get access to an object:

Some use the term "dependency injection" to refer to this. Instead of code reaching *out* and finding its dependencies by calling into something global, the dependencies are pushed *in* to the code that needs it through parameters. Others reserve "dependency injection" for more complex ways of providing dependencies to code.

- **Pass it in.** The simplest solution, and often the best, is to simply pass the object you need as an argument to the functions that need it. It's worth considering before we discard it as too cumbersome.

  Consider a function for rendering objects. In order to render, it needs access to an object that represents the graphics device and maintains the render state. It's very common to simply pass that in to all of the rendering functions, usually as a parameter named something like `context`.

  On the other hand, some objects don't belong in the signature of a method. For example, a function that handles AI may need to also write to a log file, but logging isn't its core concern. It would be strange to see `Log` show up in its argument list, so for cases like that we'll want to consider other options.

The term for things like logging that appear scattered throughout a codebase is "cross-cutting concern". Handling cross-cutting concerns gracefully is a continuing architectural challenge, especially in statically typed languages.

*Aspect-oriented programming* was designed to address these concerns.

- **Get it from the base class.** Many game architectures have shallow but wide inheritance hierarchies, often only one level deep. For example, you may have a base `GameObject` class with derived classes for each enemy or object in the game. With architectures like this, a large portion of the game code will live in these "leaf" derived classes. This means that all these classes already have access to the same thing: their `GameObject` base class. We can use that to our advantage:

```
class GameObject
{
protected:
  Log& log() { return log_; }

private:
  static Log& log_;
};
```

**84**  Singleton – **What We Can Do Instead**

```
class Enemy : public GameObject
{
  void doSomething()
  {
    getLog().write("I can log!");
  }
};
```

This ensures nothing outside of `GameObject` has access to its `Log` object, but every derived entity does using `log()`. This pattern of letting derived objects implement themselves in terms of protected methods provided to them is covered in the Subclass Sandbox chapter (p. 181).

This raises the question, "how does `GameObject` get the `Log` instance?" A simple solution is to have the base class simply create and own a static instance.

If you don't want the base class to take such an active role, you can provide an initialization function to pass it in or use the Service Locator pattern (p. 251) to find it.

- **Get it from something already global.** The goal of removing *all* global state is admirable, but rarely practical. Most codebases will still have a couple of globally available objects, such as a single `Game` or `World` object representing the entire game state.

  We can reduce the number of global classes by piggybacking on existing ones like that. Instead of making singletons out of `Log`, `FileSystem`, and `AudioPlayer`, do this:

```
class Game
{
public:
  static Game& instance() { return instance_; }

  Log&          log()         { return *log_; }
  FileSystem&   fileSystem()  { return *files_; }
  AudioPlayer&  audioPlayer() { return *audio_; }

  // Functions to set log_, et. al. ...

private:
  static Game instance_;
  Log          *log_;
  FileSystem   *files_;
  AudioPlayer  *audio_;
};
```

With this, only `Game` is globally available. Functions can get to the other systems through it:

```
Game::instance().getAudioPlayer().play(LOUD_BANG);
```

If, later, the architecture is changed to support multiple `Game` instances (perhaps for streaming or testing purposes), `Log`, `FileSystem`, and `AudioPlayer` are all unaffected—they won't even know the difference. The downside with this, of course, is that more code ends up coupled to

Purists will claim this violates the Law of Demeter. I claim that's still better than a giant pile of singletons.

`Game` itself. If a class just needs to play sound, our example still requires it to know about the world in order to get to the audio player.

We solve this with a hybrid solution. Code that already knows about `Game` can simply access `AudioPlayer` directly from it. For code that doesn't, we provide access to `AudioPlayer` using one of the other options described here.

- **Get it from a Service Locator.** So far, we're assuming the global class is some regular concrete class like `Game`. Another option is to define a class whose sole reason for being is to give global access to objects. This common pattern is called a Service Locator and gets its own chapter (p. 251).

## What's Left for Singleton

The question remains, where *should* we use the real Singleton pattern? Honestly, I've never used the full Gang of Four implementation in a game. To ensure single instantiation, I usually simply use a static class. If that doesn't work, I'll use a static flag to check at runtime that only one instance of the class is constructed.

There are a couple of other chapters in this book that can also help here. The Subclass Sandbox pattern (p. 181) gives instances of a class access to some shared state without making it globally available. The Service Locator pattern (p. 251) *does* make an object globally available, but it gives you more flexibility with how that object is configured.

# State

# 7

*"Allow an object to alter its behavior when its internal state changes. The object will appear to change its class."*

Confession time: I went a little overboard and packed way too much into this chapter. It's ostensibly about the State design pattern, but I can't talk about that and games without going into the more fundamental concept of *finite state machines* (or "FSMs"). But then once I went there, I figured I might as well introduce *hierarchical state machines* and *pushdown automata*.

That's a lot to cover, so to keep things as short as possible, the code samples here leave out a few details that you'll have to fill in on your own. I hope they're still clear enough for you to get the big picture.

Don't feel sad if you've never heard of a state machine. While well known to AI and compiler hackers, they aren't that familiar to other programming circles. I think they should be more widely known, so I'm going to throw them at a different kind of problem here.

This pairing echoes the early days of artificial intelligence. In the '50s and '60s, much of AI research was focused on language processing. Many of the techniques compilers now use for parsing programming languages were invented for parsing human languages.

## We've All Been There

We're working on a little side-scrolling platformer. Our job is to implement the heroine that is the player's avatar in the game world. That means making her respond to user input. Push the B button and she should jump. Simple enough:

```
void Heroine::handleInput(Input input)
{
  if (input == PRESS_B)
  {
    yVelocity_ = JUMP_VELOCITY;
    setGraphics(IMAGE_JUMP);
  }
}
```

Spot the bug? There's nothing to prevent "air jumping"—keep hammering B while she's in the air, and she will float forever. The simple fix is to add an isJumping_ Boolean field to Heroine that tracks when she's jumping, and then do:

There should also be code that sets isJumping_ back to false when the heroine touches the ground. I've omitted that here for brevity's sake.

```
void Heroine::handleInput(Input input)
{
  if (input == PRESS_B)
  {
    if (!isJumping_)
    {
      isJumping_ = true;
      // Jump...
    }
  }
}
```

Next, we want the heroine to duck if the player presses down while she's on the ground and stand back up when the button is released:

```
void Heroine::handleInput(Input input)
{
  if (input == PRESS_B)
  {
    // Jump if not jumping...
  }
  else if (input == PRESS_DOWN)
  {
    if (!isJumping_)
    {
      setGraphics(IMAGE_DUCK);
    }
  }
  else if (input == RELEASE_DOWN)
  {
    setGraphics(IMAGE_STAND);
  }
}
```

Spot the bug this time? With this code, the player could:

1. Press down to duck.

2. Press B to jump from a ducking position.

3. Release down while still in the air.

The heroine will switch to her standing graphic in the middle of the jump. Time for another flag...

```
void Heroine::handleInput(Input input)
{
  if (input == PRESS_B)
  {
    if (!isJumping_ && !isDucking_)
    {
      // Jump...
    }
  }
  else if (input == PRESS_DOWN)
  {
    if (!isJumping_)
    {
      isDucking_ = true;
      setGraphics(IMAGE_DUCK);
    }
  }
  else if (input == RELEASE_DOWN)
  {
    if (isDucking_)
    {
      isDucking_ = false;
      setGraphics(IMAGE_STAND);
    }
  }
}
```

Next, it would be cool if the heroine did a dive attack if the player presses down in the middle of a jump:

```
void Heroine::handleInput(Input input)
{
  if (input == PRESS_B)
  {
    if (!isJumping_ && !isDucking_)
    {
      // Jump...
    }
  }
  else if (input == PRESS_DOWN)
  {
    if (!isJumping_)
    {
      isDucking_ = true;
      setGraphics(IMAGE_DUCK);
    }
    else
    {
      isJumping_ = false;
      setGraphics(IMAGE_DIVE);
    }
  }
  else if (input == RELEASE_DOWN)
  {
    if (isDucking_)
    {
      // Stand...
    }
  }
}
```

Bug hunting time again. Find it? We check that you can't air jump while jumping, but not while diving. Yet another field…

Something is clearly wrong with our approach. Every time we touch this handful of code, we break something. We need to add a bunch more moves—we haven't even added *walking* yet—but at this rate, it will collapse into a heap of bugs before we're done with it.

## Finite State Machines to the Rescue

In a fit of frustration, you sweep everything off your desk except a pen and paper and start drawing a flowchart. You draw a box for each thing the heroine can be doing: standing, jumping, ducking, and diving. When she can respond to a button press in one of those states, you draw an arrow from that box, label it with that button, and connect it to the state she changes to.

Those coders you idolize who always seem to create flawless code aren't simply superhuman programmers. Instead, they have an intuition about which *kinds* of code are error-prone, and they steer away from them.
Complex branching and mutable state—fields that change over time—are two of those error-prone kinds of code, and the examples above have both.

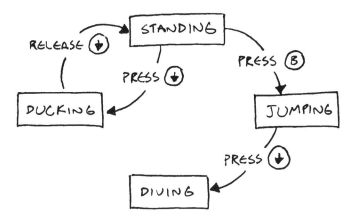

*Figure 7.1 – A flowchart for a state machine*

Congratulations, you've just created a *finite state machine*. These came out of a branch of computer science called *automata theory* whose family of data structures also includes the famous Turing machine. FSMs are the simplest member of that family. The gist is:

- **You have a fixed *set of states* that the machine can be in.** For our example, that's standing, jumping, ducking, and diving.

- **The machine can only be in *one* state at a time.** Our heroine can't be jumping and standing simultaneously. In fact, preventing that is one reason we're going to use an FSM.

- **A sequence of *inputs or events* is sent to the machine.** In our example, that's the raw button presses and releases.

- **Each state has a set of *transitions*, each associated with an input and pointing to a state.** When an input comes in, if it matches a transition for the current state, the machine changes to the state that transition points to.

  For example, pressing down while standing transitions to the ducking state. Pressing down while jumping transitions to diving. If no transition is defined for an input on the current state, the input is ignored.

In their pure form, that's the whole banana: states, inputs, and transitions. You can draw it out like a little flowchart. Unfortunately, the compiler doesn't recognize our scribbles, so how do we go about *implementing* one? The Gang of Four's State pattern is one method—which we'll get to—but let's start simpler.

My favorite analogy for FSMs is the old text adventure games like Zork. You have a world of rooms that are connected to each other by exits. You explore them by entering commands like "go north".

This maps directly to a state machine: Each room is a state. The room you're in is the current state. Each room's exits are its transitions. The navigation commands are the inputs.

## Enums and Switches

One problem our `Heroine` class has is some combinations of those Boolean fields aren't valid: `isJumping_` and `isDucking_` should never both be true, for example. When you have a handful of flags where only one is `true` at a time, that's a hint that what you really want is an `enum`.

In this case, that `enum` is exactly the set of states for our FSM, so let's define that:

```
enum State
{
  STATE_STANDING,
  STATE_JUMPING,
  STATE_DUCKING,
  STATE_DIVING
};
```

Instead of a bunch of flags, `Heroine` will just have one `state_` field. We also flip the order of our branching. In the previous code, we switched on input, *then* on state. This kept the code for handling one button press together, but it smeared around the code for one state. We want to keep that together, so we switch on state first. That gives us:

```
void Heroine::handleInput(Input input)
{
  switch (state_)
  {
    case STATE_STANDING:
      if (input == PRESS_B)
      {
        state_ = STATE_JUMPING;
        yVelocity_ = JUMP_VELOCITY;
        setGraphics(IMAGE_JUMP);
      }
      else if (input == PRESS_DOWN)
      {
        state_ = STATE_DUCKING;
        setGraphics(IMAGE_DUCK);
      }
      break;

    // Other states...
  }
}
```

We can fill in the other states like so:

```
void Heroine::handleInput(Input input)
{
  switch (state_)
  {
    // Standing state...

    case STATE_JUMPING:
      if (input == PRESS_DOWN)
      {
        state_ = STATE_DIVING;
        setGraphics(IMAGE_DIVE);
      }
      break;

    case STATE_DUCKING:
      if (input == RELEASE_DOWN)
      {
        state_ = STATE_STANDING;
        setGraphics(IMAGE_STAND);
      }
      break;
  }
}
```

This seems trivial, but it's a real improvement over the previous code. We still have some conditional branching, but we simplified the mutable state to a single field. All of the code for handling a single state is now nicely lumped together. This is the simplest way to implement a state machine and is fine for some uses.

In particular, the heroine can no longer be in an *invalid* state. With the Boolean flags, some sets of values were possible but meaningless. With the enum, each value is valid.

Your problem may outgrow this solution, though. Say we want to add a move where our heroine can duck for a while to charge up and unleash a special attack. While she's ducking, we need to track the charge time.

We add a `chargeTime_` field to `Heroine` to store how long the attack has charged. Assume we already have an `update()` that gets called each frame. In there, we add:

If you guessed that this is the Update Method pattern (p. 139), you win a prize!

```
void Heroine::update()
{
  if (state_ == STATE_DUCKING)
  {
    chargeTime_++;
    if (chargeTime_ > MAX_CHARGE)
    {
      superBomb();
    }
  }
}
```

We need to reset the timer when she starts ducking, so we modify
handleInput():

```
void Heroine::handleInput(Input input)
{
  switch (state_)
  {
    case STATE_STANDING:
      if (input == PRESS_DOWN)
      {
        state_ = STATE_DUCKING;
        chargeTime_ = 0;
        setGraphics(IMAGE_DUCK);
      }

      // Handle other inputs...
      break;

      // Other states...
  }
}
```

All in all, to add this charge attack, we had to modify two methods and
add a chargeTime_ field onto Heroine even though it's only meaningful
while in the ducking state. What we'd prefer is to have all of that code and
data nicely wrapped up in one place. The Gang of Four has us covered.

## The State Pattern

For people deeply into the object-oriented mindset, every conditional
branch is an opportunity to use dynamic dispatch (in other words a
virtual method call in C++). I think you can go too far down that rabbit
hole. Sometimes an if is all you need.

But in our example, we've reached a tipping point where something
object-oriented is a better fit. That gets us to the State pattern. The pattern
the Gang of Four describe looks like this when applied to our heroine:

### A state interface

First, we define an interface for the state. Every bit of behavior that is state-
dependent—every place we had a switch before—becomes a virtual
method in that interface. For us, that's handleInput() and update():

There's a historical basis for this. Many
of the original object-oriented apostles,
the Gang of Four, came from Smalltalk.
There, ifThen: is just a method
you invoke on the condition, which is
implemented differently by the true
and false objects.

```
class HeroineState
{
public:
  virtual ~HeroineState() {}
  virtual void handleInput(Heroine& heroine,
                           Input input) {}
  virtual void update(Heroine& heroine) {}
};
```

## Classes for each state

For each state, we define a class that implements the interface. Its methods define the heroine's behavior when in that state. In other words, take each case from the earlier switch statements and move them into their state's class. For example:

```
class DuckingState : public HeroineState
{
public:
  DuckingState()
  : chargeTime_(0)
  {}

  virtual void handleInput(Heroine& heroine,
                           Input input) {
    if (input == RELEASE_DOWN)
    {
      // Change to standing state...
      heroine.setGraphics(IMAGE_STAND);
    }
  }

  virtual void update(Heroine& heroine) {
    chargeTime_++;
    if (chargeTime_ > MAX_CHARGE)
    {
      heroine.superBomb();
    }
  }

private:
  int chargeTime_;
};
```

Note that we also moved chargeTime_ out of Heroine and into the DuckingState class. This is great—that piece of data is only meaningful while in that state, and now our object model reflects that explicitly.

### Delegate to the state

Next, we give the `Heroine` a pointer to her current state, lose each big `switch`, and delegate to the state instead:

```
class Heroine
{
public:
  virtual void handleInput(Input input)
  {
    state_->handleInput(*this, input);
  }

  virtual void update() { state_->update(*this); }

  // Other methods...
private:
  HeroineState* state_;
};
```

In order to "change state", we just need to assign `state_` to point to a different `HeroineState` object. That's the State pattern in its entirety.

## Where Are the State Objects?

I did gloss over one bit here. To change states, we need to assign `state_` to point to the new one, but where does that object come from? With our `enum` implementation, that was a no-brainer—`enum` values are primitives like numbers. But now our states are classes, which means we need an actual instance to point to. There are two common answers to this:

### Static states

If the state object doesn't have any other fields, then the only data it stores is a pointer to the internal virtual method table so that its methods can be called. In that case, there's no reason to ever have more than one instance of it. Every instance would be identical anyway.

In that case, you can make a single *static* instance. Even if you have a bunch of FSMs all going at the same time in that same state, they can all point to the same instance since it has nothing machine-specific about it.

*Where* you put that static instance is up to you. Find a place that makes sense. For no particular reason, let's put ours inside the base state class:

```
class HeroineState
{
public:
  static StandingState standing;
  static DuckingState ducking;
  static JumpingState jumping;
  static DivingState diving;

  // Other code...
};
```

Each of those static fields is the one instance of that state that the game uses. To make the heroine jump, the standing state would do something like:

```
if (input == PRESS_B)
{
  heroine.state_ = &HeroineState::jumping;
  heroine.setGraphics(IMAGE_JUMP);
}
```

### Instantiated states

Sometimes, though, this doesn't fly. A static state won't work for the ducking state. It has a `chargeTime_` field, and that's specific to the heroine that happens to be ducking. This may coincidentally work in our game if there's only one heroine, but if we try to add two-player co-op and have two heroines on screen at the same time, we'll have problems.

In that case, we have to create a state object when we transition to it. This lets each FSM have its own instance of the state. Of course, if we're allocating a *new* state, that means we need to free the *current* one. We have to be careful here, since the code that's triggering the change is in a method in the current state. We don't want to delete `this` out from under ourselves.

Instead, we'll allow `handleInput()` in `HeroineState` to optionally return a new state. When it does, `Heroine` will delete the old one and swap in the new one, like so:

When you dynamically allocate states, you may have to worry about fragmentation. The Object Pool pattern (p. 305) can help.

```
void Heroine::handleInput(Input input)
{
  HeroineState* state = state_->handleInput(
      *this, input);
  if (state != NULL)
  {
    delete state_;
    state_ = state;
  }
}
```

That way, we don't delete the previous state until we've returned from its method. Now, the standing state can transition to ducking by creating a new instance:

```
HeroineState* StandingState::handleInput(
    Heroine& heroine, Input input)
{
  if (input == PRESS_DOWN)
  {
    // Other code...
    return new DuckingState();
  }

  // Stay in this state.
  return NULL;
}
```

When I can, I prefer to use static states since they don't burn memory and CPU cycles allocating objects each state change. For states that are more, uh, *stateful*, though, this is the way to go.

## Enter and Exit Actions

The goal of the State pattern is to encapsulate all of the behavior and data for one state in a single class. We're partway there, but we still have some loose ends. When the heroine changes state, we also switch her sprite. Right now, that code is owned by the state she's switching *from*. When she goes from ducking to standing, the ducking state sets her image:

```
HeroineState* DuckingState::handleInput(
    Heroine& heroine, Input input)
{
  if (input == RELEASE_DOWN)
  {
    heroine.setGraphics(IMAGE_STAND);
    return new StandingState();
  }

  // Other code...
}
```

What we really want is each state to control its own graphics. We can handle that by giving the state an *entry action*:

```
class StandingState : public HeroineState
{
public:
  virtual void enter(Heroine& heroine)
  {
    heroine.setGraphics(IMAGE_STAND);
  }

  // Other code...
};
```

Back in `Heroine`, we modify the code for handling state changes to call
that on the new state:

```
void Heroine::handleInput(Input input)
{
  HeroineState* state = state_->handleInput(
      *this, input);
  if (state != NULL)
  {
    delete state_;
    state_ = state;

    // Call the enter action on the new state.
    state_->enter(*this);
  }
}
```

This lets us simplify the ducking code to:

```
HeroineState* DuckingState::handleInput(
    Heroine& heroine, Input input)
{
  if (input == RELEASE_DOWN)
  {
    return new StandingState();
  }

  // Other code...
}
```

All it does is switch to standing and the standing state takes care of the
graphics. Now our states really are encapsulated. One particularly nice
thing about entry actions is that they run when you enter the state
regardless of which state you're coming *from*.

Most real-world state graphs have multiple transitions into the same
state. For example, our heroine will also end up standing after she
lands a jump or dive. That means we would end up duplicating some
code everywhere that transition occurs. Entry actions give us a place to
consolidate that.

We can, of course, also extend this to support an *exit action*. This is just a method we call on the state we're *leaving* right before we switch to the new state.

## What's the Catch?

I've spent all this time selling you on FSMs, and now I'm going to pull the rug out from under you. Everything I've said so far is true, and FSMs are a good fit for some problems. But their greatest virtue is also their greatest flaw.

State machines help you untangle hairy code by enforcing a very constrained structure on it. All you've got is a fixed set of states, a single current state, and some hardcoded transitions.

If you try using a state machine for something more complex like game AI, you will slam face-first into the limitations of that model. Thankfully, our forebears have found ways to dodge some of those barriers. I'll close this chapter out by walking you through a couple of them.

A finite state machine isn't even *Turing complete*. Automata theory describes computation using a series of abstract models, each more complex than the previous. A *Turing machine* is one of the most expressive models.

"Turing complete" means a system (usually a programming language) is powerful enough to implement a Turing machine in it, which means all Turing complete languages are, in some ways, equally expressive. FSMs are not flexible enough to be in that club.

## Concurrent State Machines

We've decided to give our heroine the ability to carry a gun. When she's packing heat, she can still do everything she could before: run, jump, duck, etc. But she also needs to be able to fire her weapon while doing it.

If we want to stick to the confines of an FSM, we have to *double* the number of states we have. For each existing state, we'll need another one for doing the same thing while she's armed: standing, standing with gun, jumping, jumping with gun, you get the idea.

Add a couple of more weapons and the number of states explodes combinatorially. Not only is it a huge number of states, it's a huge amount of redundancy: the unarmed and armed states are almost identical except for the little bit of code to handle firing.

If we want to cram $n$ states for what she's doing and $m$ states for what she's carrying into a single machine, we need $n \times m$ states. With two machines, it's just $n + m$.

The problem is that we've jammed two pieces of state—what she's *doing* and what she's *carrying*—into a single machine. To model all possible combinations, we would need a state for each *pair*. The fix is obvious: have two separate state machines.

We keep our original state machine for what she's doing and leave it alone. Then we define a separate state machine for what she's carrying. Heroine will have *two* "state" references, one for each, like:

```
class Heroine
{
  // Other code...

private:
  HeroineState* state_;
  HeroineState* equipment_;
};
```

When the heroine delegates inputs to the states, she hands it to both of them:

```
void Heroine::handleInput(Input input)
{
  state_->handleInput(*this, input);
  equipment_->handleInput(*this, input);
}
```

For illustrative purposes, we're using the full State pattern for her equipment. In practice, since it only has two states, a Boolean flag would work too.

Each state machine can then respond to inputs, spawn behavior, and change its state independently of the other machine. When the two sets of states are mostly unrelated, this works well.

In practice, you'll find a few cases where the states do interact. For example, maybe she can't fire while jumping, or maybe she can't do a dive attack if she's armed. To handle that, in the code for one state, you'll probably just do some crude if tests on the *other* machine's state to coordinate them. It's not the most elegant solution, but it gets the job done.

A more full-featured system would probably have a way for one state machine to *consume* an input so that the other doesn't receive it. That would prevent both machines from erroneously trying to respond to the same input.

## Hierarchical State Machines

After fleshing out our heroine's behavior some more, she'll likely have a bunch of similar states. For example, she may have standing, walking, running, and sliding states. In any of those, pressing B jumps and pressing down ducks.

With a simple state machine implementation, we have to duplicate that code in each of those states. It would be better if we could implement that once and reuse it across all of the states.

If this was just object-oriented code instead of a state machine, one way to share code across those states would be using inheritance. We could define a class for an "on ground" state that handles jumping and ducking. Standing, walking, running, and sliding would then inherit from that and add their own additional behavior.

It turns out, this is a common structure called a *hierarchical state machine*. A state can have a *superstate* (making itself a *substate*). When

This has both good and bad implications. Inheritance is a powerful means of code reuse, but it's also a very strong coupling between two chunks of code. It's a big hammer, so swing it carefully.

an event comes in, if the substate doesn't handle it, it rolls up the chain of superstates. In other words, it works just like overriding inherited methods.

In fact, if we're using the State pattern to implement our FSM, we can use class inheritance to implement the hierarchy. Define a base class for the superstate:

```
class OnGroundState : public HeroineState
{
public:
  virtual void handleInput(Heroine& heroine,
                           Input input)
  {
    if (input == PRESS_B) // Jump...
    else if (input == PRESS_DOWN) // Duck...
    }
  }
};
```

And then each substate inherits it:

```
class DuckingState : public OnGroundState
{
public:
  virtual void handleInput(Heroine& heroine,
                           Input input)
  {
    if (input == RELEASE_DOWN)
    {
      // Stand up...
    }
    else
    {
      // Didn't handle input, so walk up hierarchy.
      OnGroundState::handleInput(heroine, input);
    }
  }
};
```

This isn't the only way to implement the hierarchy, of course. If you aren't using the Gang of Four's State pattern, this won't work. Instead, you can model the current state's chain of superstates explicitly using a *stack* of states instead of a single state in the main class.

The current state is the one on the top of the stack, under that is its immediate superstate, and then *that* state's superstate and so on. When you dish out some state-specific behavior, you start at the top of the stack and walk down until one of the states handles it. (If none do, you ignore it.)

# Pushdown Automata

There's another common extension to finite state machines that also uses a stack of states. Confusingly, the stack represents something entirely different, and is used to solve a different problem.

The problem is that finite state machines have no concept of *history*. You know what state you *are* in, but have no memory of what state you *were* in. There's no easy way to go back to a previous state.

Here's an example: Earlier, we let our fearless heroine arm herself to the teeth. When she fires her gun, we need a new state that plays the firing animation and spawns the bullet and any visual effects. So we slap together a `FiringState` and make all of the states that she can fire from transition into that when the fire button is pressed.

Since this behavior is duplicated across several states, it may also be a good place to use a hierarchical state machine to reuse that code.

The tricky part is what state she transitions to *after* firing. She can pop off a round while standing, running, jumping, and ducking. When the firing sequence is complete, she should transition back to what she was doing before.

If we're sticking with a vanilla FSM, we've already forgotten what state she was in. To keep track of it, we'd have to define a slew of nearly identical states — firing while standing, firing while running, firing while jumping, and so on — just so that each one can have a hardcoded transition that goes back to the right state when it's done.

What we'd really like is a way to *store* the state she was in before firing and then *recall* it later. Again, automata theory is here to help. The relevant data structure is called a *pushdown automaton*.

Where a finite state machine has a *single* pointer to a state, a pushdown automaton has a *stack* of them. In an FSM, transitioning to a new state *replaces* the previous one. A pushdown automaton lets you do that, but it also gives you two additional operations:

- You can *push* a new state onto the stack. The "current" state is always the one on top of the stack, so this transitions to the new state. But it leaves the previous state directly under it on the stack instead of discarding it.

- You can *pop* the topmost state off the stack. That state is discarded, and the state under it becomes the new current state.

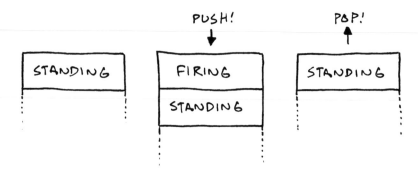

*Figure 7.2 – Pushing and popping, not the same as popping and locking*

This is just what we need for firing. We create a *single* firing state. When the fire button is pressed while in any other state, we *push* the firing state onto the stack. When the firing animation is done, we *pop* that state off, and the pushdown automaton automatically transitions us right back to the state we were in before.

## So How Useful Are They?

Even with those common extensions to state machines, they are still pretty limited. The trend these days in game AI is more toward exciting things like *behavior trees* and *planning systems*. If complex AI is what you're interested in, all this chapter has done is whet your appetite. You'll want to read other books to satisfy it.

This doesn't mean finite state machines, pushdown automata, and other simple systems aren't useful. They're a good modeling tool for certain kinds of problems. Finite state machines are useful when:

- You have an entity whose behavior changes based on some internal state.

- That state can be rigidly divided into one of a relatively small number of distinct options.

- The entity responds to a series of inputs or events over time.

In games, they are most known for being used in AI, but they are also common in implementations of user input handling, navigating menu screens, parsing text, network protocols, and other asynchronous behavior.

# Sequencing Patterns

Videogames are exciting in large part because they take us somewhere else. For a few minutes (or, let's be honest with ourselves, much longer), we become inhabitants of a virtual world. Creating these worlds is one of the supreme delights of being a game programmer.

One aspect that most of these game worlds feature is *time*—the artificial world lives and breathes at its own cadence. As world builders, we must invent time and craft the gears that drive our game's great clock.

The patterns in this section are tools for doing just that. A Game Loop (p. 123) is the central axle that the clock spins on. Objects hear its ticking through Update Methods (p. 139). We can hide the computer's sequential nature behind a facade of snapshots of moments in time using Double Buffering (p. 107) so that the world appears to update simultaneously.

# Double Buffer

# 8

*Cause a series of sequential operations to appear instantaneous or simultaneous.*

## Motivation

In their hearts, computers are sequential beasts. Their power comes from being able to break down the largest tasks into tiny steps that can be performed one after another. Often, though, our users need to see things occur in a single instantaneous step or see multiple tasks performed simultaneously.

With threading and multi-core architectures this is becoming less true, but even with several cores, only a few operations are running concurrently.

A typical example, and one that every game engine must address, is rendering. When the game draws the world the users see, it does so one piece at a time—the mountains in the distance, the rolling hills, the trees, each in its turn. If the user *watched* the view draw incrementally like that, the illusion of a coherent world would be shattered. The scene must update smoothly and quickly, displaying a series of complete frames, each appearing instantly.

Double buffering solves this problem, but to understand how, we first need to review how a computer displays graphics.

## How computer graphics work (briefly)

This explanation is, err, "simplified". If you're a low-level hardware person and you're cringing right now, feel free to skip to the next section. You already know enough to understand the rest of the chapter. If you *aren't* that person, my goal here is to give you just enough context to understand the pattern we'll discuss later.

The specific mapping between byte values and colors is described by the *pixel format* and the *color depth* of the system. In most gaming consoles today, each pixel gets 32 bits: eight each for the red, green, and blue channels, and another eight left over for various other purposes.

A video display like a computer monitor draws one pixel at a time. It sweeps across each row of pixels from left to right and then moves down to the next row. When it reaches the bottom right corner, it scans back up to the top left and starts all over again. It does this so fast — around sixty times a second—that our eyes can't see the scanning. To us, it's a single static field of colored pixels — an image.

You can think of this process like a tiny hose that pipes pixels to the display. Individual colors go into the back of the hose, and it sprays them out across the display, one bit of color to each pixel in its turn. So how does the hose know what colors go where?

In most computers, the answer is that it pulls them from a *framebuffer*. A framebuffer is an array of pixels in memory, a chunk of RAM where each couple of bytes represents the color of a single pixel. As the hose sprays across the display, it reads in the color values from this array, one byte at a time.

Ultimately, in order to get our game to appear on screen, all we do is write to that array. All of the crazy advanced graphics algorithms we have boil down to just that: setting byte values in the framebuffer. But there's a little problem.

Earlier, I said computers are sequential. If the machine is executing a chunk of our rendering code, we don't expect it to be doing anything else at the same time. That's mostly accurate, but a couple of things *do* happen in the middle of our program running. One of those is that the video display will be reading from the framebuffer *constantly* while our game runs. This can cause a problem for us.

Let's say we want a happy face to appear on screen. Our program starts looping through the framebuffer, coloring pixels. What we don't realize is that the video driver is pulling from the framebuffer right as we're writing to it. As it scans across the pixels we've written, our face starts to appear, but then it outpaces us and moves into pixels we haven't written yet. The result is *tearing*, a hideous visual bug where you see half of something drawn on screen.

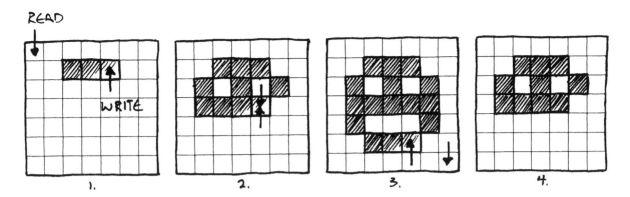

READ WRITE

1.   2.   3.   4.

*Figure 8.1 – Tearing during rendering*

This is why we need this pattern. Our program renders the pixels one at a time, but we need the display driver to see them all at once—in one frame the face isn't there, and in the next one it is. Double buffering solves this. I'll explain how by analogy.

We start drawing pixels just as the video driver starts reading from the framebuffer (1). The video driver eventually catches up to the renderer and then races past it to pixels we haven't written yet (2). We finish drawing (3), but the driver doesn't catch those new pixels.

The result (4) is that the user sees half of the drawing. The name "tearing" comes from the fact that it looks like the bottom half was torn off.

## Act 1, Scene 1

Imagine our users are watching a play produced by ourselves. As scene one ends and scene two starts, we need to change the stage setting. If we have the stagehands run on after the scene and start dragging props around, the illusion of a coherent place will be broken. We could dim the lights while we do that (which, of course, is what real theaters do), but the audience still knows *something* is going on. We want there to be no gap in time between scenes.

With a bit of real estate, we come up with this clever solution: we build *two* stages set up so the audience can see both. Each has its own set of lights. We'll call them stage A and stage B. Scene one is shown on stage A. Meanwhile, stage B is dark as the stagehands are setting up scene two. As soon as scene one ends, we cut the lights on stage A and bring them up on stage B. The audience looks to the new stage and scene two begins immediately.

At the same time, our stagehands are over on the now darkened stage *A*, striking scene one and setting up scene *three*. As soon as scene two ends, we switch the lights back to stage A again. We continue this process for the entire play, using the darkened stage as a work area where we can set up the next scene. Every scene transition, we just toggle the lights between the two stages. Our audience gets a continuous performance with no delay between scenes. They never see a stagehand.

Using a half-silvered mirror and some very smart layout, you could actually build this so that the two stages would appear to the audience in the same *place*. As soon as the lights switch, they would be looking at a different stage, but they would never have to change where they look. Building this is left as an exercise for the reader.

Not *all* games and consoles do this, though. Older and simpler consoles where memory is limited carefully sync their drawing to the video refresh instead. It's tricky.

**Back to the graphics**

That is exactly how double buffering works, and this process underlies the rendering system of just about every game you've ever seen. Instead of a single framebuffer, we have *two*. One of them represents the current frame, stage A in our analogy. It's the one the video hardware is reading from. The GPU can scan through it as much as it wants whenever it wants.

Meanwhile, our rendering code is writing to the *other* framebuffer. This is our darkened stage B. When our rendering code is done drawing the scene, it switches the lights by *swapping* the buffers. This tells the video hardware to start reading from the second buffer now instead of the first one. As long as it times that switch at the end of a refresh, we won't get any tearing, and the entire scene will appear all at once.

Meanwhile, the old framebuffer is now available for use. We start rendering the next frame onto it. Voilà!

# The Pattern

A **buffered class** encapsulates a **buffer**: a piece of state that can be modified. This buffer is edited incrementally, but we want all outside code to see the edit as a single atomic change. To do this, the class keeps *two* instances of the buffer: a **next buffer** and a **current buffer**.

When information is read *from* a buffer, it is always from the *current* buffer. When information is written *to* a buffer, it occurs on the *next* buffer. When the changes are complete, a **swap** operation swaps the next and current buffers instantly so that the new buffer is now publicly visible. The old current buffer is now available to be reused as the new next buffer.

# When to Use It

This pattern is one of those ones where you'll know when you need it. If you have a system that lacks double buffering, it will probably look visibly wrong (tearing, etc.) or will behave incorrectly. But saying, "you'll know when you need it" doesn't give you much to go on. More specifically, this pattern is appropriate when all of these are true:

- We have some state that is being modified incrementally.

- That same state may be accessed in the middle of modification.

- We want to prevent the code that's accessing the state from seeing the work in progress.

- We want to be able to read the state and we don't want to have to wait while it's being written.

## Keep in Mind

Unlike larger architectural patterns, double buffering exists at a lower implementation level. Because of this, it has fewer consequences for the rest of the codebase—most of the game won't even be aware of the difference. There are a couple of caveats, though.

### The swap itself takes time

Double-buffering requires a *swap* step once the state is done being modified. That operation must be atomic—no code can access *either* state while they are being swapped. Often, this is as quick as assigning a pointer, but if it takes longer to swap than it does to modify the state to begin with, then we haven't helped ourselves at all.

### We have to have two buffers

The other consequence of this pattern is increased memory usage. As its name implies, the pattern requires you to keep *two* copies of your state in memory at all times. On memory-constrained devices, this can be a heavy price to pay. If you can't afford two buffers, you may have to look into other ways to ensure your state isn't being accessed during modification.

## Sample Code

Now that we've got the theory, let's see how it works in practice. We'll write a very bare-bones graphics system that lets us draw pixels on a framebuffer. In most consoles and PCs, the video driver provides this low-level part of the graphics system, but implementing it by hand here will let us see what's going on. First up is the buffer itself:

```
class Framebuffer
{
public:
  // Constructor and methods...

private:
  static const int WIDTH = 160;
  static const int HEIGHT = 120;

  char pixels_[WIDTH * HEIGHT];
};
```

It has basic operations for clearing the entire buffer to a default color and setting the color of an individual pixel:

```
void Framebuffer::clear()
{
  for (int i = 0; i < WIDTH * HEIGHT; i++)
  {
    pixels_[i] = WHITE;
  }
}

void Framebuffer::draw(int x, int y)
{
  pixels_[(WIDTH * y) + x] = BLACK;
}
```

The little bit of arithmetic here maps from 2D coordinates to a linear array of pixels in row-major order.

It also has a function to expose the raw array of memory holding the pixel data:

```
const char* Framebuffer::getPixels()
{
  return pixels_;
}
```

We won't see this in the example, but the video driver will call that function frequently to stream memory from the buffer onto the screen. We wrap this raw buffer in a **Scene** class. It's job here is to render something by making a bunch of **draw()** calls on its buffer:

Specifically, it draws this artistic masterpiece:

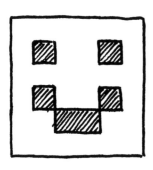

*Figure 8.2 – A face, sort of*

```
class Scene
{
public:
  void draw()
  {
    buffer_.clear();
    buffer_.draw(1, 1); buffer_.draw(4, 1);
    buffer_.draw(1, 3); buffer_.draw(2, 4);
    buffer_.draw(3, 4); buffer_.draw(4, 3);
  }

  Framebuffer& getBuffer() { return buffer_; }

private:
  Framebuffer buffer_;
};
```

Every frame, the game tells the scene to draw. The scene clears the buffer and then draws a bunch of pixels, one at a time. It also provides access to the internal buffer through **getBuffer()** so that the video driver can get to it.

This seems pretty straightforward, but if we leave it like this, we'll run into problems. The trouble is that the video driver can call `getPixels()` on the buffer at *any* point in time, even here:

```
buffer_.draw(1, 1); buffer_.draw(4, 1);
// <- Video driver reads pixels here!
buffer_.draw(1, 3); buffer_.draw(2, 4);
buffer_.draw(3, 4); buffer_.draw(4, 3);
```

When that happens, the user will see the eyes of the face, but the mouth will disappear for a single frame. In the next frame, it could get interrupted at some other point. The end result is horribly flickering graphics. We'll fix this with double buffering:

```
class Scene
{
public:
  Scene()
  : current_(&buffers_[0]),
    next_(&buffers_[1])
  {}

  void draw()
  {
    next_->clear();
    next_->draw(1, 1);
    // ...
    next_->draw(4, 3);
    swap();
  }

  Framebuffer& getBuffer() { return *current_; }

private:
  void swap()
  {
    // Just switch the pointers.
    Framebuffer* temp = current_;
    current_ = next_;
    next_ = temp;
  }

  Framebuffer  buffers_[2];
  Framebuffer* current_;
  Framebuffer* next_;
};
```

Now `Scene` has two buffers, stored in the `buffers_` array. We don't directly reference them from the array. Instead, there are two members, `next_` and `current_`, that point into the array. When we draw, we draw onto the next buffer, referenced by `next_`. When the video driver needs to get the pixels, it always accesses the *other* buffer through `current_`.

This way, the video driver never sees the buffer that we're working on. The only remaining piece of the puzzle is the call to `swap()` when the scene is done drawing the frame. That swaps the two buffers by simply switching the `next_` and `current_` references. The next time the video driver calls `getBuffer()`, it will get the new buffer we just finished drawing and put our recently drawn buffer on screen. No more tearing or unsightly glitches.

## Not just for graphics

The core problem that double buffering solves is state being accessed while it's being modified. There are two common causes of this. We've covered the first one with our graphics example—the state is directly accessed from code on another thread or interrupt.

There is another equally common cause, though: when the code *doing the modification* is accessing the same state that it's modifying. This can manifest in a variety of places, especially physics and AI where you have entities interacting with each other. Double-buffering is often helpful here too.

## Artificial unintelligence

Let's say we're building the behavioral system for, of all things, a game based on slapstick comedy. The game has a stage containing a bunch of actors that run around and get up to various hijinks and shenanigans. Here's our base actor:

```
class Actor
{
public:
  Actor() : slapped_(false) {}

  virtual ~Actor() {}
  virtual void update() = 0;

  void reset()      { slapped_ = false; }
  void slap()       { slapped_ = true; }
  bool wasSlapped() { return slapped_; }

private:
  bool slapped_;
};
```

Every frame, the game is responsible for calling `update()` on the actor so that it has a chance to do some processing. Critically, from the user's perspective, *all actors should appear to update simultaneously.*

This is an example of the Update Method pattern (p. 139).

Actors can also interact with each other, if by "interacting", we mean "they can slap each other around". When updating, the actor can call `slap()` on another actor to slap it and call `wasSlapped()` to determine if it has been slapped.

The actors need a stage where they can interact, so let's build that:

```cpp
class Stage
{
public:
  void add(Actor* actor, int index)
  {
    actors_[index] = actor;
  }

  void update()
  {
    for (int i = 0; i < NUM_ACTORS; i++)
    {
      actors_[i]->update();
      actors_[i]->reset();
    }
  }

private:
  static const int NUM_ACTORS = 3;

  Actor* actors_[NUM_ACTORS];
};
```

`Stage` lets us add actors, and provides a single `update()` call that updates each actor. To the user, actors appear to move simultaneously, but internally, they are updated one at a time.

The only other point to note is that each actor's "slapped" state is cleared immediately after updating. This is so that an actor only responds to a given slap once.

To get things going, let's define a concrete actor subclass. Our comedian here is pretty simple. He faces a single actor. Whenever he gets slapped—by anyone—he responds by slapping the actor he faces.

```
class Comedian : public Actor
{
public:
  void face(Actor* actor) { facing_ = actor; }

  virtual void update()
  {
    if (wasSlapped()) facing_->slap();
  }

private:
  Actor* facing_;
};
```

Now, let's throw some comedians on a stage and see what happens. We'll set up three comedians, each facing the next. The last one will face the first, in a big circle:

```
Stage stage;

Comedian* harry = new Comedian();
Comedian* baldy = new Comedian();
Comedian* chump = new Comedian();

harry->face(baldy);
baldy->face(chump);
chump->face(harry);

stage.add(harry, 0);
stage.add(baldy, 1);
stage.add(chump, 2);
```

The resulting stage is set up as shown in the following image. The arrows show who the actors are facing, and the numbers show their index in the stage's array.

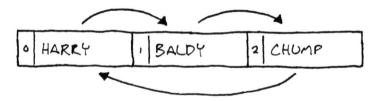

*Figure 8.3 – Violence in videogames*

We'll slap Harry to get things going and see what happens when we start processing:

```
harry->slap();
stage.update();
```

Remember that the `update()` function in `Stage` updates each actor in turn, so if we step through the code, we'll find that the following occurs:

```
Stage updates actor 0 (Harry)
  Harry was slapped, so he slaps Baldy
Stage updates actor 1 (Baldy)
  Baldy was slapped, so he slaps Chump
Stage updates actor 2 (Chump)
  Chump was slapped, so he slaps Harry
Stage update ends
```

In a single frame, our initial slap on Harry has propagated through all of the comedians. Now, to mix things up a bit, let's say we reorder the comedians within the stage's array but leave them facing each other the same way.

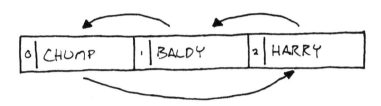

*Figure 8.4 – Violent retribution*

We'll leave the rest of the stage setup alone, but we'll replace the chunk of code where we add the actors to the stage with this:

```
stage.add(harry, 2);
stage.add(baldy, 1);
stage.add(chump, 0);
```

Let's see what happens when we run our experiment again:

```
Stage updates actor 0 (Chump)
  Chump was not slapped, so he does nothing
Stage updates actor 1 (Baldy)
  Baldy was not slapped, so he does nothing
Stage updates actor 2 (Harry)
  Harry was slapped, so he slaps Baldy
Stage update ends
```

Uh, oh. Totally different. The problem is straightforward. When we update the actors, we modify their "slapped" states, the exact same state we also *read* during the update. Because of this, changes to that state early in the update affect later parts of that *same* update step.

If you continue to update the stage, you'll see the slaps gradually cascade through the actors, one per frame. In the first frame, Harry slaps Baldy. In the next frame, Baldy slaps Chump, and so on.

The ultimate result is that an actor may respond to being slapped in either the *same* frame as the slap or in the *next* frame based entirely on how the two actors happen to be ordered on the stage. This violates our requirement that actors need to appear to run in parallel—the order that they update within a single frame shouldn't matter.

### Buffered slaps

Fortunately, our Double Buffer pattern can help. This time, instead of having two copies of a monolithic "buffer" object, we'll be buffering at a much finer granularity: each actor's "slapped" state:

```cpp
class Actor
{
public:
  Actor() : currentSlapped_(false) {}

  virtual ~Actor() {}
  virtual void update() = 0;

  void swap()
  {
    // Swap the buffer.
    currentSlapped_ = nextSlapped_;

    // Clear the new "next" buffer.
    nextSlapped_ = false;
  }

  void slap()        { nextSlapped_ = true; }
  bool wasSlapped() { return currentSlapped_; }

private:
  bool currentSlapped_;
  bool nextSlapped_;
};
```

Instead of a single `slapped_` state, each actor now has two. Just like the previous graphics example, the current state is used for reading, and the next state is used for writing.

The `reset()` function has been replaced with `swap()`. Now, right before clearing the swap state, it copies the next state into the current one, making it the new current state. This also requires a small change in `Stage`:

```
void Stage::update()
{
  for (int i = 0; i < NUM_ACTORS; i++)
  {
    actors_[i]->update();
  }

  for (int i = 0; i < NUM_ACTORS; i++)
  {
    actors_[i]->swap();
  }
}
```

The update() function now updates all of the actors and *then* swaps all of their states. The end result of this is that an actor will only see a slap in the frame *after* it was actually slapped. This way, the actors will behave the same no matter their order in the stage's array. As far as the user or any outside code can tell, all of the actors update simultaneously within a frame.

# Design Decisions

Double Buffer is pretty straightforward, and the examples we've seen so far cover most of the variations you're likely to encounter. There are two main decisions that come up when implementing this pattern.

### How are the buffers swapped?

The swap operation is the most critical step of the process since we must lock out all reading and modification of both buffers while it's occurring. To get the best performance, we want this to happen as quickly as possible.

- **Swap pointers or references to the buffer:**

  This is how our graphics example works, and it's the most common solution for double-buffering graphics.

  - *It's fast.* Regardless of how big the buffer is, the swap is simply a couple of pointer assignments. It's hard to beat that for speed and simplicity.

  - *Outside code cannot store persistent pointers to the buffer.* This is the main limitation. Since we don't actually move the *data*, what we're essentially doing is periodically telling the rest of the codebase to look somewhere else for the buffer, like in our original stage analogy. This means that the rest of the codebase can't store pointers directly to data within the buffer—they may be pointing at the wrong one a moment later.

This can be particularly troublesome on a system where the video driver expects the framebuffer to always be at a fixed location in memory. In that case, we won't be able to use this option.

- *Existing data on the buffer will be from two frames ago, not the last frame.* Successive frames are drawn on alternating buffers with no data copied between them, like so:

```
Frame 1 drawn on buffer A
Frame 2 drawn on buffer B
Frame 3 drawn on buffer A
...
```

You'll note that when we go to draw the third frame, the data already on the buffer is from frame *one*, not the more recent second frame. In most cases, this isn't an issue—we usually clear the whole buffer right before drawing. But if we intend to reuse some of the existing data on the buffer, it's important to take into account that that data will be a frame older than we might expect.

- **Copy the data between the buffers:**

  If we can't repoint users to the other buffer, the only other option is to actually copy the data from the next frame to the current frame. This is how our slapstick comedians work. In that case, we chose this method because the state—a single Boolean flag—doesn't take any longer to copy than a pointer to the buffer would.

  - *Data on the next buffer is only a single frame old.* This is the nice thing about copying the data as opposed to ping-ponging back and forth between the two buffers. If we need access to previous buffer data, this will give us more up-to-date data to work with.

  - *Swapping can take more time.* This, of course, is the big negative point. Our swap operation now means copying the entire buffer in memory. If the buffer is large, like an entire framebuffer, it can take a significant chunk of time to do this. Since nothing can read or write to *either* buffer while this is happening, that's a big limitation.

One classic use of old framebuffer data is simulating motion blur. The current frame is blended with a bit of the previously rendered frame to make a resulting image that looks more like what a real camera captures.

## What is the granularity of the buffer?

The other question is how the buffer itself is organized—is it a single monolithic chunk of data or distributed among a collection of objects? Our graphics example uses the former, and the actors use the latter.

Most of the time, the nature of what you're buffering will lead to the answer, but there's some flexibility. For example, our actors all could have stored their messages in a single message block that they all reference into by their index.

- **If the buffer is monolithic:**

  - *Swapping is simpler.* Since there is only one pair of buffers, a single swap does it. If you can swap by changing pointers, then you can swap the entire buffer, regardless of size, with just a couple of assignments.

- **If many objects have a piece of data:**

  - *Swapping is slower.* In order to swap, we need to iterate through the entire collection of objects and tell each one to swap.

    In our comedian example, that was OK since we needed to clear the next slap state anyway—every piece of buffered state needed to be touched each frame. If we don't need to otherwise touch the old buffer, there's a simple optimization we can do to get the same performance of a monolithic buffer while distributing the buffer across multiple objects.

    The idea is to get the "current" and "next" pointer concept and apply it to each of our objects by turning them into object-relative *offsets*. Like so:

```
class Actor
{
public:
  static void init() { current_ = 0; }
  static void swap() { current_ = next(); }

  void slap()      { slapped_[next()] = true; }
  bool wasSlapped() { return slapped_[current_]; }

private:
  static int current_;
  static int next()  { return 1 - current_; }

  bool slapped_[2];
};
```

Actors access their current slap state by using `current_` to index into the state array. The next state is always the other index in the array, so we can calculate that with `next()`. Swapping the state simply alternates the `current_` index. The clever bit is that `swap()` is now a *static* function—it only needs to be called once, and *every* actor's state will be swapped.

## See Also

- You can find the Double Buffer pattern in use in almost every graphics API out there. For example, OpenGL has `swapBuffers()`, Direct3D has "swap chains", and Microsoft's XNA framework swaps the framebuffers within its `endDraw()` method.

# Game Loop

# 9

*Decouple the progression of game time from user input and processor speed.*

## Motivation

If there is one pattern this book couldn't live without, this is it. Game loops are the quintessential example of a "game programming pattern". Almost every game has one, no two are exactly alike, and relatively few programs outside of games use them.

To see how they're useful, let's take a quick trip down memory lane. In the olden days of computer programming when everyone had beards, programs worked like your dishwasher. You dumped a load of code in, pushed a button, waited, and got results out. Done. These were *batch mode* programs—once the work was done, the program stopped.

Ada Lovelace and Rear Admiral Grace Hopper had honorary beards.

You still see these today, though thankfully we don't have to write them on punch cards anymore. Shell scripts, command line programs, and even the little Python script that turns a pile of Markdown into this book are all batch mode programs.

## Interview with a CPU

Eventually, programmers realized having to drop off a batch of code at the computing office and come back a few hours later for the results was a terribly slow way to get the bugs out of a program. They wanted immediate feedback. *Interactive* programs were born. Some of the first interactive programs were games:

This is Colossal Cave Adventure, the first adventure game.

```
YOU ARE STANDING AT THE END OF A ROAD BEFORE A SMALL
BRICK BUILDING . AROUND YOU IS A FOREST. A SMALL
STREAM FLOWS OUT OF THE BUILDING AND DOWN A GULLY.

> GO IN
YOU ARE INSIDE A BUILDING, A WELL HOUSE FOR A LARGE
SPRING.
```

You could have a live conversation with the program. It waited for your input, then it would respond to you. You would reply back, taking turns just like you learned to do in kindergarten. When it was your turn, it sat there doing nothing. Something like:

This loops forever, so there's no way to quit the game. A real game would do something like `while (!done)` and set `done` to exit. I've omitted that to keep things simple.

```
while (true)
{
  char* command = readCommand();
  handleCommand(command);
}
```

## Event loops

Modern graphic UI applications are surprisingly similar to old adventure games once you shuck their skin off. Your word processor usually just sits there doing nothing until you press a key or click something:

```
while (true)
{
  Event* event = waitForEvent();
  dispatchEvent(event);
}
```

Most event loops do have "idle" events so you can intermittently do stuff without user input. That's good enough for a blinking cursor or a progress bar, but too rudimentary for games.

The main difference is that instead of *text commands*, the program is waiting for *user input events*—mouse clicks and key presses. It still works basically like the old text adventures where the program *blocks* waiting for user input, which is a problem.

Unlike most other software, games keep moving even when the user isn't providing input. If you sit staring at the screen, the game doesn't freeze. Animations keep animating. Visual effects dance and sparkle. If you're unlucky, that monster keeps chomping on your hero.

This is the first key part of a real game loop: *it processes user input, but doesn't wait for it.* The loop always keeps spinning:

```
while (true)
{
  processInput();
  update();
  render();
}
```

We'll refine this later, but the basic pieces are here. `processInput()` handles any user input that has happened since the last call. Then, `update()` advances the game simulation one step. It runs AI and physics (usually in that order). Finally, `render()` draws the game so the player can see what happened.

As you might guess from the name, `update()` is a good place to use the Update Method pattern (p. 139).

## A world out of time

If this loop isn't blocking on input, that leads to the obvious question: how *fast* does it spin? Each turn through the game loop advances the state of the game by some amount. From the perspective of an inhabitant of the game world, the hand of their clock has ticked forward.

The common terms for one crank of the game loop are "tick" and "frame".

Meanwhile, the *player's* actual clock is ticking. If we measure how quickly the game loop cycles in terms of real time, we get the game's "frames per second". If the game loop cycles quickly, the FPS is high and the game moves smoothly and quickly. If it's slow, the game jerks along like a stop motion movie.

With the crude loop we have now where it just cycles as quickly as it can, two factors determine the frame rate. The first is *how much work it has to do each frame.* Complex physics, a bunch of game objects, and lots of graphic detail all will keep your CPU and GPU busy, and it will take longer to complete a frame.

The second is *the speed of the underlying platform.* Faster chips churn through more code in the same amount of time. Multiple cores, GPUs, dedicated audio hardware, and the OS's scheduler all affect how much you get done in one tick.

## Seconds per second

In early video games, that second factor was fixed. If you wrote a game for the NES or Apple IIe, you knew *exactly* what CPU your game was running on and you could (and did) code specifically for that. All you had to worry about was how much work you did each tick.

Older games were carefully coded to do just enough work each frame so that the game ran at the speed the developers wanted. But if you tried to play that same game on a faster or slower machine, then the game itself would speed up or slow down.

These days, though, few developers have the luxury of knowing exactly what hardware their game will run on. Instead, our games must intelligently adapt to a variety of devices.

This is the other key job of a game loop: *it runs the game at a consistent speed despite differences in the underlying hardware.*

This is why old PCs used to have "turbo" buttons. New PCs were faster and couldn't play old games because the games would run too fast. Turning the turbo button *off* would slow the machine down and make old games playable.

## The Pattern

A **game loop** runs continuously during gameplay. Each turn of the loop, it **processes user input** without blocking, **updates the game state**, and **renders the game**. It tracks the passage of time to **control the rate of gameplay**.

## When to Use It

Using the wrong pattern can be worse than using no pattern at all, so this section is normally here to caution against over-enthusiasm. The goal of design patterns isn't to cram as many into your codebase as you can.

But this pattern is a bit different. I can say with pretty good confidence that you *will* use this pattern. If you're using a game engine, you won't write it yourself, but it's still there.

You might think you won't need this if you're making a turn-based game. But even there, though the *game state* won't advance until the user takes their turn, the *visual* and *audible* states of the game usually do. Animation and music keep running even when the game is "waiting" for you to take your turn.

For me, this is the difference between an "engine" and a "library". With libraries, you own the main game loop and call into the library. An engine owns the loop and calls into *your* code.

## Keep in Mind

The loop we're talking about here is some of the most important code in your game. They say a program spends 90% of its time in 10% of the code. Your game loop will be firmly in that 10%. Take care with this code, and be mindful of its efficiency.

Made up statistics like this are why "real" engineers like mechanical and electrical engineers don't take us seriously.

### You may need to coordinate with the platform's event loop

If you're building your game on top of an OS or platform that has a graphic UI and an event loop built in, then you have *two* application loops in play. They'll need to play nice together.

Sometimes, you can take control and make your loop the only one. For example, if you're writing a game against the venerable Windows API, your `main()` can just have a game loop. Inside, you can call `PeekMessage()` to handle and dispatch events from the OS. Unlike `GetMessage()`, `PeekMessage()` doesn't block waiting for user input, so your game loop will keep cranking.

Other platforms don't let you opt out of the event loop so easily. If you're targeting a web browser, the event loop is deeply built into browser's execution model. There, the event loop will run the show, and you'll use it as your game loop too. You'll call something like `requestAnimationFrame()` and it will call back into your code to keep the game running.

## Sample Code

For such a long introduction, the code for a game loop is actually pretty straightforward. We'll walk through a couple of variations and go over their good and bad points.

The game loop drives AI, rendering, and other game systems, but those aren't the point of the pattern itself, so we'll just call into fictitious methods here. Actually implementing `render()`, `update()` and others is left as a (challenging!) exercise for the reader.

### Run, run as fast as you can

We've already seen the simplest possible game loop:

```
while (true)
{
  processInput();
  update();
  render();
}
```

The problem with it is you have no control over how fast the game runs. On a fast machine, that loop will spin so fast users won't be able to see what's going on. On a slow machine, the game will crawl. If you have a part of the game that's content-heavy or does more AI or physics, the game will actually play slower there.

## Take a little nap

1000 ms / FPS = ms per frame.

The first variation we'll look at adds a simple fix. Say you want your game to run at 60 FPS. That gives you about 16 milliseconds per frame. As long as you can reliably do all of your game processing and rendering in less than that time, you can run at a steady frame rate. All you do is process the frame and then *wait* until it's time for the next one, like so:

*Figure 9.1 – A dead simple game loop*

The code looks a bit like this:

```
while (true)
{
  double start = getCurrentTime();
  processInput();
  update();
  render();

  sleep(start + MS_PER_FRAME - getCurrentTime());
}
```

The `sleep()` here makes sure the game doesn't run too *fast* if it processes a frame quickly. It *doesn't* help if your game runs too *slowly*. If it takes longer than 16ms to update and render the frame, your sleep time goes *negative*. If we had computers that could travel back in time, lots of things would be easier, but we don't.

Instead, the game slows down. You can work around this by doing less work each frame—cut down on the graphics and razzle dazzle or dumb down the AI. But that impacts the quality of gameplay for all users, even ones on fast machines.

## One small step, one giant step

Let's try something a bit more sophisticated. The problem we have basically boils down to:

1. Each update advances game time by a certain amount.

2. It takes a certain amount of *real* time to process that.

If step two takes longer than step one, the game slows down. If it takes more than 16 ms of processing to advance game time by 16ms, it can't possibly keep up. But if we can advance the game by *more* than 16ms of game time in a single step, then we can update the game less frequently and still keep up.

The idea then is to choose a time step to advance based on how much *real* time passed since the last frame. The longer the frame takes, the bigger steps the game takes. It always keeps up with real time because it will take bigger and bigger steps to get there. They call this a *variable* or *fluid* time step. It looks like:

```
double lastTime = getCurrentTime();
while (true)
{
  double current = getCurrentTime();
  double elapsed = current - lastTime;
  processInput();
  update(elapsed);
  render();
  lastTime = current;
}
```

Each frame, we determine how much *real* time passed since the last game update (`elapsed`). When we update the game state, we pass that in. The engine is then responsible for advancing the game world forward by that amount of time.

Say you've got a bullet shooting across the screen. With a fixed time step, in each frame, you'll move it according to its velocity. With a variable time step, you *scale that velocity by the elapsed time*. As the time step gets bigger, the bullet moves farther in each frame. That bullet will get across the screen in the *same* amount of *real* time whether it's twenty small fast steps or four big slow ones. This looks like a winner:

- The game plays at a consistent rate on different hardware.

- Players with faster machines are rewarded with smoother gameplay.

But, alas, there's a serious problem lurking ahead: we've made the game non-deterministic and unstable. Here's one example of the trap we've set for ourselves:

Say we've got a two-player networked game and Fred has some beast of a gaming machine while George is using his grandmother's antique PC. That aforementioned bullet is flying across both of their screens. On Fred's machine, the game is running super fast, so each time step is

"Deterministic" means that every time you run the program, if you give it the same inputs, you get the exact same outputs back. As you can imagine, it's much easier to track down bugs in deterministic programs—find the inputs that caused the bug the first time, and you can cause it every time.

Computers are naturally deterministic; they follow programs mechanically. Non-determinism appears when the messy real world creeps in. For example, networking, the system clock, and thread scheduling all rely on bits of the external world outside of the program's control.

tiny. We cram, like, 50 frames in the second it takes the bullet to cross the screen. Poor George's machine can only fit in about five frames.

This means that on Fred's machine, the physics engine updates the bullet's position 50 times, but George's only does it five times. Most games use floating point numbers, and those are subject to *rounding error*. Each time you add two floating point numbers, the answer you get back can be a bit off. Fred's machine is doing ten times as many operations, so he'll accumulate a bigger error than George. The *same* bullet will end up in *different places* on their machines.

This is just one nasty problem a variable time step can cause, but there are more. In order to run in real time, game physics engines are approximations of the real laws of mechanics. To keep those approximations from blowing up, damping is applied. That damping is carefully tuned to a certain time step. Vary that, and the physics gets unstable.

This instability is bad enough that this example is only here as a cautionary tale and to lead us to something better...

### Play catch up

One part of the engine that usually *isn't* affected by a variable time step is rendering. Since the rendering engine captures an instant in time, it doesn't care how much time advanced since the last one. It renders things wherever they happen to be right then.

We can use this fact to our advantage. We'll *update* the game using a fixed time step because that makes everything simpler and more stable for physics and AI. But we'll allow flexibility in when we *render* in order to free up some processor time.

It goes like this: A certain amount of real time has elapsed since the last turn of the game loop. This is how much game time we need to simulate for the game's "now" to catch up with the player's. We do that using a *series* of *fixed* time steps. The code looks a bit like:

"Blowing up" is literal here. When a physics engine flakes out, objects can get completely wrong velocities and launch themselves into the air.

This is more or less true. Things like motion blur can be affected by time step, but if they're a bit off, the player doesn't usually notice.

```
double previous = getCurrentTime();
double lag = 0.0;
while (true)
{
  double current = getCurrentTime();
  double elapsed = current - previous;
  previous = current;
  lag += elapsed;
  processInput();

  while (lag >= MS_PER_UPDATE)
  {
    update();
    lag -= MS_PER_UPDATE;
  }
  render();
}
```

There's a few pieces here. At the beginning of each frame, we update `lag`
based on how much real time passed. This measures how far the game's
clock is behind compared to the real world. We then have an inner loop to
update the game, one fixed step at a time, until it's caught up. Once we're
caught up, we render and start over again. You can visualize it sort of like
this:

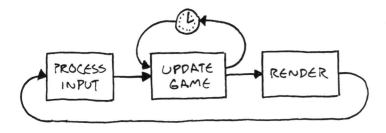

Figure 9.2 – Cutting rendering out of the core loop

Note that the time step here isn't the *visible* frame rate anymore.
`MS_PER_UPDATE` is just the *granularity* we use to update the game. The
shorter this step is, the more processing time it takes to catch up to real
time. The longer it is, the choppier the gameplay is. Ideally, you want it
pretty short, often faster than 60 FPS, so that the game simulates with
high fidelity on fast machines.

But be careful not to make it *too* short. You need to make sure the time
step is greater than the time it takes to process an `update()`, even on the
slowest hardware. Otherwise, your game simply can't catch up.

Fortunately, we've bought ourselves some breathing room here. The
trick is that we've *yanked rendering out of the update loop*. That frees up a

I left it out here, but you can safeguard
this by having the inner update loop bail
after a maximum number of iterations.
The game will slow down then, but that's
better than locking up completely.

bunch of CPU time. The end result is the game *simulates* at a constant rate using safe fixed time steps across a range of hardware. It's just that the player's *visible window* into the game gets choppier on a slower machine.

### Stuck in the middle

There's one issue we're left with, and that's residual lag. We update the game at a fixed time step, but we render at arbitrary points in time. This means that from the user's perspective, the game will often display at a point in time between two updates.

Here's a timeline:

*Figure 9.3 – A timeline showing when the game updates and renders*

As you can see, we update at a nice tight, fixed interval. Meanwhile, we render whenever we can. It's less frequent than updating, and it isn't steady either. Both of those are OK. The lame part is that we don't always render right at the point of updating. Look at the third render time. It's right between two updates:

*Figure 9.4 – Rendering right between two update frames*

Imagine a bullet is flying across the screen. On the first update, it's on the left side. The second update moves it to the right side. The game is rendered at a point in time between those two updates, so the user expects to see that bullet in the center of the screen. With our current implementation, it will still be on the left side. This means motion looks jagged or stuttery.

Conveniently, we actually know *exactly* how far between update frames we are when we render: it's stored in `lag`. We bail out of the update loop when it's less than the update time step, not when it's *zero*. That leftover amount? That's how far into the next frame we are.

When we go to render, we'll pass that in:

```
render(lag / MS_PER_UPDATE);
```

The renderer knows each game object *and its current velocity*. Say that bullet is 20 pixels from the left side of the screen and is moving right 400 pixels per frame. If we are halfway between frames, then we'll end up passing 0.5 to `render()`. So it draws the bullet half a frame ahead, at 220 pixels. Ta-da, smooth motion.

Of course, it may turn out that that extrapolation is wrong. When we calculate the next frame, we may discover the bullet hit an obstacle or slowed down or something. We rendered its position interpolated between where it was on the last frame and where we *think* it will be on the next frame. But we don't know that until we've actually done the full update with physics and AI.

So the extrapolation is a bit of a guess and sometimes ends up wrong. Fortunately, though, those kinds of corrections usually aren't noticeable. At least, they're less noticeable than the stuttering you get if you don't extrapolate at all.

We divide by `MS_PER_UPDATE` here to *normalize* the value. The value passed to `render()` will vary from 0 (right at the previous frame) to just under 1.0 (right at the next frame), regardless of the update time step. This way, the renderer doesn't have to worry about the frame rate. It just deals in values from 0 to 1.

## Design Decisions

Despite the length of this chapter, I've left out more than I've included. Once you throw in things like synchronizing with the display's refresh rate, multithreading, and GPUs, a real game loop can get pretty hairy. At a high level, though, here are a few questions you'll likely answer:

### Do you own the game loop, or does the platform?

This is less a choice you make and more one that's made for you. If you're making a game that runs in a web browser, you pretty much *can't* write your own classic game loop. The browser's event-based nature precludes it. Likewise, if you're using an existing game engine, you will probably rely on its game loop instead of rolling your own.

- **Use the platform's event loop:**

  - *It's simple.* You don't have to worry about writing and optimizing the core loop of the game.

- *It plays nice with the platform.* You don't have to worry about explicitly giving the host time to process its own events, caching events, or otherwise managing the impedance mismatch between the platform's input model and yours.

- *You lose control over timing.* The platform will call your code as it sees fit. If that's not as frequently or as smoothly as you'd like, too bad. Worse, most application event loops weren't designed with games in mind and usually *are* slow and choppy.

- **Use a game engine's loop:**

  - *You don't have to write it.* Writing a game loop can get pretty tricky. Since that core code gets executed every frame, minor bugs or performance problems can have a large impact on your game. A tight game loop is one reason to consider using an existing engine.

  - *You don't get to write it.* Of course, the flip side to that coin is the loss of control if you *do* have needs that aren't a perfect fit for the engine.

- **Write it yourself:**

  - *Total control.* You can do whatever you want with it. You can design it specifically for the needs of your game.

  - *You have to interface with the platform.* Application frameworks and operating systems usually expect to have a slice of time to process events and do other work. If you own your app's core loop, it won't get any. You'll have to explicitly hand off control periodically to make sure the framework doesn't hang or get confused.

### How do you manage power consumption?

This wasn't an issue five years ago. Games ran on things plugged into walls or on dedicated handheld devices. But with the advent of smartphones, laptops, and mobile gaming, the odds are good that you do care about this now. A game that runs beautifully but turns players' phones into space heaters before running out of juice thirty minutes later is not a game that makes people happy.

Now, you may need to think not only about making your game look great, but also use as little CPU as possible. There will likely be an *upper* bound to performance where you let the CPU sleep if you've done all the work you need to do in a frame.

- **Run as fast as it can:**

  This is what you're likely to do for PC games (though even those are increasingly being played on laptops). Your game loop will never explicitly tell the OS to sleep. Instead, any spare cycles will be spent cranking up the FPS or graphic fidelity.

  This gives you the best possible gameplay experience but, it will use as much power as it can. If the player is on a laptop, they'll have a nice lap warmer.

- **Clamp the frame rate:**

  Mobile games are often more focused on the quality of gameplay than they are on maximizing the detail of the graphics. Many of these games will set an upper limit on the frame rate (usually 30 or 60 FPS). If the game loop is done processing before that slice of time is spent, it will just sleep for the rest.

  This gives the player a "good enough" experience and then goes easy on their battery beyond that.

## How do you control gameplay speed?

A game loop has two key pieces: non-blocking user input and adapting to the passage of time. Input is straightforward. The magic is in how you deal with time. There are a near-infinite number of platforms that games can run on, and any single game may run on quite a few. How it accommodates that variation is key.

Game-making seems to be human nature, since every time we've built a machine that can compute, we've made games on it. The PDP-1 was a 2 kHz machine with only 4,096 words of memory, yet Steve Russell and friends managed to create Spacewar! on it.

- **Fixed time step with no synchronization:**

  This was our first sample code. You just run the game loop as fast as you can.

  - *It's simple.* This is its main (well, only) virtue.

  - *Game speed is directly affected by hardware and game complexity.* And its main vice is that if there's any variation, it will directly affect the game speed. It's the fixie of game loops.

- **Fixed time step with synchronization:**

  The next step up on the complexity ladder is running the game at a fixed time step but adding a delay or synchronization point at the end of the loop to keep the game from running too fast.

- *Still quite simple.* It's only one line of code more than the probably-too-simple-to-actually-work example. In most game loops, you will likely do synchronization *anyway*. You will probably double buffer (p. 107) your graphics and synchronize the buffer flip to the refresh rate of the display.

- *It's power-friendly.* This is a surprisingly important consideration for mobile games. You don't want to kill the user's battery unnecessarily. By simply sleeping for a few milliseconds instead of trying to cram ever more processing into each tick, you save power.

- *The game doesn't play too fast.* This fixes half of the speed concerns of a fixed loop.

- *The game can play too slowly.* If it takes too long to update and render a game frame, playback will slow down. Because this style doesn't separate updating from rendering, it's likely to hit this sooner than more advanced options. Instead of just dropping *rendering* frames to catch up, gameplay will slow down.

- **Variable time step:**

  I'll put this in here as an option in the solution space with the caveat that most game developers I know recommend against it. It's good to remember *why* it's a bad idea, though.

  - *It adapts to playing both too slowly and too fast.* If the game can't keep up with real time, it will just take larger and larger time steps until it does.

  - *It makes gameplay non-deterministic and unstable.* And this is the real problem, of course. Physics and networking in particular become much harder with a variable time step.

- **Fixed update time step, variable rendering:**

  The last option we covered in the sample code is the most complex, but also the most adaptable. It updates with a fixed time step, but it can drop *rendering* frames if it needs to to catch up to the player's clock.

  - *It adapts to playing both too slowly and too fast.* As long as the game can *update* in real time, the game won't fall behind. If the player's machine is top-of-the-line, it will respond with a smoother gameplay experience.

- *It's more complex.* The main downside is there is a bit more going on in the implementation. You have to tune the update time step to be both as small as possible for the high-end, while not being too slow on the low end.

## See Also

- The classic article on game loops is Glenn Fiedler's "Fix Your Timestep". This chapter wouldn't be the same without it.

- Koen Witters' article "deWiTTERS Game Loop" is a close runner-up.

- The Unity framework has a complex game loop detailed in a wonderful illustration you can find by searching for "MonoBehaviour Lifecycle".

# Update Method     **10**

*Simulate a collection of independent objects by telling each to process one frame of behavior at a time.*

## Motivation

The player's mighty valkyrie is on a quest to steal the glorious jewels resting on the bones of the long-dead sorcerer-king. She tentatively approaches his magnificent crypt and is attacked by... *nothing*. No cursed statues shooting lightning at her. No undead warriors patrolling the entrance. She just walks right in and grabs the loot. Game over. You win.

Well, that won't do. This crypt needs some guards—enemies our brave heroine can grapple with. First up, we want a re-animated skeleton warrior to patrol back and forth in front of the door. If you ignore everything you probably already know about game programming, the simplest possible code to make that skeleton lurch back and forth is something like:

> If the sorcerer-king wanted more intelligent behavior, he should have re-animated something that still had brain tissue.

```
while (true)
{
  // Patrol right.
  for (double x = 0; x < 100; x++) skeleton.setX(x);

  // Patrol left.
  for (double x = 100; x > 0; x--) skeleton.setX(x);
}
```

The problem here, of course, is that the skeleton moves back and forth, but the player never sees it. The program is locked in an infinite loop, which is not exactly a fun gameplay experience. What we actually want is for the skeleton to move one step *each frame*.

We'll have to remove those loops and rely on the outer game loop for iteration. That ensures the game keeps responding to user input and rendering while the guard is making his rounds. Like:

```
Entity skeleton;
bool patrollingLeft = false;
double x = 0;

// Main game loop:
while (true)
{
  if (patrollingLeft)
  {
    x--;
    if (x == 0) patrollingLeft = false;
  }
  else
  {
    x++;
    if (x == 100) patrollingLeft = true;
  }

  skeleton.setX(x);

  // Handle user input and render game...
}
```

I did the before/after here to show you how the code gets more complex. Patrolling left and right used to be two simple `for` loops. It kept track of which direction the skeleton was moving implicitly by which loop was executing. Now that we have to yield to the outer game loop each frame and then resume where we left off, we have to track the direction explicitly using that `patrollingLeft` variable.

But this more or less works, so we keep going. A brainless bag of bones doesn't give yon Norse maiden too much of a challenge, so the next thing we add is a couple of enchanted statues. These will fire bolts of lightning at her every so often to keep her on her toes.

Continuing our, "what's the simplest way to code this" style, we end up with:

```
// Skeleton variables...
Entity leftStatue;
Entity rightStatue;
int leftStatueFrames = 0;
int rightStatueFrames = 0;

// Main game loop:
while (true)
{
  // Skeleton code...

  if (++leftStatueFrames == 90)
  {
    leftStatueFrames = 0;
    leftStatue.shootLightning();
  }

  if (++rightStatueFrames == 80)
  {
    rightStatueFrames = 0;
    rightStatue.shootLightning();
  }

  // Handle user input and render game...
}
```

You can tell this isn't trending towards code we'd enjoy maintaining. We've got an increasingly large pile of variables and imperative code all stuffed in the game loop, each handling one specific entity in the game. To get them all up and running at the same time, we've mushed their code together.

Anytime "mushed" accurately describes your architecture, you likely have a problem.

The pattern we'll use to fix this is so simple you probably have it in mind already: *each entity in the game should encapsulate its own behavior.* This will keep the game loop uncluttered and make it easy to add and remove entities.

To do this, we need an *abstraction layer*, and we create that by defining an abstract update() method. The game loop maintains a collection of objects, but it doesn't know their concrete types. All it knows is that they can be updated. This separates each object's behavior both from the game loop and from the other objects.

Once per frame, the game loop walks the collection and calls update() on each object. This gives each one a chance to perform one frame's worth of behavior. By calling it on all objects every frame, they all behave simultaneously.

Since some stickler will call me on this, yes, they don't behave *truly concurrently*. While one object is updating, none of the others are. We'll get into this more in a bit.

The game loop has a dynamic collection of objects, so adding and removing them from the level is easy—just add and remove them from the collection. Nothing is hardcoded anymore, and we can even populate the level using some kind of data file, which is exactly what our level designers want.

## The Pattern

The **game world** maintains a **collection of objects**. Each object implements an **update method** that **simulates one frame** of the object's behavior. Each frame, the game updates every object in the collection.

## When to Use It

If the Game Loop pattern (p. 123) is the best thing since sliced bread, then the Update Method pattern is its butter. A wide swath of games featuring live entities that the player interacts with use this pattern in some form or other. If the game has space marines, dragons, Martians, ghosts, or athletes, there's a good chance it uses this pattern.

However, if the game is more abstract and the moving pieces are less like living actors and more like pieces on a chessboard, this pattern is often a poor fit. In a game like chess, you don't need to simulate all of the pieces concurrently, and you probably don't need to tell the pawns to update themselves every frame.

Update methods work well when:

- Your game has a number of objects or systems that need to run simultaneously.

- Each object's behavior is mostly independent of the others.

- The objects need to be simulated over time.

You may not need to update their *behavior* each frame, but even in a board game, you may still want to update their *animation* every frame. This pattern can help with that too.

## Keep in Mind

This pattern is pretty simple, so there aren't a lot of hidden surprises in its dark corners. Still, every line of code has its ramifications.

### Splitting code into single frame slices makes it more complex

When you compare the first two chunks of code, the second is a good bit more complex. Both simply make the skeleton guard walk back and forth, but the second one does this while yielding control to the game loop each frame.

That change is almost always necessary to handle user input, rendering, and the other stuff that the game loop takes care of, so the first example wasn't very practical. But it's worth keeping in mind that there's a big up front complexity cost when you julienne your behavioral code like this.

## You have to store state to resume where you left off each frame

In the first code sample, we didn't have any variables to indicate whether the guard was moving left or right. That was implicit based on which code was currently executing.

When we changed this to a one-frame-at-a-time form, we had to create a `patrollingLeft` variable to track that. When we return out of the code, the execution position is lost, so we need to explicitly store enough information to restore it on the next frame.

The State pattern (p. 87) can often help here. Part of the reason state machines are common in games is because (like their name implies) they store the kind of state that you need to pick up where you left off.

## Objects all simulate each frame but are not truly concurrent

In this pattern, the game loops over a collection of objects and updates each one. Inside the `update()` call, most objects are able to reach out and touch the rest of the game world, including other objects that are being updated. This means the *order* in which the objects are updated is significant.

If A comes before B in the list of objects, then when A updates, it will see B's previous state. But when B updates, it will see A's *new* state, since A has already been updated this frame. Even though from the player's perspective, everything is moving at the same time, the core of the game is still turn-based. It's just that a complete "turn" is only one frame long.

This is mostly a good thing as far as the game logic is concerned. Updating objects in parallel leads you to some unpleasant semantic corners. Imagine a game of chess where black and white moved at the same time. They both try to make a move that places a piece in the same currently empty square. How should this be resolved?

Updating sequentially solves this—each update incrementally changes the world from one valid state to the next with no period of time where things are ambiguous and need to be reconciled.

## Be careful modifying the object list while updating

When you're using this pattern, a lot of the game's behavior ends up nestled in these update methods. That often includes code that adds or removes updatable objects from the game.

I say "almost" here because sometimes you can have your cake and eat it too. You can have straight-line code that never returns for your object behavior, while simultaneously having a number of objects running concurrently and coordinating with the game loop.

What you need is a system that lets you have multiple "threads" of execution going on at the same time. If the code for an object can pause and resume in the middle of what it's doing, instead of having to *return* completely, you can write it in a more imperative form.

Actual threads are usually too heavyweight for this to work well, but if your language supports lightweight concurrency constructs like generators, coroutines, or fibers, you may be able to use those.

The Bytecode pattern (p. 155) is another option that creates threads of execution at the application level.

If, for some reason, you decide you *don't* want your game to be sequential like this, you would need to use something like the Double Buffer pattern (p. 107). That makes the order in which A and B update not matter because *both* of them will see the previous frame's state.

It also helps online play since you have a serialized set of moves that can be sent over the network.

For example, say a skeleton guard drops an item when slain. With a new object, you can usually add it to the end of the list without too much trouble. You'll keep iterating over that list and eventually get to the new one at the end and update it too.

But that does mean that the new object gets a chance to act during the frame that it was spawned, before the player has even had a chance to see it. If you don't want that to happen, one simple fix is to cache the number of objects in the list at the beginning of the update loop and only update that many before stopping:

```
int numObjectsThisTurn = numObjects_;
for (int i = 0; i < numObjectsThisTurn; i++)
{
    objects_[i]->update();
}
```

Here, `objects_` is an array of the updatable objects in the game, and `numObjects_` is its length. When new objects are added, it gets incremented. We cache the length in `numObjectsThisTurn` at the beginning of the loop so that the iteration stops before we get to any new objects added during the current frame.

A hairier problem is when objects are *removed* while iterating. You vanquish some foul beast and now it needs to get yanked out of the object list. If it happens to be before the current object you're updating in the list, you can accidentally skip an object:

```
for (int i = 0; i < numObjects_; i++)
{
    objects_[i]->update();
}
```

This simple loop increments the index of the object being updated each iteration. The left side of the illustration below shows what the array looks like while we're updating the heroine:

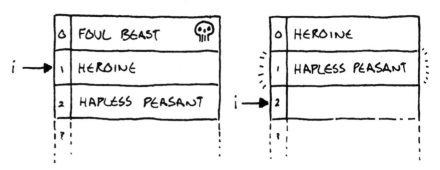

*Figure 10.1 – Removing during iteration skips over a peasant*

Since we're updating her, i is 1. She slays the foul beast so it gets removed from the array. The heroine shifts up to 0, and the hapless peasant shifts up to 1. After updating the heroine, i is incremented to 2. As you can see on the right, the hapless peasant is skipped over and never gets updated.

One fix is to just be careful when you remove objects and update any iteration variables to take the removal into account. Another is to defer removals until you're done walking the list. Mark the object as "dead", but leave it in place. During updating, make sure to skip any dead objects. Then, when that's done, walk the list again to remove the corpses.

A cheap solution is to walk the list *backwards* when you update. That way removing an object only shifts items that were already updated.

If you have multiple threads processing the items in the update loop, then you are even more likely to defer any modification to it to avoid costly thread synchronization during updates.

## Sample Code

This pattern is so straightforward that the sample code almost belabors the point. That doesn't mean the pattern isn't *useful*. It's useful in part *because* it's simple: it's a clean solution to a problem without a lot of ornamentation.

But to keep things concrete, let's walk through a basic implementation. We'll start with an Entity class that will represent the skeletons and statues:

```
class Entity
{
public:
  Entity()
  : x_(0), y_(0) {}

  virtual ~Entity() {}
  virtual void update() = 0;

  double x() const { return x_; }
  double y() const { return y_; }

  void setX(double x) { x_ = x; }
  void setY(double y) { y_ = y; }

private:
  double x_, y_;
};
```

I stuck a few things in there, but just the bare minimum we'll need later. Presumably in real code, there'd be lots of other stuff like graphics and physics. The important bit for this pattern is that it has an abstract update() method.

The game maintains a collection of these entities. In our sample, we'll put that in a class representing the game world:

```
class World
{
public:
  World()
  : numEntities_(0) {}

  void gameLoop();

private:
  Entity* entities_[MAX_ENTITIES];
  int numEntities_;
};
```

In a real-world program, you'd probably use an actual collection class, but I'm just using a vanilla array here to keep things simple.

Now that everything is set up, the game implements the pattern by updating each entity every frame:

```
void World::gameLoop()
{
  while (true)
  {
    // Handle user input...

    // Update each entity.
    for (int i = 0; i < numEntities_; i++)
    {
      entities_[i]->update();
    }

    // Physics and rendering...
  }
}
```

As the name of the method implies, this is an example of the Game Loop pattern (p. 123).

### Subclassing entities?!

There are some readers whose skin is crawling right now because I'm using inheritance on the main `Entity` class to define different behaviors. If you don't happen to see the problem, I'll provide some context.

When the game industry emerged from the primordial seas of 6502 assembly code and VBLANKs onto the shores of object-oriented languages, developers went into a software architecture fad frenzy. One of the biggest was using inheritance. Towering, Byzantine class hierarchies were built, big enough to blot out the sun.

It turns out that was a terrible idea and no one can maintain a giant class hierarchy without it crumbling around them. Even the Gang of Four knew this in 1994 when they wrote, *"Favor 'object composition' over 'class inheritance'."*

When this realization percolated through the game industry, the solution that emerged was the Component pattern (p. 213). Using that,

Between you and me, I think the pendulum has swung a bit too far *away* from subclassing. I generally avoid it, but being dogmatic about *not* using inheritance is as bad as being dogmatic about using it. You can use it in moderation without having to be a teetotaler.

`update()` would be on the entity's *components* and not on `Entity` itself. That lets you avoid creating complicated class hierarchies of entities to define and reuse behavior. Instead, you just mix and match components.

If I were making a real game, I'd probably do that too. But this chapter isn't about components. It's about `update()` methods, and the simplest way I can show them, with as few moving parts as possible, is by putting that method right on `Entity` and making a few subclasses.

The Component chapter (p. 213) is.

## Defining entities

OK, back to the task at hand. Our original motivation was to be able to define a patrolling skeleton guard and some lightning-bolt-unleashing magical statues. Let's start with our bony friend. To define his patrolling behavior, we make a new entity that implements `update()` appropriately:

```
class Skeleton : public Entity
{
public:
  Skeleton()
  : patrollingLeft_(false) {}

  virtual void update()
  {
    if (patrollingLeft_)
    {
      setX(x() - 1);
      if (x() == 0) patrollingLeft_ = false;
    }
    else
    {
      setX(x() + 1);
      if (x() == 100) patrollingLeft_ = true;
    }
  }

private:
  bool patrollingLeft_;
};
```

As you can see, we pretty much just cut that chunk of code from the game loop earlier in the chapter and pasted it into `Skeleton`'s `update()` method. The one minor difference is that `patrollingLeft_` has been made into a field instead of a local variable. That way, its value sticks around between calls to `update()`.

Game Programming Patterns – Sequencing Patterns **147**

Let's do this again with the statue:

```cpp
class Statue : public Entity
{
public:
  Statue(int delay)
  : frames_(0),
    delay_(delay)
  {}

  virtual void update()
  {
    if (++frames_ == delay_)
    {
      shootLightning();

      // Reset the timer.
      frames_ = 0;
    }
  }

private:
  int frames_;
  int delay_;

  void shootLightning()
  {
    // Shoot the lightning...
  }
};
```

Again, most of the change is moving code from the game loop into the class and renaming some stuff. In this case, though, we've actually made the codebase simpler. In the original nasty imperative code, there were separate local variables for each statue's frame counter and rate of fire.

Now that those have been moved into the Statue class itself, you can create as many as you want and each instance will have its own little timer. That's really the motivation behind this pattern—it's now much easier to add new entities to the game world because each one brings along everything it needs to take care of itself.

This pattern lets us separate *populating* the game world from *implementing* it. This in turn gives us the flexibility to populate the world using something like a separate data file or level editor.

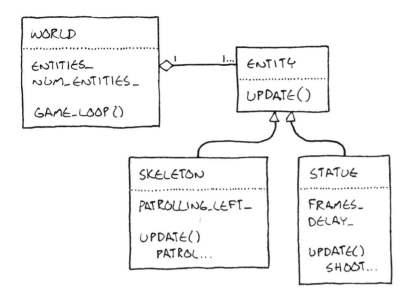

*Figure 10.2 – A UML diagram of what we just created, in case you care about UML*

## Passing time

That's the key pattern, but I'll just touch on a common refinement. So far, we've assumed every call to `update()` advances the state of the game world by the same fixed unit of time.

I happen to prefer that, but many games use a *variable time step*. In those, each turn of the game loop may simulate a larger or smaller slice of time depending on how long it took to process and render the previous frame.

That means that each `update()` call needs to know how far the hand of the virtual clock has swung, so you'll often see the elapsed time passed in. For example, we can make our patrolling skeleton handle a variable time step like so:

The Game Loop chapter (p. 123) has a lot more on the advantages and disadvantages of fixed and variable time steps.

```
void Skeleton::update(double elapsed)
{
  if (patrollingLeft_)
  {
    x -= elapsed;
    if (x <= 0)
    {
      patrollingLeft_ = false;
      x = -x;
    }
  }
  else
  {
    x += elapsed;
    if (x >= 100)
    {
      patrollingLeft_ = true;
      x = 100 - (x - 100);
    }
  }
}
```

Now, the distance the skeleton moves increases as the elapsed time grows. You can also see the additional complexity of dealing with a variable time step. The skeleton may overshoot the bounds of its patrol with a large time slice, and we have to handle that carefully.

## Design Decisions

With a simple pattern like this, there isn't too much variation, but there are still a couple of knobs you can turn.

### What class does the update method live on?

The most obvious and most important decision you'll make is what class to put update() on.

- **The entity class:**

  This is the simplest option if you already have an entity class since it doesn't bring any additional classes into play. This may work if you don't have too many kinds of entities, but the industry is generally moving away from this.

  Having to subclass Entity every time you want a new behavior is brittle and painful when you have a large number of different kinds. You'll eventually find yourself wanting to reuse pieces of code in a way that doesn't gracefully map to a single inheritance hierarchy, and then you're stuck.

- **The component class:**

  If you're already using the Component pattern (p. 213), this is a no-brainer. It lets each component update itself independently. In the same way that the Update Method pattern in general lets you decouple game entities from each other in the game world, this lets you decouple *parts of a single entity* from each other. Rendering, physics, and AI can all take care of themselves.

- **A delegate class:**

  There are other patterns that involve delegating part of a class's behavior to another object. The State pattern (p. 87) does this so that you can change an object's behavior by changing what it delegates to. The Type Object pattern (p. 193) does this so that you can share behavior across a bunch of entities of the same "kind".

  If you're using one of those patterns, it's natural to put `update()` on that delegated class. In that case, you may still have the `update()` method on the main class, but it will be non-virtual and will simply forward to the delegated object. Something like:

  ```
  void Entity::update()
  {
    // Forward to state object.
    state_->update();
  }
  ```

  Doing this lets you define new behavior by changing out the delegated object. Like using components, it gives you the flexibility to change behavior without having to define an entirely new subclass.

## How are dormant objects handled?

You often have a number of objects in the world that, for whatever reason, temporarily don't need to be updated. They could be disabled, or off-screen, or not unlocked yet. If a large number of objects are in this state, it can be a waste of CPU cycles to walk over them each frame only to do nothing.

One alternative is to maintain a separate collection of just the "live" objects that do need updating. When an object is disabled, it's removed from the collection. When it gets re-enabled, it's added back. This way, you only iterate over items that actually have real work do to.

In addition to wasted CPU cycles checking if the object is enabled and skipping past it, pointlessly iterating over objects can blow your data cache. CPUs optimize reads by loading memory from RAM into much faster on-chip caches. They do this speculatively by assuming you're likely to read memory right after a location you just read.

When you skip over an object, you can skip past the end of the cache, forcing it to go and slowly pull in another chunk of main memory.

The Data Locality chapter (p. 269) goes into this exact issue in detail.

- **If you use a single collection containing inactive objects:**

  - *You waste time.* For inactive objects, you'll end up either checking some "am I enabled" flag or calling a method that does nothing.

- **If you use a separate collection of only active objects:**

  - *You use extra memory to maintain the second collection.* There's still usually another master collection of all entities for cases where you need them all. In that case, this collection is technically redundant. When speed is tighter than memory (which it often is), this can still be a worthwhile trade-off.

    Another option to mitigate this is to have two collections, but have the other collection only contain the *inactive* entities instead of all of them.

  - *You have to keep the collections in sync.* When objects are created or completely destroyed (and not just made temporarily inactive), you have to remember to modify both the master collection and active object one.

The metric that should guide your approach here is how many inactive objects you tend to have. The more you have, the more useful it is to have a separate collection that avoids them during your core game loop.

## See Also

- This pattern, along with Game Loop (p. 123) and Component (p. 213), is part of a trinity that often forms the nucleus of a game engine.

- When you start caring about the cache performance of updating a bunch of entities or components in a loop each frame, the Data Locality pattern (p. 269) can help make that faster.

- The Unity framework uses this pattern in several classes, including `MonoBehaviour`.

- Microsoft's XNA platform uses this pattern both in the `Game` and `GameComponent` classes.

- The Quintus JavaScript game engine uses this pattern on its main `Sprite` class.

# Behavioral Patterns    IV.

Once you've built your game's set and festooned it with actors and props, all that remains is to start the scene. For this, you need behavior—the screenplay that tells each entity in your game what to do.

Of course all code is "behavior", and all software is defining behavior, but what's different about games is often the *breadth* of it that you have to implement. While your word processor may have a long list of features, it pales in comparison with the number of inhabitants, items, and quests in your average role-playing game.

The patterns in this chapter help to quickly define and refine a large quantity of maintainable behavior. Type Objects (p. 193) create categories of behavior without the rigidity of defining an actual class. A Subclass Sandbox (p. 181) gives you a safe set of primitives you can use to define a variety of behaviors. The most advanced option is Bytecode (p. 155), which moves behavior out of code entirely and into data.

# Bytecode

# 11

*Give behavior the flexibility of data by encoding it as instructions for a virtual machine.*

## Motivation

Making games may be fun, but it certainly ain't easy. Modern games require enormous, complex codebases. Console manufacturers and app marketplace gatekeepers have stringent quality requirements, and a single crash bug can prevent your game from shipping.

At the same time, we're expected to squeeze every drop of performance out of the platform. Games push hardware like nothing else, and we have to optimize relentlessly just to keep pace with the competition.

To handle these high stability and performance requirements, we reach for heavyweight languages like C++ that have both low-level expressiveness to make the most of the hardware and rich type systems to prevent or at least corral bugs.

We pride ourselves on our skill at this, but it has its cost. Being a proficient programmer takes years of dedicated training, after which you must contend with the sheer scale of your codebase. Build times for large games can vary somewhere between "go get a coffee" and "go roast

I worked on a game that had six million lines of C++ code. For comparison, the software controlling the Mars Curiosity rover is less than half that.

your own beans, hand-grind them, pull an espresso, foam some milk, and practice your latte art in the froth".

On top of these challenges, games have one more nasty constraint: *fun*. Players demand a play experience that's both novel and yet carefully balanced. That requires constant iteration, but if every tweak requires bugging an engineer to muck around in piles of low-level code and then waiting for a glacial recompile, you've killed your creative flow.

### Spell fight!

Let's say we're working on a magic-based fighting game. A pair of wizards square off and fling enchantments at each other until a victor is pronounced. We could define these spells in code, but that means an engineer has to be involved every time one is modified. When a designer wants to tweak a few numbers and get a feel for them, they have to recompile the entire game, reboot it, and get back into a fight.

Like most games these days, we also need to be able to update the game after it ships, both to fix bugs and to add new content. If all of these spells are hard-coded, then updating them means patching the actual game executable.

Let's take things a bit further and say that we also want to support *modding*. We want *users* to be able to create their own spells. If those are in code, that means every modder needs a full compiler toolchain to build the game, and we have to release the sources. Worse, if they have a bug in their spell, it can crash the game on some other player's machine.

### Data > code

It's pretty clear that our engine's implementation language isn't the right fit. We need spells to be safely sandboxed from the core game. We want them to be easy to modify, easy to reload, and physically separate from the rest of the executable.

I don't know about you, but to me that sounds a lot like *data*. If we can define our behavior in separate data files that the game engine loads and "executes" in some way, we can achieve all of our goals.

We just need to figure out what "execute" means for data. How do you make some bytes in a file express behavior? There are a few ways to do this. I think it will help you get a picture of *this* pattern's strengths and weaknesses if we compare it to another one: the Interpreter pattern.

## The Interpreter pattern

I could write a whole chapter on this pattern, but four other guys already covered that for me. Instead, I'll cram the briefest of introductions in here. It starts with a language—think *programming* language—that you want to execute. Say, for example, it supports arithmetic expressions like this:

I'm referring, of course, to the Interpreter pattern in *Design Patterns*.

```
(1 + 2) * (3 - 4)
```

Then, you take each piece of that expression, each rule in the language's grammar, and turn it into an *object*. The number literals will be objects:

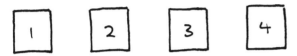

*Figure 11.1 – Four little number literals, all in a row*

Basically, they're little wrappers around the raw value. The operators will be objects too, and they'll have references to their operands. If you take into account the parentheses and precedence, that expression magically turns into a little tree of objects like so:

What "magic" is this? It's simple—*parsing*. A parser takes a string of characters and turns it into an *abstract syntax tree*, a collection of objects representing the grammatical structure of the text.

Whip up one of these and you've got yourself half of a compiler.

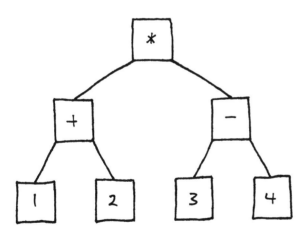

*Figure 11.2 – An abstract syntax tree for a nested expression*

The Interpreter pattern isn't about *creating* that tree; it's about *executing* it. The way it works is pretty clever. Each object in the tree is an expression or a subexpression. In true object-oriented fashion, we'll let expressions evaluate themselves.

First, we define a base interface that all expressions implement:

```
class Expression
{
public:
  virtual ~Expression() {}
  virtual double evaluate() = 0;
};
```

Then, we define a class that implements this interface for each kind of expression in our language's grammar. The simplest one is numbers:

```
class NumberExpression : public Expression
{
public:
  NumberExpression(double value)
  : value_(value)
  {}

  virtual double evaluate() { return value_; }

private:
  double value_;
};
```

A literal number expression simply evaluates to its value. Addition and multiplication are a bit more complex because they contain subexpressions. Before they can evaluate themselves, they need to recursively evaluate their subexpressions. Like so:

I'm sure you can figure out what the implementation of multiply looks like.

```
class AdditionExpression : public Expression
{
public:
  AdditionExpression(Expression* left,
                     Expression* right)
  : left_(left),
    right_(right)
  {}

  virtual double evaluate()
  {
    // Evaluate the operands.
    double left = left_->evaluate();
    double right = right_->evaluate();

    // Add them.
    return left + right;
  }

private:
  Expression* left_;
  Expression* right_;
};
```

Pretty neat right? Just a couple of simple classes and now we can represent and evaluate arbitrarily complex arithmetic expressions. We just need to create the right objects and wire them up correctly.

It's a beautiful, simple pattern, but it has some problems. Look back at the illustration. What do you see? Lots of little boxes, and lots of arrows between them. Code is represented as a sprawling fractal tree of tiny objects. That has some unpleasant consequences:

- Loading it from disk requires instantiating and wiring up tons of these small objects.

- Those objects and the pointers between them use a lot of memory. On a 32-bit machine, that little arithmetic expression up there takes up at least 68 bytes, not including padding.

- Traversing the pointers into subexpressions is murder on your data cache. Meanwhile, all of those virtual method calls wreak carnage on your instruction cache.

Put those together, and what do they spell? S-L-O-W. There's a reason most programming languages in wide use aren't based on the Interpreter pattern. It's just too slow, and it uses up too much memory.

## Machine code, virtually

Consider our game. When we run it, the player's computer doesn't traverse a bunch of C++ grammar tree structures at runtime. Instead, we compile it ahead of time to machine code, and the CPU runs that. What's machine code got going for it?

- *It's dense.* It's a solid, contiguous blob of binary data, and no bit goes to waste.

- *It's linear.* Instructions are packed together and executed one right after another. No jumping around in memory (unless you're doing actual control flow, of course).

- *It's low-level.* Each instruction does one relatively minimal thing, and interesting behavior comes from *composing* them.

- *It's fast.* As a consequence of all of these (well, and the fact that it's implemented directly in hardware), machine code runs like the wind.

This sounds swell, but we don't want actual machine code for our spells. Letting users provide machine code which our game executes is just

Ruby was implemented like this for something like 15 years. At version 1.9, they switched to bytecode like this chapter describes. Look how much time I'm saving you!

If you're playing along at home, don't forget to take into account the vtable pointers.

See the chapter on Data Locality (p. 269) for more on what the cache is and how it affects your performance.

This is why many game consoles and iOS don't allow programs to execute machine code loaded or generated at runtime. That's a drag because the fastest programming language implementations do exactly that. They contain a "just-in-time" compiler, or *JIT*, that translates the language to optimized machine code on the fly.

In programming language circles, "virtual machine" and "interpreter" are synonymous, and I use them interchangeably here. When I refer to the Gang of Four's Interpreter pattern, I'll use "pattern" to make it clear.

begging for security problems. What we need is a compromise between the performance of machine code and the safety of the Interpreter pattern.

What if instead of loading actual machine code and executing it directly, we defined our own *virtual* machine code? We'd then write a little emulator for it in our game. It would be similar to machine code—dense, linear, relatively low-level—but would also be handled entirely by our game so we could safely sandbox it.

We'd call our little emulator a *virtual machine* (or "VM" for short), and the synthetic binary machine code it runs *bytecode*. It's got the flexibility and ease of use of defining things in data, but it has better performance than higher-level representations like the Interpreter pattern.

This sounds daunting, though. My goal for the rest of this chapter is to show you that if you keep your feature list pared down, it's actually pretty approachable. Even if you end up not using this pattern yourself, you'll at least have a better understanding of Lua and many other languages which are implemented using it.

## The Pattern

An **instruction set** defines the low-level operations that can be performed. A series of instructions is encoded as a **sequence of bytes**. A **virtual machine** executes these instructions one at a time, using a **stack for intermediate values**. By combining instructions, complex high-level behavior can be defined.

## When to Use It

This is the most complex pattern in this book, and it's not something to throw into your game lightly. Use it when you have a lot of behavior you need to define and your game's implementation language isn't a good fit because:

- It's too low-level, making it tedious or error-prone to program in.

- Iterating on it takes too long due to slow compile times or other tooling issues.

- It has too much trust. If you want to ensure the behavior being defined can't break the game, you need to sandbox it from the rest of the codebase.

Of course, that list describes a bunch of your game. Who doesn't want a faster iteration loop or more safety? However, that doesn't come for free. Bytecode is slower than native code, so it isn't a good fit for performance-critical parts of your engine.

# Keep in Mind

There's something seductive about creating your own language or system-within-a-system. I'll be doing a minimal example here, but in the real world, these things tend to grow like vines.

Every time I see someone define a little language or a scripting system, they say, "Don't worry, it will be tiny." Then, inevitably, they add more and more little features until it's a full-fledged language. Except, unlike some other languages, it grew in an ad-hoc, organic fashion and has all of the architectural elegance of a shanty town.

Of course, there's nothing *wrong* with making a full-fledged language. Just make sure you do so deliberately. Otherwise, be very careful to control the scope of what your bytecode can express. Put a short leash on it before it runs away from you.

For me, game development is seductive in the same way. In both cases, I'm striving to create a virtual space for others to play and be creative in.

For example, see every templating language ever.

## You'll need a front-end

Low-level bytecode instructions are great for performance, but a binary bytecode format is *not* what your users are going to author. One reason we're moving behavior out of code is so that we can express it at a *higher* level. If C++ is too low-level, making your users effectively write in assembly language—even one of your own design—isn't an improvement!

Much like the Gang of Four's Interpreter pattern, it's assumed that you also have some way to *generate* the bytecode. Usually, users author their behavior in some higher-level format, and a tool translates that to the bytecode that our virtual machine understands. In other words, a compiler.

I know, that sounds scary. That's why I'm mentioning it here. If you don't have the resources to build an authoring tool, then bytecode isn't for you. But as we'll see later, it may not be as bad as you think.

Challenging that assertion is the venerable game RoboWar. In that game, *players* write little programs to control a robot in a language very similar to assembly and the kind of instruction sets we'll be discussing here.

It was my first introduction to assembly-like languages.

## You'll miss your debugger

Programming is hard. We know what we want the machine to do, but we don't always communicate that correctly—we write bugs. To help find and fix those, we've amassed a pile of tools to understand what our code is doing wrong, and how to right it. We have debuggers, static analyzers, decompilers, etc. All of those tools are designed to work with some existing language: either machine code or something higher level.

When you define your own bytecode VM, you leave those tools behind. Sure, you can step through the VM in your debugger, but that tells you what the VM *itself* is doing, and not what the bytecode it's interpreting is up to. It certainly doesn't help you map that bytecode back to the high-level form it was compiled from.

If the behavior you're defining is simple, you can scrape by without too much tooling to help you debug it. But as the scale of your content grows, plan to invest real time into features that help users see what their bytecode is doing. Those features might not ship in your game, but they'll be critical to ensure that you actually *can* ship your game.

## Sample Code

After the previous couple of sections, you might be surprised how straightforward the implementation is. First, we need to craft an instruction set for our VM. Before we start thinking about bytecode and stuff, let's just think about it like an API.

### A magical API

If we were defining spells in straight C++ code, what kind of API would we need for that code to call into? What are the basic operations in the game engine that spells are defined in terms of? Most spells ultimately change one of the stats of a wizard, so we'll start with a couple for that:

```
void setHealth(int wizard, int amount);
void setWisdom(int wizard, int amount);
void setAgility(int wizard, int amount);
```

The first parameter identifies which wizard is affected, say 0 for the player's and 1 for their opponent. This way, healing spells can affect the player's own wizard, while damaging attacks harm their nemesis. These three little methods cover a surprisingly wide variety of magical effects.

If the spells just silently tweaked stats, the game logic would be fine, but playing it would bore players to tears. Let's fix that:

```
void playSound(int soundId);
void spawnParticles(int particleType);
```

These don't affect gameplay, but they crank up the intensity of the gameplay *experience*. We could add more for camera shake, animation, etc., but this is enough to get us started.

Of course, if you want your game to be moddable, then you *will* ship those features, and they'll be even more important.

## A magical instruction set

Now let's see how we'd turn this *programmatic* API into something that can be controlled from data. Let's start small and then we'll work our way up to the whole shebang. For now, we'll ditch all of the parameters to these methods. We'll say the set___() methods always affect the player's own wizard and always max out the stat. Likewise, the FX operations always play a single hard-coded sound and particle effect.

Given that, a spell is just a series of instructions. Each one identifies which operation you want to perform. We can enumerate them:

```
enum Instruction
{
  INST_SET_HEALTH      = 0x00,
  INST_SET_WISDOM      = 0x01,
  INST_SET_AGILITY     = 0x02,
  INST_PLAY_SOUND      = 0x03,
  INST_SPAWN_PARTICLES = 0x04
};
```

To encode a spell in data, we store an array of **enum** values. We've only got a few different primitives, so the range of **enum** values easily fits into a byte. This means the code for a spell is just a list of bytes—ergo "bytecode".

To execute a single instruction, we see which primitive it is and dispatch to the right API method:

```
switch (instruction)
{
  case INST_SET_HEALTH:
    setHealth(0, 100);
    break;

  case INST_SET_WISDOM:
    setWisdom(0, 100);
    break;

  case INST_SET_AGILITY:
    setAgility(0, 100);
    break;

  case INST_PLAY_SOUND:
    playSound(SOUND_BANG);
    break;

  case INST_SPAWN_PARTICLES:
    spawnParticles(PARTICLE_FLAME);
    break;
}
```

Some bytecode VMs use more than a single byte for each instruction and have more complicated rules for how they are decoded. Actual machine code on common chips like x86 is a good bit more complex.

But a single byte is good enough for the Java Virtual Machine and Microsoft's Common Language Runtime, which forms the backbone of the .NET platform, and it's good enough for us.

In this way, our interpreter forms the bridge between code world and data world. We can wrap this in a little VM that executes an entire spell like so:

```
class VM
{
public:
  void interpret(char bytecode[], int size)
  {
    for (int i = 0; i < size; i++)
    {
      char instruction = bytecode[i];
      switch (instruction)
      {
        // Cases for each instruction...
      }
    }
  }
};
```

Type that in and you'll have written your first virtual machine. Unfortunately, it's not very flexible. We can't define a spell that touches the player's opponent or lowers a stat. We can only play one sound!

To get something that starts to have the expressive feel of an actual language, we need to get parameters in here.

### A stack machine

To execute a complex nested expression, you start with the innermost subexpressions. You calculate those, and the results flow outward as arguments to the expressions that contain them until eventually, the whole expression has been evaluated.

The Interpreter pattern models this explicitly as a tree of nested objects, but we want the speed of a flat list of instructions. We still need to ensure results from subexpressions flow to the right surrounding expressions. But, since our data is flattened, we'll have to use the *order* of the instructions to control that. We'll do it the same way your CPU does—with a stack.

This architecture is unimaginatively called a *stack machine*. Programming languages like Forth, PostScript, and Factor expose this model directly to the user.

```
class VM
{
public:
  VM() : stackSize_(0) {}

  // Other stuff...

private:
  static const int MAX_STACK = 128;
  int stackSize_;
  int stack_[MAX_STACK];
};
```

The VM maintains an internal stack of values. In our example, the only kinds of values our instructions work with are numbers, so we can use a simple array of ints. Whenever a bit of data needs to work its way from one instruction to another, it gets there through the stack.

Like the name implies, values can be pushed onto or popped off of the stack, so let's add a couple of methods for that:

```
class VM
{
private:
  void push(int value)
  {
    // Check for stack overflow.
    assert(stackSize_ < MAX_STACK);
    stack_[stackSize_++] = value;
  }

  int pop()
  {
    // Make sure the stack isn't empty.
    assert(stackSize_ > 0);
    return stack_[--stackSize_];
  }

  // Other stuff...
};
```

When an instruction needs to receive parameters, it pops them off the stack like so:

```
switch (instruction)
{
  case INST_SET_HEALTH:
  {
    int amount = pop();
    int wizard = pop();
    setHealth(wizard, amount);
    break;
  }

  // Similar for SET_WISDOM and SET_AGILITY...

  case INST_PLAY_SOUND:
    playSound(pop());
    break;

  case INST_SPAWN_PARTICLES:
    spawnParticles(pop());
    break;
}
```

To get some values *onto* that stack, we need one more instruction: a literal. It represents a raw integer value. But where does *it* get its value from? How do we avoid some turtles-all-the-way-down infinite regress here?

The trick is to take advantage of the fact that our instruction stream is a sequence of bytes—we can stuff the number directly in the byte array. We define another instruction type for a number literal like so:

```
switch (instruction)
{
  // Other instruction cases...

  case INST_LITERAL:
  {
    // Read the next byte from the bytecode.
    int value = bytecode[++i];
    push(value);
    break;
  }
}
```

Here, I'm reading a single byte for the value to avoid the fiddly code required to decode a multiple-byte integer, but in a real implementation, you'll want to support literals that cover your full numeric range.

It reads the next byte in the bytecode stream *as a number* and pushes it onto the stack.

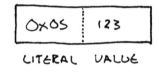

*Figure 11.3 – A literal in bytecode*

Let's string a few of these instructions together and watch the interpreter execute them to get a feel for how the stack works.

We start with an empty stack and the interpreter pointing to the first instruction:

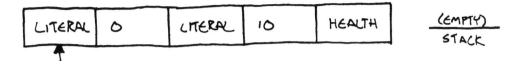

*Figure 11.4 - Before executing any instructions*

First, it executes the first `INST_LITERAL`. That reads the next byte from the bytecode (0) and pushes it onto the stack:

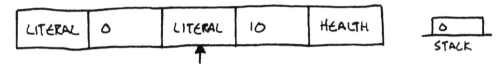

*Figure 11.5 – After executing the first literal*

Then, it executes the second `INST_LITERAL`. That reads the 10 and pushes it:

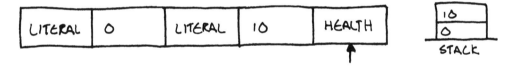

*Figure 11.6 – About to execute the last instruction*

Finally, it executes `INST_SET_HEALTH`. That pops 10 and stores it in `amount`, then pops 0 and stores it in `wizard`. Then, it calls `setHealth()` with those parameters.

Ta-da! We've got a spell that sets the player's wizard's health to ten points. Now, we've got enough flexibility to define spells that set either wizard's stats to whatever amounts we want. We can also play different sounds and spawn particles.

But... this still feels like a *data* format. We can't, for example, raise a wizard's health by half of their wisdom. Our designers want to be able to express *rules* for spells, not just *values*.

### Behavior = composition

If we think of our little VM like a programming language, all it supports now is a couple of built-in functions and constant parameters for them. To get bytecode to feel like *behavior*, what we're missing is *composition*.

Our designers need to be able to create expressions that combine different values in interesting ways. For a simple example, they want spells that modify a stat *by* a certain amount instead of *to* a certain amount. That requires taking into account a stat's current value. We have instructions for *writing* a stat, but we need to add a couple to *read* stats:

```
case INST_GET_HEALTH:
{
  int wizard = pop();
  push(getHealth(wizard));
  break;
}

case INST_GET_WISDOM:
case INST_GET_AGILITY:
  // You get the idea...
```

As you can see, these work with the stack in both directions. They pop a parameter to determine which wizard to get the stat for, and then they look up the stat's value and push that back onto the stack.

This lets us write spells that copy stats around. We could create a spell that set a wizard's agility to their wisdom or a strange incantation that set one wizard's health to mirror his opponent's.

Better, but still quite limited. Next, we need arithmetic. It's time our baby VM learned how to add 1 + 1. We'll add a few more instructions. By now, you've probably got the hang of it and can guess how they look. I'll just show addition:

```
case INST_ADD:
{
  int b = pop();
  int a = pop();
  push(a + b);
  break;
}
```

Like our other instructions, it pops a couple of values, does a bit of work, and then pushes the result back. Up until now, every new instruction gave us an incremental improvement in expressiveness, but we just made a big leap. It isn't obvious, but we can now handle all sorts of complicated, deeply nested arithmetic expressions.

Let's walk through a slightly more complex example. Say we want a spell that increases the player's wizard's health by the average of their agility and wisdom. In code, that's:

```
setHealth(0, getHealth(0) +
    (getAgility(0) + getWisdom(0)) / 2);
```

You might think we'd need instructions to handle the explicit grouping that parentheses give you in the expression here, but the stack supports that implicitly. Here's how you could evaluate this by hand:

1. Get the wizard's current health and remember it.

2. Get the wizard's agility and remember it.

3. Do the same for their wisdom.

4. Get those last two, add them, and remember the result.

5. Divide that by two and remember the result.

6. Recall the wizard's health and add it to that result.

7. Take that result and set the wizard's health to that value.

Do you see all of those "remembers" and "recalls"? Each "remember" corresponds to a push, and the "recalls" are pops. That means we can translate this to bytecode pretty easily. For example, the first line to get the wizard's current health is:

```
LITERAL 0
GET_HEALTH
```

This bit of bytecode pushes the wizard's health onto the stack. If we mechanically translate each line like that, we end up with a chunk of bytecode that evaluates our original expression. To give you a feel for how the instructions compose, I've done that on the next page.

To show how the stack changes over time, we'll walk through a sample execution where the wizard's current stats are 45 health, 7 agility, and 11 wisdom. Next to each instruction is what the stack looks like after executing it and then a little comment explaining the instruction's purpose:

```
LITERAL 0    [0]                # Wizard index
LITERAL 0    [0, 0]             # Wizard index
GET_HEALTH   [0, 45]            # getHealth()
LITERAL 0    [0, 45, 0]         # Wizard index
GET_AGILITY  [0, 45, 7]         # getAgility()
LITERAL 0    [0, 45, 7, 0]      # Wizard index
GET_WISDOM   [0, 45, 7, 11]     # getWisdom()
ADD          [0, 45, 18]        # Add agility and wisdom
LITERAL 2    [0, 45, 18, 2]     # Divisor
DIVIDE       [0, 45, 9]         # Average them
ADD          [0, 54]            # Add average to health
SET_HEALTH   []                 # Set health to result
```

If you watch the stack at each step, you can see how data flows through it almost like magic. We push 0 for the wizard index at the beginning, and it just hangs around at the bottom of the stack until we finally need it for the last SET_HEALTH at the end.

## A virtual machine

I could keep going, adding more and more instructions, but this is a good place to stop. As it is, we've got a nice little VM that lets us define fairly open-ended behavior using a simple, compact data format. While "bytecode" and "virtual machines" sound intimidating, you can see they're often as simple as a stack, a loop, and a switch statement.

Remember our original goal to have behavior be nicely sandboxed? Now that you've seen exactly how the VM is implemented, it's obvious that we've accomplished that. The bytecode can't do anything malicious or reach out into weird parts of the game engine because we've only defined a few instructions that touch the rest of the game.

We control how much memory it uses by how big of a stack we create, and we're careful to make sure it can't overflow that. We can even control how much *time* it uses. In our instruction loop, we can track how many we've executed and bail out if it goes over some limit.

There's just one problem left: actually creating the bytecode. So far, we've taken bits of pseudocode and compiled them to bytecode by hand. Unless you've got a *lot* of free time, that's not going to work in practice.

Maybe my threshold for "magic" is a little too low here.

Controlling execution time isn't necessary in our sample because we don't have any instructions for looping. We could limit execution time by limiting the total size of the bytecode. This also means our bytecode isn't Turing-complete.

## Spellcasting tools

One of our initial goals was to have a *higher*-level way to author behavior, but we've gone and created something *lower*-level than C++. It has the runtime performance and safety we want, but absolutely none of the designer-friendly usability.

To fill that gap, we need some tooling. We need a program that lets users define the high-level behavior of a spell and then takes that and generates the appropriate low-level stack machine bytecode.

That probably sounds way harder than making the VM. Many programmers were dragged through a compilers class in college and took away from it nothing but PTSD triggered by the sight of a book with a dragon on the cover or the words "lex" and "yacc".

I'm referring, of course, to the classic text *Compilers: Principles, Techniques, and Tools.*

In truth, compiling a text-based language isn't that bad, though it's a *bit* too broad of a topic to cram in here. However, you don't have to do that. What I said we need is a *tool*—it doesn't have to be a *compiler* whose input format is a *text file*.

On the contrary, I encourage you to consider building a graphical interface to let users define their behavior, especially if the people using it won't be highly technical. Writing text that's free of syntax errors is difficult for people who haven't spent years getting used to a compiler yelling at them.

Instead, you can build an app that lets users "script" by clicking and dragging little boxes, pulling down menu items, or whatever else makes sense for the kind of behavior you want them to create.

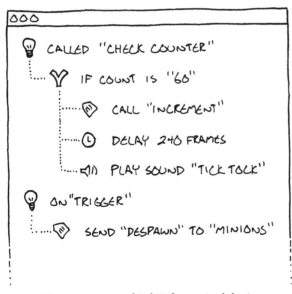

The scripting system I wrote for Henry Hatsworth in the Puzzling Adventure worked like this.

*Figure 11.7 – A graphical UI for creating behavior*

The nice thing about this is that your UI can make it impossible for users to create "invalid" programs. Instead of vomiting error messages on them, you can proactively disable buttons or provide default values to ensure that the thing they've created is valid at all points in time.

This spares you from designing a grammar and writing a parser for a little language. But, I know, some of you find UI programming equally unpleasant. Well, in that case, I don't have any good news for you.

Ultimately, this pattern is about expressing behavior in a user-friendly, high-level way. You have to craft the user experience. To execute the behavior efficiently, you then need to translate that into a lower-level form. It is real work, but if you're up to the challenge, it can pay off.

## Design Decisions

I tried to keep this chapter as simple as I could, but what we're really doing is creating a language. That's a pretty open-ended design space. Exploring it can be tons of fun, so make sure you don't forget to finish your game.

### How do instructions access the stack?

Bytecode VMs come in two main flavors: stack-based and register-based. In a stack-based VM, instructions always work from the top of the stack, like in our sample code. For example, INST_ADD pops two values, adds them, and pushes the result.

Register-based VMs still have a stack. The only difference is that instructions can read their inputs from deeper in the stack. Instead of INST_ADD always *popping* its operands, it has two indexes stored in the bytecode that identify where in the stack to read the operands from.

- **With a stack-based VM:**

  - *Instructions are small.* Since each instruction implicitly finds its arguments on top of the stack, you don't need to encode any data for that. This means each instruction can be pretty small, usually a single byte.

  - *Code generation is simpler.* When you get around to writing the compiler or tool that outputs bytecode, you'll find it simpler to generate stack-based bytecode. Since each instruction implicitly works from the top of the stack, you just need to output instructions in the right order to pass parameters between them.

- *You have more instructions.* Each instruction only sees the very top of the stack. This means that to generate code for something like a = b + c, you need separate instructions to move b and c to the top of the stack, perform the operation, then move the result into a.

- **With a register-based VM:**

  - *Instructions are larger.* Since instructions need arguments for stack offsets, a single instruction needs more bits. For example, an instruction in Lua—probably the most well-known register-based VM—is a full 32-bits. It uses 6 bits for the instruction type, and the rest are arguments.

    The Lua folks don't specify Lua's bytecode format, and it changes from version to version. What I'm describing here is true as of Lua 5.1. For an absolutely amazing deep dive into Lua's internals, look up "A No-Frills Introduction to Lua 5.1 VM Instructions".

  - *You have fewer instructions.* Since each instruction can do more work, you don't need as many of them. Some say you get a performance improvement since you don't have to shuffle values around in the stack as much.

So which should you do? My recommendation is to stick with a stack-based VM. They're simpler to implement and much simpler to generate code for. Register-based VMs got a reputation for being a bit faster after Lua converted to that style, but it depends *deeply* on your actual instructions and on lots of other details of your VM.

## What instructions do you have?

Your instruction set defines the boundaries of what can and cannot be expressed in bytecode, and it also has a big impact on the performance of your VM. Here's a laundry list of the different kinds of instructions you may want:

- **External primitives.** These are the ones that reach out of the VM into the rest of the game engine and do stuff that the user can see. They control what kinds of real behavior can be expressed in bytecode. Without these, your VM can't do anything more than burn CPU cycles.

- **Internal primitives.** These manipulate values inside the VM—things like literals, arithmetic, comparison operators, and instructions that juggle the stack around.

- **Control flow.** Our example didn't cover these, but when you want behavior that's imperative and conditionally executes instructions or loops and executes instructions more than once, you need control flow. In the low-level language of bytecode, they're surprisingly simple: jumps.

In our instruction loop, we had an index to track where we were in the bytecode. All a jump instruction does is modify that variable and change where we're currently executing. In other words, it's a `goto`. You can build all kinds of higher-level control flow using that.

- **Abstraction.** If your users start defining a *lot* of stuff in data, eventually they'll want to start reusing bits of bytecode instead of having to copy and paste it. You may want something like callable procedures.

  In their simplest form, procedures aren't much more complex than a jump. The only difference is that the VM maintains a second *return* stack. When it executes a "call" instruction, it pushes the current instruction index onto the return stack and then jumps to the called bytecode. When it hits a "return", the VM pops the index from the return stack and jumps back to it.

### How are values represented?

Our sample VM only works with one kind of value, integers. That makes answering this easy — the stack is just a stack of `int`s. A more full-featured VM will support different data types: strings, objects, lists, etc. You'll have to decide how those are stored internally.

- **A single datatype:**

  - *It's simple.* You don't have to worry about tagging, conversions, or type-checking.

  - *You can't work with different data types.* This is the obvious downside. Cramming different types into a single representation—think storing numbers as strings—is asking for pain.

- **A tagged variant:**

  This is the common representation for dynamically typed languages. Every value has two pieces. The first is a type tag—an `enum`—that identifies what data type is being stored.

  ```
  enum ValueType
  {
    TYPE_INT,
    TYPE_DOUBLE,
    TYPE_STRING
  };
  ```

The rest of the bits are then interpreted appropriately according to that type, like:

```
struct Value
{
  ValueType type;
  union
  {
    int    intValue;
    double doubleValue;
    char*  stringValue;
  };
};
```

- *Values know their type.* The nice thing about this representation is that you can check the type of a value at runtime. That's important for dynamic dispatch and for ensuring that you don't try to perform operations on types that don't support it.

- *It takes more memory.* Every value has to carry around a few extra bits with it to identify its type. In something as low-level as a VM, a few bits here and there add up quickly.

- **An untagged union:**

  This uses a union like the previous form, but it does *not* have a type tag that goes along with it. You have a little blob of bits that could represent more than one type, and it's up to you to ensure you don't misinterpret them.

  This is how statically typed languages represent things in memory. Since the type system ensures at compile time that you aren't misinterpreting values, you don't need to validate it at runtime.

  This is also how *untyped* languages like assembly and Forth store values. Those languages leave it to the *user* to make sure they don't write code that misinterprets a value's type. Not for the faint of heart!

  - *It's compact.* You can't get any more efficient than storing just the bits you need for the value itself.

  - *It's fast.* Not having type tags implies you're not spending cycles checking them at runtime either. This is one of the reasons statically typed languages tend to be faster than dynamic ones.

  - *It's unsafe.* This is the real cost, of course. A bad chunk of bytecode that causes you to misinterpret a value and treat a number like a pointer or vice versa can violate the security of your game or make it crash.

  If your bytecode was compiled from a statically typed language, you might think you're safe here because the compiler won't generate unsafe bytecode. That may be true, but remember that malicious users may hand-craft evil bytecode without going through your compiler.

  That's why, for example, the Java Virtual Machine has to do *bytecode verification* when it loads a program.

- **An interface:**

  The object-oriented solution for a value that maybe be one of several different types is through polymorphism. An interface provides virtual methods for the various type tests and conversions, along the lines of:

  ```
  class Value
  {
  public:
    virtual ~Value() {}

    virtual ValueType type() = 0;

    virtual int asInt() {
      // Can only call this on ints.
      assert(false);
      return 0;
    }

    // Other conversion methods...
  };
  ```

  Then you have concrete classes for each specific data type, like:

  ```
  class IntValue : public Value
  {
  public:
    IntValue(int value)
    : value_(value)
    {}

    virtual ValueType type() { return TYPE_INT; }
    virtual int asInt() { return value_; }

  private:
    int value_;
  };
  ```

- *It's open-ended.* You can define new value types outside of the core VM as long as they implement the base interface.

- *It's object-oriented.* If you adhere to OOP principles, this does things the "right" way and uses polymorphic dispatch for type-specific behavior instead of something like switching on a type tag.

- *It's verbose.* You have to define a separate class with all of the associated ceremonial verbiage for each data type. Note that in the previous examples, we showed the entire definition of *all* of the value types. Here, we only cover one!

- *It's inefficient.* To get polymorphism, you have to go through a pointer, which means even tiny values like Booleans and numbers get wrapped in objects that are allocated on the heap. Every time you touch a value, you have to do a virtual method call.

  In something like the core of a virtual machine, small performance hits like this quickly add up. In fact, this suffers from many of the problems that caused us to avoid the Interpreter pattern, except now the problem is in our *values* instead of our *code*.

My recommendation is that if you can stick with a single data type, do that. Otherwise, do a tagged union. That's what almost every language interpreter in the world does.

### How is the bytecode generated?

I saved the most important question for last. I've walked you through the code to *consume* and *interpret* bytecode, but it's up to you to build something to *produce* it. The typical solution here is to write a compiler, but it's not the only option.

- **If you define a text-based language:**

  - *You have to define a syntax.* Both amateur and professional language designers categorically underestimate how difficult this is to do. Defining a grammar that makes parsers happy is easy. Defining one that makes *users* happy is *hard*.

    Syntax design is user interface design, and that process doesn't get easier when you constrain the user interface to a string of characters.

  - *You have to implement a parser.* Despite their reputation, this part is pretty easy. Either use a parser generator like ANTLR or Bison, or — like I do—hand-roll a little recursive descent one, and you're good to go.

  - *You have to handle syntax errors.* This is one of the most important and most difficult parts of the process. When users make syntax and semantic errors—which they will, constantly—it's your job to guide them back onto the right path. Giving helpful feedback isn't easy when all you know is that your parser is sitting on some unexpected punctuation.

- *It will likely turn off non-technical users.* We programmers like text files. Combined with powerful command-line tools, we think of them as the LEGO blocks of computing—simple, but easily composable in a million ways.

  Most non-programmers don't think of plaintext like that. To them, text files feel like filling in tax forms for an angry robotic auditor that yells at them if they forget a single semicolon.

- **If you define a graphical authoring tool:**

  - *You have to implement a user interface.* Buttons, clicks, drags, stuff like that. Some cringe at the idea of this, but I personally love it. If you go down this route, it's important to treat designing the user interface as a core part of doing your job well—not just an unpleasant task to be muddled through.

    Every little bit of extra work you do here will make your tool easier and more pleasant to use, and that directly leads to better content in your game. If you look behind many of the games you love, you'll often find the secret was fun authoring tools.

  - *You have fewer error cases.* Because the user is building behavior interactively one step at a time, your application can guide them away from mistakes as soon as they happen.

    With a text-based language, the tool doesn't see *any* of the user's content until they throw an entire file at it. That makes it harder to prevent and handle errors.

  - *Portability is harder.* The nice thing about text compilers is that text files are universal. A simple compiler just reads in one file and writes one out. Porting that across operating systems is trivial.

    When you're building a UI, you have to choose which framework to use, and many of those are specific to one OS. There are cross-platform UI toolkits too, but those often get ubiquity at the expense of familiarity—they feel equally foreign on all of platforms.

Except for line endings. And encodings.

# See Also

- This pattern's close sister is the Gang of Four's Interpreter pattern. Both give you a way to express composable behavior in terms of data. In fact, you'll often end up using *both* patterns. The tool you use to generate bytecode will have an internal tree of objects that represents the code. This is exactly what the Interpreter pattern expects.

  In order to compile that to bytecode, you'll recursively walk the tree, just like you do to interpret it with the Interpreter pattern. The *only* difference is that instead of executing a primitive piece of behavior immediately, you output the bytecode instruction to perform that later.

- The Lua programming language is the most widely used scripting language in games. It's implemented internally as a very compact register-based bytecode VM.

- Kismet is a graphical scripting tool built into UnrealEd, the editor for the Unreal engine.

- My own little scripting language, Wren, is a simple stack-based bytecode interpreter.

# Subclass Sandbox                12

*Define behavior in a subclass using a set of operations provided by its base class.*

## Motivation

Every kid has dreamed of being a superhero, but unfortunately, cosmic rays are in short supply here on Earth. Games that let you pretend to be a superhero are the closest approximation. Because our game designers have never learned to say, "no", *our* superhero game aims to feature dozens, if not hundreds, of different superpowers that heroes may choose from.

Our plan is that we'll have a `Superpower` base class. Then, we'll have a derived class that implements each superpower. We'll divvy up the design doc among our team of programmers and get coding. When we're done, we'll have a hundred superpower classes.

We want to immerse our players in a world teeming with variety. Whatever power they dreamed up when they were a kid, we want in our game. That means these superpower subclasses will be able to do just about everything: play sounds, spawn visual effects, interact with AI, create and destroy other game entities, and mess with physics. There's no corner of the codebase that they won't touch.

When you find yourself with a *lot* of subclasses, like in this example, that often means a data-driven approach is better. Instead of lots of *code* for defining different powers, try finding a way to define that behavior in *data* instead.

Patterns like Type Object (p. 193), Bytecode (p. 155), and Interpreter can all help.

Let's say we unleash our team and get them writing superpower classes. What's going to happen?

- *There will be lots of redundant code.* While the different powers will be wildly varied, we can still expect plenty of overlap. Many of them will spawn visual effects and play sounds in the same way. A freeze ray, heat ray, and Dijon mustard ray are all pretty similar when you get down to it. If the people implementing those don't coordinate, there's going to be a lot of duplicate code and effort.

- *Every part of the game engine will get coupled to these classes.* Without knowing better, people will write code that calls into subsystems that were never meant to be tied directly to the superpower classes. If our renderer is organized into several nice neat layers, only one of which is intended to be used by code outside of the graphics engine, we can bet that we'll end up with superpower code that pokes into every one of them.

- *When these outside systems need to change, odds are good some random superpower code will get broken.* Once we have different superpower classes coupling themselves to various and sundry parts of the game engine, it's inevitable that changes to those systems will impact the power classes. That's no fun because your graphics, audio, and UI programmers probably don't want to also have to be gameplay programmers *too*.

- *It's hard to define invariants that all superpowers obey.* Let's say we want to make sure that all audio played by our powers gets properly queued and prioritized. There's no easy way to do that if our hundred classes are all directly calling into the sound engine on their own.

What we want is to give each of the gameplay programmers who is implementing a superpower a set of primitives they can play with. You want your power to play a sound? Here's your `playSound()` function. You want particles? Here's `spawnParticles()`. We'll make sure these operations cover everything you need to do so that you don't need to `#include` random headers and nose your way into the rest of the codebase.

We do this by making these operations *protected methods of the* `Superpower` *base class*. Putting them in the base class gives every power subclass direct, easy access to the methods. Making them protected (and likely non-virtual) communicates that they exist specifically to be *called* by subclasses.

Once we have these toys to play with, we need a place to use them. For that, we'll define a *sandbox method*, an abstract protected method that subclasses must implement. Given those, to implement a new kind of power, you:

1. Create a new class that inherits from `Superpower`.

2. Override `activate()`, the sandbox method.

3. Implement the body of that by calling the protected methods that `Superpower` provides.

We can fix our redundant code problem now by making those provided operations as high-level as possible. When we see code that's duplicated between lots of the subclasses, we can always roll it up into `Superpower` as a new operation that they can all use.

We've addressed our coupling problem by constraining the coupling to one place. `Superpower` itself will end up coupled to the different game systems, but our hundred derived classes will not. Instead, they are *only* coupled to their base class. When one of those game systems changes, modification to `Superpower` may be necessary, but dozens of subclasses shouldn't have to be touched.

This pattern leads to an architecture where you have a shallow but wide class hierarchy. Your inheritance chains aren't *deep*, but there are a *lot* of classes that hang off `Superpower`. By having a single class with a lot of direct subclasses, we have a point of leverage in our codebase. Time and love that we put into `Superpower` can benefit a wide set of classes in the game.

Lately, you find a lot of people criticizing inheritance in object-oriented languages. Inheritance *is* problematic—there's really no deeper coupling in a codebase than the one between a base class and its subclass—but I find *wide* inheritance trees to be easier to work with than *deep* ones.

## The Pattern

A **base class** defines an abstract **sandbox method** and several **provided operations**. Marking them protected makes it clear that they are for use by derived classes. Each derived **sandboxed subclass** implements the sandbox method using the provided operations.

## When to Use It

The Subclass Sandbox pattern is a very simple, common pattern lurking in lots of codebases, even outside of games. If you have a non-virtual protected method laying around, you're probably already using something like this. Subclass Sandbox is a good fit when:

- You have a base class with a number of derived classes.

- The base class is able to provide all of the operations that a derived class may need to perform.

- There is behavioral overlap in the subclasses and you want to make it easier to share code between them.

- You want to minimize coupling between those derived classes and the rest of the program.

## Keep in Mind

"Inheritance" is a bad word in many programming circles these days, and one reason is that base classes tend to accrete more and more code. This pattern is particularly susceptible to that.

Since subclasses go through their base class to reach the rest of the game, the base class ends up coupled to every system *any* derived class needs to talk to. Of course, the subclasses are also intimately tied to their base class. That spiderweb of coupling makes it very hard to change the base class without breaking something—you've got the *brittle base class problem*.

The flip side of the coin is that since most of your coupling has been pushed up to the base class, the derived classes are now much more cleanly separated from the rest of the world. Ideally, most of your behavior will be in those subclasses. That means much of your codebase is isolated and easier to maintain.

Still, if you find this pattern is turning your base class into a giant bowl of code stew, consider pulling some of the provided operations out into separate classes that the base class can dole out responsibility to. The Component pattern (p. 213) can help here.

## Sample Code

Because this is such a simple pattern, there isn't much to the sample code. That doesn't mean it isn't useful—the pattern is about the *intent*, not the complexity of its implementation.

We'll start with our **Superpower** base class:

```
class Superpower
{
public:
  virtual ~Superpower() {}

protected:
  virtual void activate() = 0;

  void move(double x, double y, double z)
  {
    // Code here...
  }

  void playSound(SoundId sound)
  {
    // Code here...
  }

  void spawnParticles(ParticleType type, int count)
  {
    // Code here...
  }
};
```

The `activate()` method is the sandbox method. Since it is virtual and abstract, subclasses *must* override it. This makes it clear to someone creating a power subclass where their work has to go.

The other protected methods, `move()`, `playSound()`, and `spawnParticles()`, are the provided operations. These are what the subclasses will call in their implementation of `activate()`.

We didn't implement the provided operations in this example, but an actual game would have real code there. Those methods are where `Superpower` gets coupled to other systems in the game—`move()` may call into physics code, `playSound()` will talk to the audio engine, etc. Since this is all in the *implementation* of the base class, it keeps that coupling encapsulated within `Superpower` itself.

OK, now let's get our radioactive spiders out and create a power. Here's one:

```
class SkyLaunch : public Superpower
{
protected:
  virtual void activate()
  {
    move(0, 0, 20); // Spring into the air.
    playSound(SOUND_SPROING);
    spawnParticles(PARTICLE_DUST, 10);
  }
};
```

OK, maybe being able to *jump* isn't all that *super*, but I'm trying to keep things basic here.

This power springs the superhero into the air, playing an appropriate sound and kicking up a little cloud of dust. If all of the superpowers were this simple — just a combination of sound, particle effect, and motion—then we wouldn't need this pattern at all. Instead, Superpower could have a baked-in implementation of activate() that accesses fields for the sound ID, particle type, and movement. But that only works when every power essentially works the same way with only some differences in data. Let's elaborate on it a bit:

```
class Superpower
{
protected:
  double getHeroX() { /* Code here... */ }
  double getHeroY() { /* Code here... */ }
  double getHeroZ() { /* Code here... */ }

  // Existing stuff...
};
```

Here, we've added a couple of methods to get the hero's position. Our SkyLaunch subclass can now use those:

```
class SkyLaunch : public Superpower
{
protected:
  virtual void activate()
  {
    if (getHeroZ() == 0)
    {
      // On the ground, so spring into the air.
      playSound(SOUND_SPROING);
      spawnParticles(PARTICLE_DUST, 10);
      move(0, 0, 20);
    }
    else if (getHeroZ() < 10.0f)
    {
      // Near the ground, so do a double jump.
      playSound(SOUND_SWOOP);
      move(0, 0, getHeroZ() - 20);
    }
    else
    {
      // Way up in the air, so do a dive attack.
      playSound(SOUND_DIVE);
      spawnParticles(PARTICLE_SPARKLES, 1);
      move(0, 0, -getHeroZ());
    }
  }
};
```

Since we have access to some state, now our sandbox method can do actual, interesting control flow. Here, it's still just a couple of simple `if` statements, but you can do anything you want. By having the sandbox method be an actual full-fledged method that contains arbitrary code, the sky's the limit.

Earlier, I suggested a data-driven approach for powers. This is one reason why you may decide *not* to do that. If your behavior is complex and imperative, it is more difficult to define in data.

## Design Decisions

As you can see, Subclass Sandbox is a fairly "soft" pattern. It describes a basic idea, but it doesn't have a lot of detailed mechanics. That means you'll be making some interesting choices each time you apply it. Here are some questions to consider.

### What operations should be provided?

This is the biggest question. It deeply affects how this pattern feels and how well it works. At the minimal end of the spectrum, the base class doesn't provide *any* operations. It just has a sandbox method. To implement it, you'll have to call into systems outside of the base class. If you take that angle, it's probably not even fair to say you're using this pattern.

On the other end of the spectrum, the base class provides *every* operation that a subclass may need. Subclasses are *only* coupled to the base class and don't call into any outside systems whatsoever.

Concretely, this means each source file for a subclass would only need a single `#include`—the one for its base class.

Between these two points, there's a wide middle ground where some operations are provided by the base class and others are accessed directly from the outside system that defines it. The more operations you provide, the less coupled subclasses are to outside systems, but the *more* coupled the base class is. It removes coupling from the derived classes, but it does so by pushing that up to the base class itself.

That's a win if you have a bunch of derived classes that were all coupled to some outside system. By moving the coupling up into a provided operation, you've centralized it into one place: the base class. But the more you do this, the bigger and harder to maintain that one class becomes.

So where should you draw the line? Here are a few rules of thumb:

- If a provided operation is only used by one or a few subclasses, you don't get a lot of bang for your buck. You're adding complexity to the base class, which affects everyone, but only a couple of classes benefit.

  This may be worth it to make the operation consistent with other provided operations, or it may be simpler and cleaner to let those special case subclasses call out to the external systems directly.

- When you call a method in some other corner of the game, it's less intrusive if that method doesn't modify any state. It still creates a coupling, but it's a "safe" coupling because it can't break anything in the game.

  Calls that do modify state, on the other hand, more deeply tie you to those parts of the codebase, and you need to be much more cognizant of that. That makes them good candidates for being rolled up into provided operations in the more visible base class.

- If the implementation of a provided operation only forwards a call to some outside system, then it isn't adding much value. In that case, it may be simpler to call the outside method directly.

  However, even simple forwarding can still be useful—those methods often access state that the base class doesn't want to directly expose to subclasses. For example, let's say `Superpower` provided this:

```
void playSound(SoundId sound)
{
  soundEngine_.play(sound);
}
```

It's just forwarding the call to some `soundEngine_` field in `Superpower`. The advantage, though, is that it keeps that field encapsulated in `Superpower` so subclasses can't poke at it.

### Should methods be provided directly, or through objects that contain them?

The challenge with this pattern is that you can end up with a painfully large number of methods crammed into your base class. You can mitigate that by moving some of those methods over to other classes. The provided operations in the base class then just return one of those objects.

For example, to let a power play sounds, we could add these directly to `Superpower`:

```
class Superpower
{
protected:
  void playSound(SoundId sound) { /* Code... */ }
  void stopSound(SoundId sound) { /* Code... */ }
  void setVolume(SoundId sound) { /* Code... */ }

  // Sandbox method and other operations...
};
```

But if `Superpower` is already getting large and unwieldy, we might want to avoid that. Instead, we create a `SoundPlayer` class that exposes that functionality:

```
class SoundPlayer
{
  void playSound(SoundId sound) { /* Code... */ }
  void stopSound(SoundId sound) { /* Code... */ }
  void setVolume(SoundId sound) { /* Code... */ }
};
```

Then `Superpower` provides access to it:

```
class Superpower
{
protected:
  SoundPlayer& getSoundPlayer()
  {
    return soundPlayer_;
  }

  // Sandbox method and other operations...

private:
  SoundPlayer soundPlayer_;
};
```

Shunting provided operations into auxiliary classes like this can do a few things for you:

- *It reduces the number of methods in the base class.* In the example here, we went from three methods to just a single getter.

- *Code in the helper class is usually easier to maintain.* Core base classes like `Superpower`, despite our best intentions, tend to be tricky to change since so much depends on them. By moving functionality over to a less coupled secondary class, we make that code easier to poke at without breaking things.

- *It lowers the coupling between the base class and other systems.* When `playSound()` was a method directly on `Superpower`, our base class was directly tied to `SoundId` and whatever audio code the implementation called into. Moving that over to `SoundPlayer` reduces `Superpower`'s coupling to the single `SoundPlayer` class, which then encapsulates all of its other dependencies.

### How does the base class get the state that it needs?

Your base class will often need some data that it wants to encapsulate and keep hidden from its subclasses. In our first example, the `Superpower` class provided a `spawnParticles()` method. If the implementation of that needs some particle system object, how would it get one?

- **Pass it to the base class constructor:**

  The simplest solution is to have the base class take it as a constructor argument:

  ```
  class Superpower
  {
  public:
    Superpower(ParticleSystem* particles)
    : particles_(particles) {}
    // Sandbox method and other operations...
  private:
    ParticleSystem* particles_;
  };
  ```

  This safely ensures that every superpower does have a particle system by the time it's constructed. But let's look at a derived class:

  ```
  class SkyLaunch : public Superpower
  {
  public:
    SkyLaunch(ParticleSystem* particles)
    : Superpower(particles) {}
  };
  ```

  Here we see the problem. Every derived class will need to have a constructor that calls the base class one and passes along that argument. That exposes every derived class to a piece of state that we don't want them to know about.

  This is also a maintenance headache. If we later add another piece of state to the base class, every constructor in each of our derived classes will have to be modified to pass it along.

- **Do two-stage initialization:**

  To avoid passing everything through the constructor, we can split initialization into two steps. The constructor will take no parameters and just create the object. Then, we call a separate method defined directly on the base class to pass in the rest of the data that it needs:

  ```
  Superpower* power = new SkyLaunch();
  power->init(particles);
  ```

Note here that since we aren't passing anything into the constructor for `SkyLaunch`, it isn't coupled to anything we want to keep private in `Superpower`. The trouble with this approach, though, is that you have to make sure you always remember to call `init()`. If you ever forget, you'll have a power that's in some twilight half-created state and won't work.

You can fix that by encapsulating the entire process into a single function, like so:

```
Superpower* createSkyLaunch(
    ParticleSystem* particles)
{
  Superpower* power = new SkyLaunch();
  power->init(particles);
  return power;
}
```

With a little trickery like private constructors and friend classes, you can ensure this `createSkylaunch()` function is the *only* function that can actually create powers. That way, you can't forget any of the initialization stages.

- **Make the state static:**

  In the previous example, we were initializing each `Superpower` *instance* with a particle system. That makes sense when every power needs its own unique state. But let's say that the particle system is a singleton (p. 73), and every power will be sharing the same state.

  In that case, we can make the state private to the base class and also make it *static*. The game will still have to make sure that it initializes the state, but it only has to initialize the `Superpower` *class* once for the entire game, and not each instance.

  ```
  class Superpower
  {
  public:
    static void init(ParticleSystem* particles)
    {
      particles_ = particles;
    }

    // Sandbox method and other operations...
  private:
    static ParticleSystem* particles_;
  };
  ```

  Note here that `init()` and `particles_` are both static. As long as the game calls `Superpower::init()` once early on, every power can access the particle system. At the same time, `Superpower` instances can be created freely by calling the right derived class's constructor.

Keep in mind that this still has many of the problems of a singleton. You've got some state shared between lots and lots of objects (all of the Superpower instances). The particle system is encapsulated, so it isn't globally *visible*, which is good, but it can still make reasoning about powers harder because they can all poke at the same object.

Even better, now that `particles_` is a *static* variable, we don't have to store it for each instance of Superpower, so we've made the class use less memory.

- **Use a service locator:**

The previous option requires that outside code specifically remembers to push in the state that the base class needs before it needs it. That places the burden of initialization on the surrounding code. Another option is to let the base class handle it by pulling in the state it needs. One way to do that is by using the Service Locator pattern (p. 251):

```
class Superpower
{
protected:
  void spawnParticles(ParticleType type, int count)
  {
    ParticleSystem& particles =
        Locator::getParticles();
    particles.spawn(type, count);
  }

  // Sandbox method and other operations...
};
```

Here, `spawnParticles()` needs a particle system. Instead of being *given* one by outside code, it fetches one itself from the service locator.

## See Also

- When you apply the Update Method pattern (p. 139), your update method will often also be a sandbox method.

- This pattern is a role reversal of the Template Method pattern. In both patterns, you implement a method using a set of primitive operations. With Subclass Sandbox, the method is in the derived class and the primitive operations are in the base class. With Template Method, the *base* class has the method and the primitive operations are implemented by the *derived* class.

- You can also consider this a variation on the Facade pattern. That pattern hides a number of different systems behind a single simplified API. With Subclass Sandbox, the base class acts as a facade that hides the entire game engine from the subclasses.

# Type Object

# 13

*Allow the flexible creation of new "classes" by creating a class,
each instance of which represents a different type of object.*

## Motivation

Imagine we're working on a fantasy role-playing game. Our task is to
write the code for the hordes of vicious monsters that seek to slay our
brave hero. Monsters have a bunch of different attributes: health, attacks,
graphics, sounds, etc., but for example purposes we'll just worry about the
first two.

Each monster in the game has a value for its current health. It starts out
full, and each time the monster is wounded, it diminishes. Monsters also
have an attack string. When the monster attacks our hero, that text will be
shown to the user somehow. (We don't care how here.)

The designers tell us that monsters come in a variety of different *breeds*,
like "dragon" or "troll". Each breed describes a *kind* of monster that exists
in the game, and there can be multiple monsters of the same breed
running around in the dungeon at the same time.

The breed determines a monster's starting health—dragons start off
with more than trolls, making them harder to kill. It also determines the
attack string — all monsters of the same breed attack the same way.

## The typical OOP answer

With that game design in mind, we fire up our text editor and start coding. According to the design, a dragon is a kind of monster, a troll is another kind, and so on with the other breeds. Thinking object-oriented, that leads us to a `Monster` base class:

```
class Monster
{
public:
  virtual ~Monster() {}
  virtual const char* getAttack() = 0;

protected:
  Monster(int startingHealth)
  : health_(startingHealth) {}

private:
  int health_; // Current health.
};
```

The public `getAttack()` function lets the combat code get the string that should be displayed when the monster attacks the hero. Each derived breed class will override this to provide a different message.

The constructor is protected and takes the starting health for the monster. We'll have derived classes for each breed that provide their own public constructors that call this one, passing in the starting health that is appropriate for that breed. Now let's see a couple of breed subclasses:

```
class Dragon : public Monster
{
public:
  Dragon() : Monster(230) {}

  virtual const char* getAttack()
  {
    return "The dragon breathes fire!";
  }
};
```

```
class Troll : public Monster
{
public:
  Troll() : Monster(48) {}

  virtual const char* getAttack()
  {
    return "The troll clubs you!";
  }
};
```

Each class derived from `Monster` passes in the starting health and overrides `getAttack()` to return the attack string for that breed. Everything works as expected, and before long, we've got our hero running around slaying a variety of beasties. We keep slinging code, and before we know it, we've got dozens of monster subclasses, from acidic slimes to zombie goats.

Then, strangely, things start to bog down. Our designers ultimately want to have *hundreds* of breeds, and we find ourselves spending all of our time writing these little seven-line subclasses and recompiling. It gets worse—the designers want to start tuning the breeds we've already coded. Our formerly productive workday degenerates to:

1. Get email from designer asking to change health of troll from 48 to 52.

2. Check out and change `Troll.h`.

3. Recompile game.

4. Check in change.

5. Reply to email.

6. Repeat.

We spend the day frustrated because we've turned into data monkeys. Our designers are frustrated because it takes them forever to get a simple number tuned. What we need is the ability to change breed stats without having to recompile the whole game every time. Even better, we'd like designers to be able to create and tune breeds without *any* programmer intervention at all.

## A class for a class

At a very high level, the problem we're trying to solve is pretty simple. We have a bunch of different monsters in the game, and we want to share certain attributes between them. A horde of monsters are beating on the hero, and we want some of them to use the same text for their attack. We define that by saying that all of those monsters are the same "breed", and that the breed determines the attack string.

We decided to implement this concept using inheritance since it lines up with our intuition of classes. A dragon is a monster, and each dragon in the game is an instance of this dragon "class". Defining each breed as a subclass of an abstract base `Monster` class, and having each monster in the game be an instance of that derived breed class mirrors that. We end up with a class hierarchy like this:

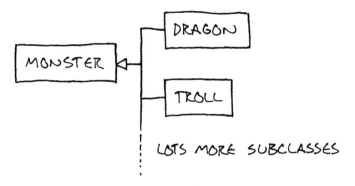

Here, the ◁— means "inherits from".

*Figure 13.1 – So many subclasses.*

Each instance of a monster in the game will be of one of the derived monster types. The more breeds we have, the bigger the class hierarchy. That's the problem of course: adding new breeds means adding new code, and each breed has to be compiled in as its own type.

This works, but it isn't the only option. We could also architect our code so that each monster *has* a breed. Instead of subclassing Monster for each breed, we have a single Monster class and a single Breed class:

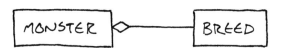

Here, the ◇— means "is referenced by".

*Figure 13.2 – Two classes, infinite breeds.*

That's it. Two classes. Notice that there's no inheritance at all. With this system, each monster in the game is simply an instance of class Monster. The Breed class contains the information that's shared between all monsters of the same breed: starting health and the attack string.

To associate monsters with breeds, we give each Monster instance a reference to a Breed object containing the information for that breed. To get the attack string, a monster just calls a method on its breed. The Breed class essentially defines a monster's "type". Each breed instance is an *object* that represents a different conceptual *type*, hence the name of the pattern: Type Object.

What's especially powerful about this pattern is that now we can define new *types* of things without complicating the codebase at all. We've essentially lifted a portion of the type system out of the hard-coded class hierarchy into data we can define at runtime.

We can create hundreds of different breeds by instantiating more instances of `Breed` with different values. If we create breeds by initializing them from data read from some configuration file, we have the ability to define new types of monsters completely in data. So easy, a designer could do it!

## The Pattern

Define a **type object** class and a **typed object** class. Each type object instance represents a different logical type. Each typed object stores a **reference to the type object that describes its type**.

Instance-specific data is stored in the typed object instance, and data or behavior that should be shared across all instances of the same conceptual type is stored in the type object. Objects referencing the same type object will function as if they were the same type. This lets us share data and behavior across a set of similar objects, much like subclassing lets us do, but without having a fixed set of hard-coded subclasses.

## When to Use It

This pattern is useful anytime you need to define a variety of different "kinds" of things, but baking the kinds into your language's type system is too rigid. In particular, it's useful when either of these is true:

- You don't know what types you will need up front. (For example, what if our game needed to support downloading content that contained new breeds of monsters?)

- You want to be able to modify or add new types without having to recompile or change code.

## Keep in Mind

This pattern is about moving the definition of a "type" from the imperative but rigid language of code into the more flexible but less behavioral world of objects in memory. The flexibility is good, but you lose some things by hoisting your types into data.

## The type objects have to be tracked manually

Under the hood, C++ virtual methods are implemented using something called a "virtual function table", or just "vtable". A vtable is a simple `struct` containing a set of function pointers, one for each virtual method in a class. There is one vtable in memory for each class. Each instance of a class has a pointer to the vtable for its class.

One advantage of using something like C++'s type system is that the compiler handles all of the bookkeeping for the classes automatically. The data that defines each class is automatically compiled into the static memory segment of the executable and just works.

With the Type Object pattern, we are now responsible for managing not only our monsters in memory, but also their *types*—we have to make sure all of the breed objects are instantiated and kept in memory as long as our monsters need them. Whenever we create a new monster, it's up to us to ensure that it's correctly initialized with a reference to a valid breed.

When you call a virtual function, the code first looks up the vtable for the object, then it calls the function stored in the appropriate function pointer in the table.

We've freed ourselves from some of the limitations of the compiler, but the cost is that we have to re-implement some of what it used to be doing for us.

Sound familiar? The vtable is our breed object, and the pointer to the vtable is the reference the monster holds to its breed. C++ classes are the Type Object pattern applied to C, handled automatically by the compiler.

## It's harder to define *behavior* for each type

With subclassing, you can override a method and do whatever you want to — calculate values procedurally, call other code, etc. The sky is the limit. We could define a monster subclass whose attack string changed based on the phase of the moon if we wanted to. (Handy for werewolves, I suppose.)

When we use the Type Object pattern instead, we replace an overridden method with a member variable. Instead of having monster subclasses that override a method to *calculate* an attack string using different *code*, we have a breed object that *stores* an attack string in a different *variable*.

This makes it very easy to use type objects to define type-specific *data*, but hard to define type-specific *behavior*. If, for example, different breeds of monster needed to use different AI algorithms, using this pattern becomes more challenging.

There are a couple of ways we can get around this limitation. A simple solution is to have a fixed set of pre-defined behaviors and then use data in the type object to simply *select* one of them. For example, let's say our monster AI will always be either "stand still", "chase hero", or "whimper and cower in fear" (hey, they can't all be mighty dragons). We can define functions to implement each of those behaviors. Then, we can associate an AI algorithm with a breed by having it store a pointer to the appropriate function.

Sound familiar again? Now we're back to really implementing vtables in *our* type objects.

Another more powerful solution is to actually support defining behavior completely in data. The Interpreter and Bytecode (p. 155) patterns both let us build objects that represent behavior. If we read in a data file and use that to create a data structure for one of these patterns, we've moved the behavior's definition completely out of code and into content.

## Sample Code

For our first pass at an implementation, let's start simple and build the basic system described in the motivation section. We'll start with the `Breed` class:

```
class Breed
{
public:
  Breed(int health, const char* attack)
  : health_(health),
    attack_(attack)
  {}

  int getHealth() { return health_; }
  const char* getAttack() { return attack_; }

private:
  int health_; // Starting health.
  const char* attack_;
};
```

Very simple. It's basically just a container for two data fields: the starting health and the attack string. Let's see how monsters use it:

```
class Monster
{
public:
  Monster(Breed& breed)
  : health_(breed.getHealth()),
    breed_(breed)
  {}

  const char* getAttack()
  {
    return breed_.getAttack();
  }

private:
  // Current health.
  int health_;
  Breed& breed_;
};
```

When we construct a monster, we give it a reference to a breed object. This defines the monster's breed instead of the subclasses we were previously using. In the constructor, `Monster` uses the breed to determine its starting

Over time, games are getting more data-driven. Hardware gets more powerful, and we find ourselves limited more by how much content we can author than how hard we can push the hardware. With a 64K cartridge, the challenge was *cramming* the gameplay into it. With a double-sided DVD, the challenge is *filling* it with gameplay.

Scripting languages and other higher-level ways of defining game behavior can give us a much needed productivity boost, at the expense of less optimal runtime performance. Since hardware keeps getting better but our brainpower doesn't, that trade-off starts to make more and more sense.

health. To get the attack string, the monster simply forwards the call to its breed.

This very simple chunk of code is the core idea of the pattern. Everything from here on out is bonus.

### Making type objects more like types: constructors

With what we have now, we construct a monster directly and are responsible for passing in its breed. This is a bit backwards from how regular objects are instantiated in most OOP languages—we don't usually allocate a blank chunk of memory and then *give* it its class. Instead, we call a constructor function on the class itself, and it's responsible for giving us a new instance.

"Pattern" is the right word here. What we're talking about is one of the classic patterns from Design Patterns: Factory Method.

In some languages, this pattern is applied for constructing *all* objects. In Ruby, Smalltalk, Objective-C, and other languages where classes are objects, you construct new instances by calling a method on the class object itself.

We can apply this same pattern to our type objects:

```
class Breed
{
public:
  Monster* newMonster()
  {
    return new Monster(*this);
  }

  // Previous Breed code...
};
```

And the class that uses them:

```
class Monster
{
  friend class Breed;

public:
  const char* getAttack()
  {
    return breed_.getAttack();
  }

private:
  Monster(Breed& breed)
  : health_(breed.getHealth()),
    breed_(breed)
  {}

  int health_; // Current health.
  Breed& breed_;
};
```

The key difference is the `newMonster()` function in `Breed`. That's our "constructor" factory method. With our original implementation, creating a monster looked like:

```
Monster* monster = new Monster(someBreed);
```

After our changes, it's like this:

```
Monster* monster = someBreed.newMonster();
```

So, why do this? There are two steps to creating an object: allocation and initialization. `Monster`'s constructor lets us do all of the initialization we need. In our example, that's only storing the breed, but a full game would be loading graphics, initializing the monster's AI, and doing other set-up work.

However, that all happens *after* allocation. We've already got a chunk of memory to put our monster into before its constructor is called. In games, we often want to control that aspect of object creation too: we'll typically use things like custom allocators or the Object Pool pattern (p. 305) to control where in memory our objects end up.

Defining a "constructor" function in `Breed` gives us a place to put that logic. Instead of simply calling `new`, the `newMonster()` function can pull the memory from a pool or custom heap before passing control off to `Monster` for initialization. By putting this logic inside `Breed`, in the *only* function that has the ability to create monsters, we ensure that all monsters go through the memory management scheme we want.

There's another minor difference here. Because the sample code is in C++, we can use a handy little feature: *friend classes*.

We've made `Monster`'s constructor private, which prevents anyone from calling it directly. Friend classes sidestep that restriction so `Breed` can still access it. This means the *only* way to create monsters is by going through `newMonster()`.

### Sharing data through inheritance

What we have so far is a perfectly serviceable type object system, but it's pretty basic. Our game will eventually have *hundreds* of different breeds, each with dozens of attributes. If a designer wants to tune all of the thirty different breeds of troll to make them a little stronger, she's got a lot of tedious data entry ahead of her.

What would help is the ability to share attributes across multiple *breeds* in the same way that breeds let us share attributes across multiple *monsters*. Just like we did with our original OOP solution, we can solve this using inheritance. Only, this time, instead of using our language's inheritance mechanism, we'll implement it ourselves within our type objects.

To keep things simple, we'll only support single inheritance. In the same way that a class can have a parent base class, we'll allow a breed to have a parent breed:

```
class Breed
{
public:
  Breed(Breed* parent, int health,
        const char* attack)
  : parent_(parent),
    health_(health),
    attack_(attack)
  {}

  int         getHealth();
  const char* getAttack();

private:
  Breed*      parent_;
  int         health_; // Starting health.
  const char* attack_;
};
```

When we construct a breed, we give it a parent that it inherits from. We can pass in NULL for a base breed that has no ancestors.

To make this useful, a child breed needs to control which attributes are inherited from its parent and which attributes it overrides and specifies itself. For our example system, we'll say that a breed overrides the monster's health by having a non-zero value and overrides the attack by having a non-NULL string. Otherwise, the attribute will be inherited from its parent.

There are two ways we can implement this. One is to handle the delegation dynamically every time the attribute is requested, like this:

```
int Breed::getHealth()
{
  // Override.
  if (health_ != 0 || parent_ == NULL)
  {
    return health_;
  }

  // Inherit.
  return parent_->getHealth();
}
```

```
const char* Breed::getAttack()
{
  // Override.
  if (attack_ != NULL || parent_ == NULL)
  {
    return attack_;
  }

  // Inherit.
  return parent_->getAttack();
}
```

This has the advantage of doing the right thing if a breed is modified at runtime to no longer override, or no longer inherit some attribute. On the other hand, it takes a bit more memory (it has to retain a pointer to its parent), and it's slower. It has to walk the inheritance chain each time you look up an attribute.

If we can rely on a breed's attributes not changing, a faster solution is to apply the inheritance at *construction time*. This is called "copy-down" delegation because we *copy* inherited attributes *down* into the derived type when it's created. It looks like this:

```
Breed(Breed* parent, int health, const char* attack)
: health_(health),
  attack_(attack)
{
  // Inherit non-overridden attributes.
  if (parent != NULL)
  {
    if (health == 0) health_ = parent->getHealth();

    if (attack == NULL)
    {
      attack_ = parent->getAttack();
    }
  }
}
```

Note that we no longer need a field for the parent breed. Once the constructor is done, we can forget the parent since we've already copied all of its attributes in. To access a breed's attribute, now we just return the field:

```
int         getHealth() { return health_; }
const char* getAttack() { return attack_; }
```

Nice and fast!

Let's say our game engine is set up to create the breeds by loading a JSON file that defines them. It could look like:

```json
{
  "Troll": {
    "health": 25,
    "attack": "The troll hits you!"
  },
  "Troll Archer": {
    "parent": "Troll",
    "health": 0,
    "attack": "The troll archer fires an arrow!"
  },
  "Troll Wizard": {
    "parent": "Troll",
    "health": 0,
    "attack": "The troll wizard casts a spell!"
  }
}
```

We'd have a chunk of code that reads each breed entry and instantiates a new breed instance with its data. As you can see from the `"parent": "Troll"` fields, the `Troll Archer` and `Troll Wizard` breeds inherit from the base `Troll` breed.

Since both of them have zero for their health, they'll inherit it from the base `Troll` breed instead. This means now our designer can tune the health in `Troll` and all three breeds will be updated. As the number of breeds and the number of different attributes each breed has increase, this can be a big time-saver. Now, with a pretty small chunk of code, we have an open-ended system that puts control in our designers' hands and makes the best use of their time. Meanwhile, we can get back to coding other features.

## Design Decisions

The Type Object pattern lets us build a type system as if we were designing our own programming language. The design space is wide open, and we can do all sorts of interesting stuff.

In practice, a few things curtail our fancy. Time and maintainability will discourage us from anything particularly complicated. More importantly, whatever type object system we design, our users (often non-programmers) will need to be able to easily understand it. The simpler we can make it, the more usable it will be. So what we'll cover here is the well-trodden design space, and we'll leave the far reaches for the academics and explorers.

## Is the type object encapsulated or exposed?

In our sample implementation, `Monster` has a reference to a breed, but it doesn't publicly expose it. Outside code can't get directly at the monster's breed. From the codebase's perspective, monsters are essentially typeless, and the fact that they have breeds is an implementation detail.

We can easily change this and allow `Monster` to return its `Breed`:

```
class Monster
{
public:
  Breed& getBreed() { return breed_; }

  // Existing code...
};
```

As in other examples in this book, we're following a convention where we return objects by reference instead of pointer to indicate to users that NULL will never be returned.

Doing this changes the design of `Monster`. The fact that all monsters have breeds is now a publicly visible part of its API. There are benefits with either choice.

- **If the type object is encapsulated:**

  - *The complexity of the Type Object pattern is hidden from the rest of the codebase.* It becomes an implementation detail that only the typed object has to worry about.

  - *The typed object can selectively override behavior from the type object.* Let's say we wanted to change the monster's attack string when it's near death. Since the attack string is always accessed through `Monster`, we have a convenient place to put that code:

    ```
    const char* Monster::getAttack()
    {
      if (health_ < LOW_HEALTH)
      {
        return "The monster flails weakly.";
      }

      return breed_.getAttack();
    }
    ```

    If outside code was calling `getAttack()` directly on the breed, we wouldn't have the opportunity to insert that logic.

  - *We have to write forwarding methods for everything the type object exposes.* This is the tedious part of this design. If our type object class has a large number of methods, the object class will have to have its own methods for each of the ones that we want to be publicly visible.

- **If the type object is exposed:**

  - *Outside code can interact with type objects without having an instance of the typed class.* If the type object is encapsulated, there's no way to use it without also having a typed object that wraps it. This prevents us, for example, from using our constructor pattern where new monsters are created by calling a method on the breed. If users can't get to breeds directly, they wouldn't be able to call it.

  - *The type object is now part of the object's public API.* In general, narrow interfaces are easier to maintain than wide ones—the less you expose to the rest of the codebase, the less complexity and maintenance you have to deal with. By exposing the type object, we widen the object's API to include everything the type object provides.

### How are typed objects created?

With this pattern, each "object" is now a pair of objects: the main object and the type object it uses. So how do we create and bind the two together?

- **Construct the object and pass in its type object:**

  - *Outside code can control allocation.* Since the calling code is constructing both objects itself, it can control where in memory that occurs. If we want our objects to be usable in a variety of different memory scenarios (different allocators, on the stack, etc.) this gives us the flexibility to do that.

- **Call a "constructor" function on the type object:**

  - *The type object controls memory allocation.* This is the other side of the coin. If we *don't* want users to choose where in memory our objects are created, requiring them to go through a factory method on the type object gives us control over that. This can be useful if we want to ensure all of our objects come from a certain object pool (p. 305) or other memory allocator.

### Can the type change?

So far, we've presumed that once an object is created and bound to its type object that that binding will never change. The type an object is created with is the type it dies with. This isn't strictly necessary. We *could* allow an object to change its type over time.

Let's look back at our example. When a monster dies, the designers tell us sometimes they want its corpse to become a reanimated zombie. We could implement this by spawning a new monster with a zombie breed when a monster dies, but another option is to simply get the existing monster and change its breed to a zombie one.

- **If the type doesn't change:**

  - *It's simpler both to code and to understand.* At a conceptual level, "type" is something most people probably will not expect to change. This codifies that assumption.

  - *It's easier to debug.* If we're trying to track down a bug where a monster gets into some weird state, it simplifies our job if we can take for granted that the breed we're looking at *now* is the breed the monster has always had.

- **If the type can change:**

  - *There's less object creation.* In our example, if the type can't change, we'll be forced to burn CPU cycles creating a new zombie monster, copying over any attributes from the original monster that need to be preserved, and then deleting it. If we can change the type, all that work gets replaced by a simple assignment.

  - *We need to be careful that assumptions are met.* There's a fairly tight coupling between an object and its type. For example, a breed might assume that a monster's *current* health is never above the starting health that comes from the breed.

    If we allow the breed to change, we need to make sure that the new type's requirements are met by the existing object. When we change the type, we will probably need to execute some validation code to make sure the object is now in a state that makes sense for the new type.

## What kind of inheritance is supported?

- **No inheritance:**

  - *It's simple.* Simplest is often best. If you don't have a ton of data that needs sharing between your type objects, why make things hard on yourself?

  - *It can lead to duplicated effort.* I've yet to see an authoring system where designers *didn't* want some kind of inheritance. When you've got fifty different kinds of elves, having to tune their health by changing the same number in fifty different places *sucks*.

- **Single inheritance:**

  - *It's still relatively simple.* It's easy to implement, but, more importantly, it's also pretty easy to understand. If non-technical users are going to be working with the system, the fewer moving parts, the better. There's a reason a lot of programming languages only support single inheritance. It seems to be a sweet spot between power and simplicity.

  - *Looking up attributes is slower.* To get a given piece of data from a type object, we might need to walk up the inheritance chain to find the type that ultimately decides the value. If we're in performance-critical code, we may not want to spend time on this.

- **Multiple inheritance:**

  - *Almost all data duplication can be avoided.* With a good multiple inheritance system, users can build a hierarchy for their type objects that has almost no redundancy. When it comes time to tune numbers, we can avoid a lot of copy and paste.

  - *It's complex.* Unfortunately, the benefits for this seem to be more theoretical than practical. Multiple inheritance is hard to understand and reason about.

    If our Zombie Dragon type inherits both from Zombie and Dragon, which attributes come from Zombie and which come from Dragon? In order to use the system, users will need to understand how the inheritance graph is traversed and have the foresight to design an intelligent hierarchy.

    Most C++ coding standards I see today tend to ban multiple inheritance, and Java and C# lack it completely. That's an acknowledgement of a sad fact: it's so hard to get it right that it's often best to not use it at all. While it's worth thinking about, it's rare that you'll want to use multiple inheritance for the type objects in your games. As always, simpler is better.

# See Also

- The high-level problem this pattern addresses is sharing data and behavior between several objects. Another pattern that addresses the same problem in a different way is Prototype (p. 59).

- Type Object is a close cousin to Flyweight (p. 33). Both let you share data across instances. With Flyweight, the intent is on saving memory, and the shared data may not represent any conceptual "type" of object. With the Type Object pattern, the focus is on organization and flexibility.

- There's a lot of similarity between this pattern and the State pattern (p. 87). Both patterns let an object delegate part of what defines itself to another object. With a type object, we're usually delegating what the object *is*: invariant data that broadly describes the object. With State, we delegate what an object *is right now*: temporal data that describes an object's current configuration.

  When we discussed having an object change its type, you can look at that as having our Type Object serve double duty as a State too.

# Decoupling Patterns  **V.**

Once you get the hang of a programming language, writing code to do what you want is actually pretty easy. What's hard is writing code that's easy to adapt when your requirements *change*. Rarely do we have the luxury of a perfect feature set before we've fired up our editor.

A powerful tool we have for making change easier is *decoupling*. When we say two pieces of code are "decoupled", we mean a change in one usually doesn't require a change in the other. When you change some feature in your game, the fewer places in code you have to touch, the easier it is.

Components (p. 213) decouple different domains in your game from each other within a single entity that has aspects of all of them. Event Queues (p. 233) decouple two objects communicating with each other, both statically and *in time*. Service Locators (p. 251) let code access a facility without being bound to the code that provides it.

# Component

# 14

*Allow a single entity to span multiple domains without coupling the domains to each other.*

## Motivation

Let's say we're building a platformer. The Italian plumber demographic is covered, so ours will star a Danish baker, Bjørn. It stands to reason that we'll have a class representing our friendly pastry chef, and it will contain everything he does in the game.

Since the player controls him, that means reading controller input and translating that input into motion. And, of course, he needs to interact with the level, so some physics and collision go in there. Once that's done, he's got to show up on screen, so toss in animation and rendering. He'll probably play some sounds too.

Hold on a minute; this is getting out of control. Software Architecture 101 tells us that different domains in a program should be kept isolated from each other. If we're making a word processor, the code that handles printing shouldn't be affected by the code that loads and saves documents. A game doesn't have the same domains as a business app, but the rule still applies.

Brilliant game ideas like this are why I'm a programmer and not a designer.

As much as possible, we don't want AI, physics, rendering, sound and other domains to know about each other, but now we've got all of that crammed into one class. We've seen where this road leads to: a 5,000-line dumping ground source file so big that only the bravest ninja coders on your team even dare to go in there.

This is great job security for the few who can tame it, but it's hell for the rest of us. A class that big means even the most seemingly trivial changes can have far-reaching implications. Soon, the class collects *bugs* faster than it collects *features*.

### The Gordian knot

Even worse than the simple scale problem is the coupling one. All of the different systems in our game have been tied into a giant knotted ball of code like:

```
if (collidingWithFloor() &&
    (getRenderState() != INVISIBLE))
{
  playSound(HIT_FLOOR);
}
```

Any programmer trying to make a change in code like that will need to know something about physics, graphics, and sound just to make sure they don't break anything.

These two problems compound each other; the class touches so many domains that every programmer will have to work on it, but it's so huge that doing so is a nightmare. If it gets bad enough, coders will start putting hacks in other parts of the codebase just to stay out of the hairball that this `Bjorn` class has become.

### Cutting the knot

We can solve this like Alexander the Great—with a sword. We'll take our monolithic `Bjorn` class and slice it into separate parts along domain boundaries. For example, we'll take all of the code for handling user input and move it into a separate `InputComponent` class. `Bjorn` will then own an instance of this component. We'll repeat this process for each of the domains that `Bjorn` touches.

When we're done, we'll have moved almost everything out of `Bjorn`. All that remains is a thin shell that binds the components together. We've solved our huge class problem by simply dividing it up into multiple smaller classes, but we've accomplished more than just that.

While coupling like this sucks in *any* game, it's even worse on modern games that use concurrency. On multi-core hardware, it's vital that code is running on multiple threads simultaneously. One common way to split a game across threads is along domain boundaries—run AI on one core, sound on another, rendering on a third, etc.

Once you do that, it's critical that those domains stay decoupled in order to avoid deadlocks or other fiendish concurrency bugs. Having a single class with an `UpdateSounds()` method that must be called from one thread and a `RenderGraphics()` method that must be called from another is begging for those kinds of bugs to happen.

## Loose ends

Our component classes are now decoupled. Even though `Bjorn` has a `PhysicsComponent` and a `GraphicsComponent`, the two don't know about each other. This means the person working on physics can modify their component without needing to know anything about graphics and vice versa.

In practice, the components will need to have *some* interaction between themselves. For example, the AI component may need to tell the physics component where Bjørn is trying to go. However, we can restrict this to the components that *do* need to talk instead of just tossing them all in the same playpen together.

## Tying back together

Another feature of this design is that the components are now reusable packages. So far, we've focused on our baker, but let's consider a couple of other kinds of objects in our game world. *Decorations* are things in the world the player sees but doesn't interact with: bushes, debris and other visual detail. *Props* are like decorations but can be touched: boxes, boulders, and trees. *Zones* are the opposite of decorations—invisible but interactive. They're useful for things like triggering a cutscene when Bjørn enters an area.

Now, consider how we'd set up an inheritance hierarchy for those classes if we weren't using components. A first pass might look like:

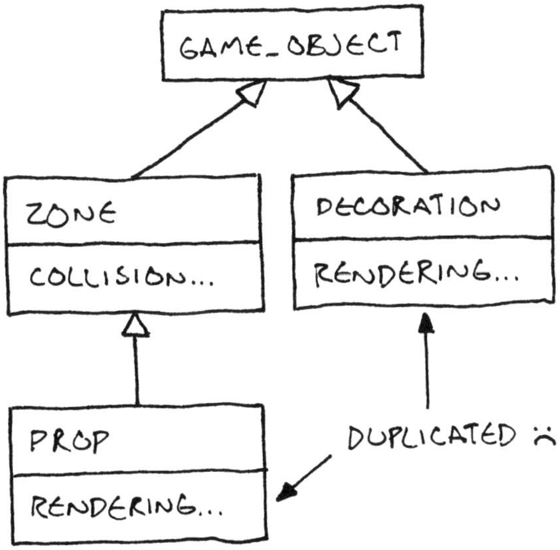

When object-oriented programming first hit the scene, inheritance was the shiniest tool in its toolbox. It was considered the ultimate code-reuse hammer, and coders swung it often. Since then, we've learned the hard way that it's a heavy hammer indeed. Inheritance has its uses, but it's often too cumbersome for simple code reuse.

Instead, the growing trend in software design is to use composition instead of inheritance when possible. Instead of sharing code between two classes by having them *inherit* from the same class, we do so by having them both *own an instance* of the same class.

Figure 14.1 – There's no way to reuse along two axes with single inheritance

We have a base `GameObject` class that has common stuff like position and orientation. `Zone` inherits from that and adds collision detection. Likewise, `Decoration` inherits from `GameObject` and adds rendering. `Prop` inherits from `Zone`, so it can reuse the collision code. However, `Prop` can't *also* inherit from `Decoration` to reuse the *rendering* code without running into the Deadly Diamond.

We could flip things around so that `Prop` inherits from `Decoration`, but then we end up having to duplicate the *collision* code. Either way, there's no clean way to reuse the collision and rendering code between the classes that need it without resorting to multiple inheritance. The only other option is to push everything up into `GameObject`, but then `Zone` is wasting memory on rendering data it doesn't need and `Decoration` is doing the same with physics.

Now, let's try it with components. Our subclasses disappear completely. Instead, we have a single `GameObject` class and two component classes: `PhysicsComponent` and `GraphicsComponent`. A decoration is simply a `GameObject` with a `GraphicsComponent` but no `PhysicsComponent`. A zone is the opposite, and a prop has both components. No code duplication, no multiple inheritance, and only three classes instead of four.

Components are basically plug-and-play for objects. They let us build complex entities with rich behavior by plugging different reusable component objects into sockets on the entity. Think software Voltron.

## The Pattern

A **single entity spans multiple domains**. To keep the domains isolated, the code for each is placed in its own **component class**. The entity is reduced to a simple **container of components**.

## When to Use It

Components are most commonly found within the core class that defines the entities in a game, but they may be useful in other places as well. This pattern can be put to good use when any of these are true:

- You have a class that touches multiple domains which you want to keep decoupled from each other.

- A class is getting massive and hard to work with.

The "Deadly Diamond" occurs in class hierarchies with multiple inheritance where there are two different paths to the same base class. The pain that causes is a bit out of the scope of this book, but understand that they named it "deadly" for a reason.

A restaurant menu is a good analogy. If each entity is a monolithic class, it's like you can only order combos. We need to have a separate class for each possible *combination* of features. To satisfy every customer, we would need dozens of combos.

Components are à la carte dining—each customer can select just the dishes they want, and the menu is a list of the dishes they can choose from.

"Component", like "Object", is one of those words that means everything and nothing in programming. Because of that, it's been used to describe a few concepts. In business software, there's a "Component" design pattern that describes decoupled services that communicate over the web.

I tried to find a different name for this unrelated pattern found in games, but "Component" seems to be the most common term for it. Since design patterns are about documenting existing practices, I don't have the luxury of coining a new term. So, following in the footsteps of XNA, Delta3D, and others, "Component" it is.

- You want to be able to define a variety of objects that share different capabilities, but using inheritance doesn't let you pick the parts you want to reuse precisely enough.

## Keep in Mind

The Component pattern adds a good bit of complexity over simply making a class and putting code in it. Each conceptual "object" becomes a cluster of objects that must be instantiated, initialized, and correctly wired together. Communication between the different components becomes more challenging, and controlling how they occupy memory is more complex.

For a large codebase, this complexity may be worth it for the decoupling and code reuse it enables, but take care to ensure you aren't over-engineering a "solution" to a non-existent problem before applying this pattern.

Another consequence of using components is that you often have to hop through a level of indirection to get anything done. Given the container object, first you have to get the component you want, *then* you can do what you need. In performance-critical inner loops, this pointer following may lead to poor performance.

There's a flip side to this coin. The Component pattern can often *improve* performance and cache coherence. Components make it easier to use the Data Locality pattern (p. 269) to organize your data in the order that the CPU wants it.

## Sample Code

One of the biggest challenges for me in writing this book is figuring out how to isolate each pattern. Many design patterns exist to contain code that itself isn't part of the pattern. In order to distill the pattern down to its essence, I try to cut as much of that out as possible, but at some point it becomes a bit like explaining how to organize a closet without showing any clothes.

The Component pattern is a particularly hard one. You can't get a real feel for it without seeing some code for each of the domains that it decouples, so I'll have to sketch in a bit more of Bjørn's code than I'd like. The pattern is really only the component *classes* themselves, but the code in them should help clarify what the classes are for. It's fake code—it calls into other classes that aren't presented here—but it should give you an idea of what we're going for.

## A monolithic class

To get a clearer picture of how this pattern is applied, we'll start by showing a monolithic `Bjorn` class that does everything we need but *doesn't* use this pattern:

```
class Bjorn
{
public:
  Bjorn() : velocity_(0), x_(0), y_(0) {}

  void update(World& world, Graphics& graphics);

private:
  static const int WALK_ACCELERATION = 1;

  int velocity_;
  int x_, y_;

  Volume volume_;

  Sprite spriteStand_;
  Sprite spriteWalkLeft_;
  Sprite spriteWalkRight_;
};
```

`Bjorn` has an `update()` method that gets called once per frame by the game:

```
void Bjorn::update(World& world, Graphics& graphics)
{
  // Apply user input to hero's velocity.
  switch (Controller::getJoystickDirection())
  {
    case DIR_LEFT:
      velocity_ -= WALK_ACCELERATION;
      break;

    case DIR_RIGHT:
      velocity_ += WALK_ACCELERATION;
      break;
  }

  // Modify position by velocity.
  x_ += velocity_;
  world.resolveCollision(volume_, x_, y_, velocity_);

  // Draw the appropriate sprite.
  Sprite* sprite = &spriteStand_;
  if (velocity_ < 0) sprite = &spriteWalkLeft_;
  else if (velocity_ > 0) sprite = &spriteWalkRight_;
  graphics.draw(*sprite, x_, y_);
}
```

It reads the joystick to determine how to accelerate the baker. Then it resolves its new position with the physics engine. Finally, it draws Bjørn onto the screen.

The sample implementation here is trivially simple. There's no gravity, animation, or any of the dozens of other details that make a character fun to play. Even so, we can see that we've got a single function that several different coders on our team will probably have to spend time in, and it's starting to get a bit messy. Imagine this scaled up to a thousand lines and you can get an idea of how painful it can become.

## Splitting out a domain

Starting with one domain, let's pull a piece out of `Bjorn` and push it into a separate component class. We'll start with the first domain that gets processed: input. The first thing `Bjorn` does is read in user input and adjust his velocity based on it. Let's move that logic out into a separate class:

```
class InputComponent
{
public:
  void update(Bjorn& bjorn)
  {
    switch (Controller::getJoystickDirection())
    {
      case DIR_LEFT:
        bjorn.velocity -= WALK_ACCELERATION;
        break;

      case DIR_RIGHT:
        bjorn.velocity += WALK_ACCELERATION;
        break;
    }
  }

private:
  static const int WALK_ACCELERATION = 1;
};
```

Pretty simple. We've taken the first section of `Bjorn`'s `update()` method and put it into this class. The changes to `Bjorn` are also straightforward:

```
class Bjorn
{
public:
  int velocity;
  int x, y;

  void update(World& world, Graphics& graphics)
  {
    input_.update(*this);

    // Modify position by velocity.
    x += velocity;
    world.resolveCollision(volume_, x, y, velocity);

    // Draw the appropriate sprite.
    Sprite* sprite = &spriteStand_;
    if (velocity_ < 0)
    {
      sprite = &spriteWalkLeft_;
    }
    else if (velocity_ > 0)
    {
      sprite = &spriteWalkRight_;
    }
    graphics.draw(*sprite, x, y);
  }

private:
  InputComponent input_;

  Volume volume_;

  Sprite spriteStand_;
  Sprite spriteWalkLeft_;
  Sprite spriteWalkRight_;
};
```

Bjorn now owns an InputComponent object. Where before he was handling user input directly in the update() method, now he delegates to the component:

```
input_.update(*this);
```

We've only started, but already we've gotten rid of some coupling—the main Bjorn class no longer has any reference to Controller. This will come in handy later.

### Splitting out the rest

Now, let's go ahead and do the same cut-and-paste job on the physics and graphics code. Here's our new `PhysicsComponent`:

```
class PhysicsComponent
{
public:
  void update(Bjorn& bjorn, World& world)
  {
    bjorn.x += bjorn.velocity;
    world.resolveCollision(volume_,
        bjorn.x, bjorn.y, bjorn.velocity);
  }

private:
  Volume volume_;
};
```

In addition to moving the physics *behavior* out of the main `Bjorn` class, you can see we've also moved out the *data* too: The `Volume` object is now owned by the component.

Last but not least, here's where the rendering code lives now:

```
class GraphicsComponent
{
public:
  void update(Bjorn& bjorn, Graphics& graphics)
  {
    Sprite* sprite = &spriteStand_;
    if (bjorn.velocity < 0)
    {
      sprite = &spriteWalkLeft_;
    }
    else if (bjorn.velocity > 0)
    {
      sprite = &spriteWalkRight_;
    }

    graphics.draw(*sprite, bjorn.x, bjorn.y);
  }

private:
  Sprite spriteStand_;
  Sprite spriteWalkLeft_;
  Sprite spriteWalkRight_;
};
```

We've yanked almost everything out, so what's left of our humble pastry chef? Not much:

```
class Bjorn
{
public:
  int velocity;
  int x, y;

  void update(World& world, Graphics& graphics)
  {
    input_.update(*this);
    physics_.update(*this, world);
    graphics_.update(*this, graphics);
  }

private:
  InputComponent input_;
  PhysicsComponent physics_;
  GraphicsComponent graphics_;
};
```

The `Bjorn` class now basically does two things: it holds the set of components that actually define it, and it holds the state that is shared across multiple domains. Position and velocity are still in the core `Bjorn` class for two reasons. First, they are "pan-domain" state—almost every component will make use of them, so it isn't clear which component *should* own them if we did want to push them down.

Secondly, and more importantly, it gives us an easy way for the components to communicate without being coupled to each other. Let's see if we can put that to use.

### Robo-Bjørn

So far, we've pushed our behavior out to separate component classes, but we haven't *abstracted* the behavior out. `Bjorn` still knows the exact concrete classes where his behavior is defined. Let's change that.

We'll take our component for handling user input and hide it behind an interface. We'll turn `InputComponent` into an abstract base class:

```
class InputComponent
{
public:
  virtual ~InputComponent() {}
  virtual void update(Bjorn& bjorn) = 0;
};
```

Then, we'll take our existing user input handling code and push it down into a class that implements that interface:

```
class PlayerInputComponent : public InputComponent
{
public:
  virtual void update(Bjorn& bjorn)
  {
    switch (Controller::getJoystickDirection())
    {
      case DIR_LEFT:
        bjorn.velocity -= WALK_ACCELERATION;
        break;

      case DIR_RIGHT:
        bjorn.velocity += WALK_ACCELERATION;
        break;
    }
  }

private:
  static const int WALK_ACCELERATION = 1;
};
```

We'll change Bjorn to hold a pointer to the input component instead of having an inline instance:

```
class Bjorn
{
public:
  int velocity;
  int x, y;

  Bjorn(InputComponent* input)
  : input_(input)
  {}

  void update(World& world, Graphics& graphics)
  {
    input_->update(*this);
    physics_.update(*this, world);
    graphics_.update(*this, graphics);
  }

private:
  InputComponent* input_;
  PhysicsComponent physics_;
  GraphicsComponent graphics_;
};
```

Now, when we instantiate `Bjorn`, we can pass in an input component for it to use, like so:

```
Bjorn* bjorn = new Bjorn(new PlayerInputComponent());
```

This instance can be any concrete type that implements our abstract `InputComponent` interface. We pay a price for this—`update()` is now a virtual method call, which is a little slower. What do we get in return for this cost?

Most consoles require a game to support "demo mode." If the player sits at the main menu without doing anything, the game will start playing automatically, with the computer standing in for the player. This keeps the game from burning the main menu into your TV and also makes the game look nicer when it's running on a kiosk in a store.

Hiding the input component class behind an interface lets us get that working. We already have our concrete `PlayerInputComponent` that's normally used when playing the game. Now, let's make another one:

```
class DemoInputComponent : public InputComponent
{
public:
  virtual void update(Bjorn& bjorn)
  {
    // AI to automatically control Bjorn...
  }
};
```

When the game goes into demo mode, instead of constructing Bjørn like we did earlier, we'll wire him up with our new component:

```
Bjorn* bjorn = new Bjorn(new DemoInputComponent());
```

And now, just by swapping out a component, we've got a fully functioning computer-controlled player for demo mode. We're able to reuse all of the other code for Bjørn—physics and graphics don't even know there's a difference. Maybe I'm a bit strange, but it's stuff like this that gets me up in the morning.

That, and coffee. Sweet, steaming hot coffee.

### No Bjørn at all?

If you look at our `Bjorn` class now, you'll notice there's nothing really "Bjørn" about it—it's just a component bag. In fact, it looks like a pretty good candidate for a base "game object" class that we can use for *every* object in the game. All we need to do is pass in *all* the components, and we can build any kind of object by picking and choosing parts like Dr. Frankenstein.

Let's take our two remaining concrete components—physics and graphics—and hide them behind interfaces like we did with input:

```
class PhysicsComponent
{
public:
  virtual ~PhysicsComponent() {}
  virtual void update(GameObject& object,
                      World& world) = 0;
};

class GraphicsComponent
{
public:
  virtual ~GraphicsComponent() {}
  virtual void update(GameObject& object,
                      Graphics& graphics) = 0;
};
```

Then we re-christen Bjorn into a generic GameObject class that uses those interfaces:

```
class GameObject
{
public:
  int velocity;
  int x, y;

  GameObject(InputComponent* input,
             PhysicsComponent* physics,
             GraphicsComponent* graphics)
  : input_(input),
    physics_(physics),
    graphics_(graphics)
  {}

  void update(World& world, Graphics& graphics)
  {
    input_->update(*this);
    physics_->update(*this, world);
    graphics_->update(*this, graphics);
  }

private:
  InputComponent* input_;
  PhysicsComponent* physics_;
  GraphicsComponent* graphics_;
};
```

Some component systems take this even further. Instead of a GameObject that contains its components, the game entity is just an ID, a number. Then, you maintain separate collections of components where each one knows the ID of the entity its attached to.

These *entity component systems* take decoupling components to the extreme and let you add new components to an entity without the entity even knowing. The Data Locality chapter (p. 269) has more details.

Our existing concrete classes will get renamed and implement those interfaces:

```
class BjornPhysicsComponent : public PhysicsComponent
{
public:
  virtual void update(GameObject& obj, World& world)
  {
    // Physics code...
  }
};

class BjornGraphicsComponent
    : public GraphicsComponent
{
public:
  virtual void update(GameObject& obj,
                          Graphics& graphics)
  {
    // Graphics code...
  }
};
```

And now we can build an object that has all of Bjørn's original behavior without having to actually create a class for him, just like this:

This createBjorn() function is, of course, an example of the classic Gang of Four Factory Method pattern.

```
GameObject* createBjorn()
{
  return new GameObject(
      new PlayerInputComponent(),
      new BjornPhysicsComponent(),
      new BjornGraphicsComponent());
}
```

By defining other functions that instantiate GameObjects with different components, we can create all of the different kinds of objects our game needs.

## Design Decisions

The most important design question you'll need to answer with this pattern is, "What set of components do I need?" The answer there is going to depend on the needs and genre of your game. The bigger and more complex your engine is, the more finely you'll likely want to slice your components. Beyond that, there are a couple of more specific options to consider:

## How does the object get its components?

Once we've split up our monolithic object into a few separate component parts, we have to decide who puts the parts back together.

- **If the object creates its own components:**

  - *It ensures that the object always has the components it needs.* You never have to worry about someone forgetting to wire up the right components to the object and breaking the game. The container object itself takes care of it for you.

  - *It's harder to reconfigure the object.* One of the powerful features of this pattern is that it lets you build new kinds of objects simply by recombining components. If our object always wires itself with the same set of hard-coded components, we aren't taking advantage of that flexibility.

- **If outside code provides the components:**

  - *The object becomes more flexible.* We can completely change the behavior of the object by giving it different components to work with. Taken to its fullest extent, our object becomes a generic component container that we can reuse over and over again for different purposes.

  - *The object can be decoupled from the concrete component types.* If we're allowing outside code to pass in components, odds are good that we're also letting it pass in *derived* component types. At that point, the object only knows about the component *interfaces* and not the concrete types themselves. This can make for a nicely encapsulated architecture.

## How do components communicate with each other?

Perfectly decoupled components that function in isolation is a nice ideal, but it doesn't really work in practice. The fact that these components are part of the *same* object implies that they are part of a larger whole and need to coordinate. That means communication.

So how can the components talk to each other? There are a couple of options, but unlike most design "alternatives" in this book, these aren't exclusive—you will likely support more than one at the same time in your designs.

- **By modifying the container object's state:**

  - *It keeps the components decoupled.* When our `InputComponent` set Bjørn's velocity and the `PhysicsComponent` later used it, the two components had no idea that the other even existed. For all they knew, Bjørn's velocity could have changed through black magic.

  - *It requires any information that components need to share to get pushed up into the container object.* Often, there's state that's really only needed by a subset of the components. For example, an animation and a rendering component may need to share information that's graphics-specific. Pushing that information up into the container object where *every* component can get to it muddies the object class.

    Worse, if we use the same container object class with different component configurations, we can end up wasting memory on state that isn't needed by *any* of the object's components. If we push some rendering-specific data into the container object, any invisible object will be burning memory on it with no benefit.

  - *It makes communication implicit and dependent on the order that components are processed.* In our sample code, the original monolithic `update()` method had a very carefully laid out order of operations. The user input modified the velocity, which was then used by the physics code to modify the position, which in turn was used by the rendering code to draw Bjørn at the right spot. When we split that code out into components, we were careful to preserve that order of operations.

    If we hadn't, we would have introduced subtle, hard-to-track bugs. For example, if we'd updated the graphics component *first*, we would wrongly render Bjørn at his position on the *last* frame, not this one. If you imagine several more components and lots more code, then you can get an idea of how hard it can be to avoid bugs like this.

- **By referring directly to each other:**

  The idea here is that components that need to talk will have direct references to each other without having to go through the container object at all. Let's say we want to let Bjørn jump. The graphics code needs to know if he should be drawn using a jump sprite or not. It can determine this by asking the physics engine if he's currently on the ground. An easy way to do this is by letting the graphics component know about the physics component directly:

Shared mutable state like this where lots of code is reading and writing the same data is notoriously hard to get right. That's a big part of why academics are spending time researching pure functional languages like Haskell where there is no mutable state at all.

```
class BjornGraphicsComponent
{
public:
  BjornGraphicsComponent(
      BjornPhysicsComponent* physics)
  : physics_(physics)
  {}

  void Update(GameObject& obj, Graphics& graphics)
  {
    Sprite* sprite;
    if (!physics_->isOnGround())
    {
      sprite = &spriteJump_;
    }
    else
    {
      // Existing graphics code...
    }

    graphics.draw(*sprite, obj.x, obj.y);
  }

private:
  BjornPhysicsComponent* physics_;

  Sprite spriteStand_;
  Sprite spriteWalkLeft_;
  Sprite spriteWalkRight_;
  Sprite spriteJump_;
};
```

When we construct Bjørn's `GraphicsComponent`, we'll give it a reference to his corresponding `PhysicsComponent`.

- *It's simple and fast.* Communication is a direct method call from one object to another. The component can call any method that is supported by the component it has a reference to. It's a free-for-all.

- *The two components are tightly coupled.* The downside of the free-for-all. We've basically taken a step back towards our monolithic class. It's not quite as bad as the original single class though, since we're at least restricting the coupling to only the component pairs that need to interact.

- **By sending messages:**

This is the most complex alternative. We can actually build a little messaging system into our container object and let the components broadcast information to each other.

Here's one possible implementation. We'll start by defining a base Component interface that all of our components will implement:

```
class Component
{
public:
  virtual ~Component() {}
  virtual void receive(int message) = 0;
};
```

It has a single receive() method that component classes implement in order to listen to an incoming message. Here, we're just using an int to identify the message, but a fuller implementation could attach additional data to the message.

Then, we'll add a method to our container object for sending messages:

```
class ContainerObject
{
public:
  void send(int message)
  {
    for (int i = 0; i < MAX_COMPONENTS; i++)
    {
      if (components_[i] != NULL)
      {
        components_[i]->receive(message);
      }
    }
  }

private:
  static const int MAX_COMPONENTS = 10;
  Component* components_[MAX_COMPONENTS];
};
```

If you really want to get fancy, you can even make this message system *queue* messages to be delivered later. For more on this, see Event Queue (p. 233).

Now, if a component has access to its container, it can send messages to the container, which will rebroadcast the message to all of the contained components. (That inclues the original component that sent the message; be careful that you don't get stuck in a feedback loop!) This has a couple of consequences:

The Gang of Four call this the Mediator pattern — two or more objects communicate with each other indirectly by routing the message through an intermediate object. In this case, the container object itself is the mediator.

- *Sibling components are decoupled.* By going through the parent container object, like our shared state alternative, we ensure that the components are still decoupled from each other. With this system, the only coupling they have is the message values themselves.

- *The container object is simple.* Unlike using shared state where the container object itself owns and knows about data used by the components, here, all it does is blindly pass the messages along. That can be useful for letting two components pass very domain-specific information between themselves without having that bleed into the container object.

Unsurprisingly, there's no one best answer here. What you'll likely end up doing is using a bit of all of them. Shared state is useful for the really basic stuff that you can take for granted that every object has—things like position and size.

Some domains are distinct but still closely related. Think animation and rendering, user input and AI, or physics and collision. If you have separate components for each half of those pairs, you may find it easiest to just let them know directly about their other half.

Messaging is useful for "less important" communication. Its fire-and-forget nature is a good fit for things like having an audio component play a sound when a physics component sends a message that the object has collided with something.

As always, I recommend you start simple and then add in additional communication paths if you need them.

## See Also

- The Unity framework's core `GameObject` class is designed entirely around components.

- The open source Delta3D engine has a base `GameActor` class that implements this pattern with the appropriately named `ActorComponent` base class.

- Microsoft's XNA game framework comes with a core `Game` class. It owns a collection of `GameComponent` objects. Where our example uses components at the individual game entity level, XNA implements the pattern at the level of the main game object itself, but the purpose is the same.

- This pattern bears resemblance to the Gang of Four's Strategy pattern. Both patterns are about taking part of an object's behavior and delegating it to a separate subordinate object. The difference is that with the Strategy pattern, the separate "strategy" object is usually stateless—it encapsulates an algorithm, but no data. It defines *how* an object behaves, but not *what* it is.

Components are a bit more self-important. They often hold state that describes the object and helps define its actual identity. However, the line may blur. You may have some components that don't need any local state. In that case, you're free to use the same component *instance* across multiple container objects. At that point, it really is behaving more akin to a strategy.

# Event Queue

# 15

*Decouple when a message or event is sent from when it is processed.*

## Motivation

Unless you live under one of the few rocks that still lack Internet access, you've probably already heard of an "event queue". If not, maybe "message queue", or "event loop", or "message pump" rings a bell. To refresh your memory, let's walk through a couple of common manifestations of the pattern.

For most of the chapter, I use "event" and "message" interchangeably. Where the distinction matters, I'll make it obvious.

### GUI event loops

If you've ever done any user interface programming, then you're well acquainted with *events*. Every time the user interacts with your program—clicks a button, pulls down a menu, or presses a key—the operating system generates an event. It throws this object at your app, and your job is to grab it and hook it up to some interesting behavior.

In order to receive these missives, somewhere deep in the bowels of your code is an *event loop*. It looks roughly like this:

This application style is so common, it's considered a paradigm: *event-driven programming*.

```
while (running)
{
  Event event = getNextEvent();
  // Handle event...
}
```

The call to `getNextEvent()` pulls a bit of unprocessed user input into your app. You route it to an event handler and, like magic, your application comes to life. The interesting part is that the application *pulls* in the event when *it* wants it. The operating system doesn't just immediately jump to some code in your app when the user pokes a peripheral.

That means when user input comes in, it needs to go somewhere so that the operating system doesn't lose it between when the device driver reported the input and when your app gets around to calling `getNextEvent()`. That "somewhere" is a *queue*.

In contrast, *interrupts* from the operating system *do* work like that. When an interrupt happens, the OS stops whatever your app was doing and forces it to jump to an interrupt handler. This abruptness is why interrupts are so hard to work with.

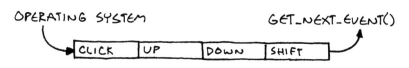

Figure 15.1 – A queue of events pumped from the OS to your app

When user input comes in, the OS adds it to a queue of unprocessed events. When you call `getNextEvent()`, that pulls the oldest event off the queue and hands it to your application.

### Central event bus

If you want to know *why* they aren't event-driven, crack open the Game Loop chapter (p. 123).

Most games aren't event-driven like this, but it is common for a game to have its own event queue as the backbone of its nervous system. You'll often hear "central", "global", or "main" used to describe it. It's used for high level communication between game systems that want to stay decoupled.

Say your game has a tutorial system to display help boxes after specific in-game events. For example, the first time the player vanquishes a foul beastie, you want to show a little balloon that says, "Press X to grab the loot!"

Tutorial systems are a pain to implement gracefully, and most players will spend only a fraction of their time using in-game help, so it feels like they aren't worth the effort. But that fraction where they *are* using the tutorial can be invaluable for easing the player into your game.

Your gameplay and combat code are likely complex enough as it is. The last thing you want to do is stuff a bunch of checks for triggering tutorials in there. Instead, you could have a central event queue. Any game system can send to it, so the combat code can add an "enemy died" event every time you slay a foe.

Likewise, any game system can *receive* events from the queue. The tutorial engine registers itself with the queue and indicates it wants to receive "enemy died" events. This way, knowledge of an enemy dying makes its way from the combat system over to the tutorial engine without the two being directly aware of each other.

This model where you have a shared space that entities can post information to and get notified by is similar to *blackboard systems* in the AI field.

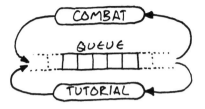

*Figure 15.2 – Combat and tutorials interact through a shared queue*

I thought about using this as the example for the rest of the chapter, but I'm not generally a fan of big global systems. Event queues don't have to be for communicating across the entire game engine. They can be just as useful within a single class or domain.

## Say what?

So, instead, let's add sound to our game. Humans are mainly visual animals, but hearing is deeply connected to our emotions and our sense of physical space. The right simulated echo can make a black screen feel like an enormous cavern, and a well-timed violin adagio can make your heartstrings hum in sympathetic resonance.

To get our game wound for sound, we'll start with the simplest possible approach and see how it goes. We'll add a little "audio engine" that has an API for playing a sound given an identifier and a volume:

While I almost always shy away from the Singleton pattern (p. 73), this is one of the places where it may fit since the machine likely only has one set of speakers. I'm taking a simpler approach and just making the method static.

```
class Audio
{
public:
  static void playSound(SoundId id, int volume);
};
```

It's responsible for loading the appropriate sound resource, finding an available channel to play it on, and starting it up. This chapter isn't about some platform's real audio API, so I'll conjure one up that we can presume is implemented elsewhere. Using it, we write our method like so:

```
void Audio::playSound(SoundId id, int volume)
{
  ResourceId resource = loadSound(id);
  int channel = findOpenChannel();
  if (channel == -1) return;
  startSound(resource, channel, volume);
}
```

We check that in, create a few sound files, and start sprinkling playSound() calls through our codebase like some magical audio fairy. For example, in our UI code, we play a little bloop when the selected menu item changes:

```
class Menu
{
public:
  void onSelect(int index)
  {
    Audio::playSound(SOUND_BLOOP, VOL_MAX);
    // Other stuff...
  }
};
```

After doing this, we notice that sometimes when you switch menu items, the whole screen freezes for a few frames. We've hit our first issue:

- **Problem 1: The API blocks the caller until the audio engine has completely processed the request.**

Our playSound() method is *synchronous*—it doesn't return back to the caller until bloops are coming out of the speakers. If a sound file has to be loaded from disc first, that may take a while. In the meantime, the rest of the game is frozen.

Ignoring that for now, we move on. In the AI code, we add a call to let out a wail of anguish when an enemy takes damage from the player. Nothing warms a gamer's heart like inflicting simulated pain on a virtual living being.

It works, but sometimes when the hero does a mighty attack, it hits two enemies in the exact same frame. That causes the game to play the wail sound twice simultaneously. If you know anything about audio, you know mixing multiple sounds together sums their waveforms. When those are the *same* waveform, it's the same as *one* sound played *twice as loud*. It's jarringly loud.

We have a related problem in boss fights when piles of minions are running around causing mayhem. The hardware can only play so many sounds at one time. When we go over that limit, sounds get ignored or cut off.

To handle these issues, we need to look at the entire *set* of sound calls to aggregate and prioritize them. Unfortunately, our audio API handles each playSound() call independently. It sees requests through a pinhole, one at a time.

I ran into this exact issue working on Henry Hatsworth in the Puzzling Adventure. My solution there is similar to what we'll cover here.

- **Problem 2: Requests cannot be processed in aggregate.**

These problems seem like mere annoyances compared to the next issue that falls in our lap. By now, we've strewn `playSound()` calls throughout the codebase in lots of different game systems. But our game engine is running on modern multi-core hardware. To take advantage of those cores, we distribute those systems on different threads—rendering on one, AI on another, etc.

Since our API is synchronous, it runs on the *caller's* thread. When we call it from different game systems, we're hitting our API concurrently from multiple threads. Look at that sample code. See any thread synchronization? Me neither.

This is particularly egregious because we intended to have a *separate* thread for audio. It's just sitting there totally idle while these other threads are busy stepping all over each other and breaking things.

- **Problem 3: Requests are processed on the wrong thread.**

The common theme to these problems is that the audio engine interprets a call to `playSound()` to mean, "Drop everything and play the sound right now!" *Immediacy* is the problem. Other game systems call `playSound()` at *their* convenience, but not necessarily when it's convenient for the audio engine to handle that request. To fix that, we'll decouple *receiving* a request from *processing* it.

# The Pattern

A **queue** stores a series of **notifications or requests** in first-in, first-out order. Sending a notification **enqueues the request and returns**. The request processor then **processes items from the queue** at a later time. Requests can be **handled directly** or **routed to interested parties**. This **decouples the sender from the receiver** both **statically** and **in time**.

# When to Use It

If you only want to decouple *who* receives a message from its sender, patterns like Observer (p. 43) and Command (p. 21) will take care of this with less complexity. You only need a queue when you want to decouple something *in time*.

I mention this in nearly every chapter, but it's worth emphasizing. Complexity slows you down, so treat simplicity as a precious resource.

I think of it in terms of pushing and pulling. You have some code A that wants another chunk B to do some work. The natural way for A to initiate that is by *pushing* the request to B.

Meanwhile, the natural way for B to process that request is by *pulling* it in at a convenient time in *its* run cycle. When you have a push model on one end and a pull model on the other, you need a buffer between them. That's what a queue provides that simpler decoupling patterns don't.

Queues give control to the code that pulls from it—the receiver can delay processing, aggregate requests, or discard them entirely. But queues do this by taking control *away* from the sender. All the sender can do is throw a request on the queue and hope for the best. This makes queues a poor fit when the sender needs a response.

## Keep in Mind

Unlike some more modest patterns in this book, event queues are complex and tend to have a wide-reaching effect on the architecture of our games. That means you'll want to think hard about how—or if—you use one.

### A central event queue is a global variable

One common use of this pattern is for a sort of Grand Central Station that all parts of the game can route messages through. It's a powerful piece of infrastructure, but *powerful* doesn't always mean *good*.

It took a while, but most of us learned the hard way that global variables are bad. When you have a piece of state that any part of the program can poke at, all sorts of subtle interdependencies creep in. This pattern wraps that state in a nice little protocol, but it's still a global, with all of the danger that entails.

### The state of the world can change under you

Say some AI code posts an "entity died" event to a queue when a virtual minion shuffles off its mortal coil. That event hangs out in the queue for who knows how many frames until it eventually works its way to the front and gets processed.

Meanwhile, the experience system wants to track the heroine's body count and reward her for her grisly efficiency. It receives each "entity died" event and determines the kind of entity slain and the difficulty of the kill so it can dish out an appropriate reward.

That requires various pieces of state in the world. We need the entity that died so we can see how tough it was. We may want to inspect its surroundings to see what other obstacles or minions were nearby. But if the event isn't received until later, that stuff may be gone. The entity may have been deallocated, and other nearby foes may have wandered off.

When you receive an event, you have to be careful not to assume the *current* state of the world reflects how the world was *when the event was raised*. This means queued events tend to be more data heavy than events in synchronous systems. With the latter, the notification can say "something happened" and the receiver can look around for the details. With a queue, those ephemeral details must be captured when the event is sent so they can be used later.

### You can get stuck in feedback loops
All event and message systems have to worry about cycles:

1. A sends an event.

2. B receives it and responds by sending an event.

3. That event happens to be one that A cares about, so it receives it. In response, it sends an event...

4. Go to 2.

When your messaging system is *synchronous*, you find cycles quickly—they overflow the stack and crash your game. With a queue, the asynchrony unwinds the stack, so the game may keep running even though spurious events are sloshing back and forth in there. A common rule to avoid this is to avoid *sending* events from within code that's *handling* one.

A little debug logging in your event system is probably a good idea too.

## Sample Code

We've already seen some code. It's not perfect, but it has the right basic functionality—the public API we want and the right low-level audio calls. All that's left for us to do now is fix its problems.

The first is that our API *blocks*. When a piece of code plays a sound, it can't do anything else until `playSound()` finishes loading the resource and actually starts making the speaker wiggle.

We want to defer that work until later so that `playSound()` can return quickly. To do that, we need to *reify* the request to play a sound. We need a little structure that stores the details of a pending request so we can keep it around until later:

```
struct PlayMessage
{
  SoundId id;
  int volume;
};
```

Next, we need to give `Audio` some storage space to keep track of these pending play messages. Now, your algorithms professor might tell you to use some exciting data structure here like a Fibonacci heap or a skip list, or, hell, at least a *linked* list. But in practice, the best way to store a bunch of homogenous things is almost always a plain old array:

Algorithm researchers get paid to publish analyses of novel data structures. They aren't exactly incentivized to stick to the basics.

- No dynamic allocation.

- No memory overhead for bookkeeping information or pointers.

For lots more on what being "cache friendly" means, see the chapter on Data Locality (p. 269).

- Cache-friendly contiguous memory usage.

So let's do that:

```
class Audio
{
public:
  static void init() { numPending_ = 0; }

  // Other stuff...
private:
  static const int MAX_PENDING = 16;

  static PlayMessage pending_[MAX_PENDING];
  static int numPending_;
};
```

We can tune the array size to cover our worst case. To play a sound, we simply slot a new message in there at the end:

```
void Audio::playSound(SoundId id, int volume)
{
  assert(numPending_ < MAX_PENDING);

  pending_[numPending_].id = id;
  pending_[numPending_].volume = volume;
  numPending_++;
}
```

This lets `playSound()` return almost instantly, but we do still have to play the sound, of course. That code needs to go somewhere, and that somewhere is an `update()` method:

As the name implies, this is the Update Method pattern (p. 139).

```
class Audio
{
public:
  static void update()
  {
    for (int i = 0; i < numPending_; i++)
    {
      ResourceId resource = loadSound(
          pending_[i].id);
      int channel = findOpenChannel();
      if (channel == -1) return;
      startSound(resource, channel,
          pending_[i].volume);
    }

    numPending_ = 0;
  }

  // Other stuff...
};
```

Now, we need to call that from somewhere convenient. What "convenient" means depends on your game. It may mean calling it from the main game loop (p. 123) or from a dedicated audio thread.

This works fine, but it does presume we can process *every* sound request in a single call to `update()`. If you're doing something like processing a request asynchronously after its sound resource is loaded, that won't work. For `update()` to work on one request at a time, it needs to be able to pull requests out of the buffer while leaving the rest. In other words, we need an actual queue.

## A ring buffer

There are a bunch of ways to implement queues, but my favorite is called a *ring buffer*. It preserves everything that's great about arrays while letting us incrementally remove items from the front of the queue.

Now, I know what you're thinking. If we remove items from the beginning of the array, don't we have to shift all of the remaining items over? Isn't that slow?

This is why they made us learn linked lists—you can remove nodes from them without having to shift things around. Well, it turns out you can implement a queue without any shifting in an array too. I'll walk you through it, but first let's get precise on some terms:

- The **head** of the queue is where requests are *read* from. The head is the oldest pending request.

- The **tail** is the other end. It's the slot in the array where the next enqueued request will be *written*. Note that it's just *past* the end of the queue. You can think of it as a half-open range, if that helps.

Since `playSound()` appends new requests at the end of the array, the head starts at element zero and the tail grows to the right.

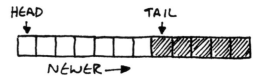

*Figure 15.3 – Filling the array with events*

Let's code that up. First, we'll tweak our fields a bit to make these two markers explicit in the class:

```
class Audio
{
public:
  static void init()
  {
    head_ = 0;
    tail_ = 0;
  }

  // Methods...
private:
  static int head_;
  static int tail_;

  // Array...
};
```

In the implementation of `playSound()`, `numPending_` has been replaced with `tail_`, but otherwise it's the same:

```
void Audio::playSound(SoundId id, int volume)
{
  assert(tail_ < MAX_PENDING);

  // Add to the end of the list.
  pending_[tail_].id = id;
  pending_[tail_].volume = volume;
  tail_++;
}
```

The more interesting change is in `update()`:

```
void Audio::update()
{
  // If there are no pending requests, do nothing.
  if (head_ == tail_) return;

  ResourceId resource = loadSound(
      pending_[head_].id);
  int channel = findOpenChannel();
  if (channel == -1) return;
  startSound(resource, channel,
      pending_[head_].volume);

  head_++;
}
```

We process the request at the head and then discard it by advancing the head pointer to the right. We detect an empty queue by seeing if there's any distance between the head and tail.

Now we've got a queue—we can add to the end and remove from the front. There's an obvious problem, though. As we run requests through the queue, the head and tail keep crawling to the right. Eventually, `tail_` hits the end of the array, and party time is over. This is where it gets clever.

This is why we made the tail one *past* the last item. It means that the queue will be empty if the head and tail are the same index.

Do you want party time to be over? No. You do not.

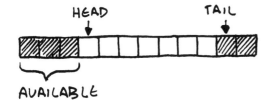

*Figure 15.4 – The queue crawls through the array leaving empty cells behind*

Notice that while the tail is creeping forward, the *head* is too. That means we've got array elements at the *beginning* of the array that aren't being used anymore. So what we do is wrap the tail back around to the beginning of the array when it runs off the end. That's why it's called a *ring* buffer—it acts like a circular array of cells.

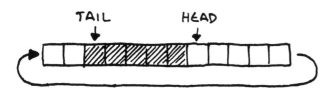

*Figure 15.5 – The tail loops back to the beginning of the array*

Implementing that is remarkably easy. When we enqueue an item, we just need to make sure the tail wraps around to the beginning of the array when it reaches the end:

```
void Audio::playSound(SoundId id, int volume)
{
  assert((tail_ + 1) % MAX_PENDING != head_);

  // Add to the end of the list.
  pending_[tail_].id = id;
  pending_[tail_].volume = volume;
  tail_ = (tail_ + 1) % MAX_PENDING;
}
```

Replacing `tail_++` with an increment modulo the array size wraps the tail back around. The other change is the assertion. We need to ensure the queue doesn't overflow. As long as there are fewer than `MAX_PENDING` requests in the queue, there will be a little gap of unused cells between the head and the tail. If the queue fills up, those will be gone and, like some weird backwards Ouroboros, the tail will collide with the head and start overwriting it. The assertion ensures that this doesn't happen.

In `update()`, we wrap the head around too:

```
void Audio::update()
{
  // If there are no pending requests, do nothing.
  if (head_ == tail_) return;

  ResourceId resource = loadSound(
      pending_[head_].id);

  int channel = findOpenChannel();
  if (channel == -1) return;
  startSound(resource, channel,
      pending_[head_].volume);

  head_ = (head_ + 1) % MAX_PENDING;
}
```

If the maximum capacity bugs you, you can use a growable array. When the queue gets full, allocate a new array twice the size of the current array (or some other multiple), then copy the items over.

Even though you copy when they array grows, enqueuing an item still has constant *amortized* complexity.

There you go—a queue with no dynamic allocation, no copying elements around, and the cache-friendliness of a simple array.

### Aggregating requests

Now that we've got a queue in place, we can move onto the other problems. The first is that multiple requests to play the same sound end up too loud. Since we know which requests are waiting to be processed now, all we need to do is merge a request if it matches an already pending one:

```
void Audio::playSound(SoundId id, int volume)
{
  // Walk the pending requests.
  for (int i = head_; i != tail_;
       i = (i + 1) % MAX_PENDING)
  {
    if (pending_[i].id == id)
    {
      // Use the larger of the two volumes.
      pending_[i].volume = max(volume,
          pending_[i].volume);

      // Don't need to enqueue.
      return;
    }
  }

  // Previous code...
}
```

When we get two requests to play the same sound, we collapse them to a single request for whichever is loudest. This "aggregation" is pretty rudimentary, but we could use the same idea to do more interesting batching.

Note that we're merging when the request is *enqueued*, not when it's *processed*. That's easier on our queue since we don't waste slots on redundant requests that will end up being collapsed later. It's also simpler to implement.

It does, however, put the processing burden on the caller. A call to `playSound()` will walk the entire queue before it returns, which could be slow if the queue is large. It may make more sense to aggregate in `update()` instead.

Another way to avoid the *O(n)* cost of scanning the queue is to use a different data structure. If we use a hash table keyed on the SoundId, then we can check for duplicates in constant time.

There's something important to keep in mind here. The window of "simultaneous" requests that we can aggregate is only as big as the queue. If we process requests more quickly and the queue size stays small, then we'll have fewer opportunities to batch things together. Likewise, if processing lags behind and the queue gets full, we'll find more things to collapse.

This pattern insulates the requester from knowing when the request gets processed, but when you treat the entire queue as a live data structure to be played with, then lag between making a request and processing it can visibly affect behavior. Make sure you're OK with that before doing this.

### Spanning threads

Finally, the most pernicious problem. With our synchronous audio API, whatever thread called `playSound()` was the thread that processed the request. That's often not what we want.

On today's multi-core hardware, you need more than one thread if you want to get the most out of your chip. There are infinite ways to distribute code across threads, but a common strategy is to move each domain of the game onto its own thread—audio, rendering, AI, etc.

We're in good shape to do that now that we have three critical pieces:

1. The code for requesting a sound is decoupled from the code that plays it.

2. We have a queue for marshalling between the two.

3. The queue is encapsulated from the rest of the program.

All that's left is to make the methods that modify the queue—`playSound()` and `update()`—thread-safe. Normally, I'd whip up some concrete code to do that, but since this is a book about architecture, I don't want to get mired in the details of any specific API or locking mechanism.

At a high level, all we need to do is ensure that the queue isn't modified concurrently. Since `playSound()` does a very small amount of work—basically just assigning a few fields—it can lock without blocking processing for long. In `update()`, we wait on something like a condition variable so that we don't burn CPU cycles until there's a request to process.

## Design Decisions

Many games use event queues as a key part of their communication structure, and you can spend a ton of time designing all sorts of complex routing and filtering for messages. But before you go off and build something like the Los Angeles telephone switchboard, I encourage you to start simple. Here's a few starter questions to consider:

### What goes in the queue?

I've used "event" and "message" interchangeably so far because it mostly doesn't matter. You get the same decoupling and aggregation abilities regardless of what you're stuffing in the queue, but there are some conceptual differences.

Straight-line code only runs on a single core at a time. If you don't use threads, even if you do the asynchronous-style programming that's in vogue, the best you'll do is keep one core busy, which is a fraction of your CPU's abilities.

Server programmers compensate for that by splitting their application into multiple independent *processes*. That lets the OS run them concurrently on different cores. Games are almost always a single process, so a bit of threading really helps.

- **If you queue events:**

  An "event" or "notification" describes something that *already* happened, like "monster died". You queue it so that other objects can *respond* to the event, sort of like an asynchronous Observer pattern (p. 43).

  - *You are likely to allow multiple listeners.* Since the queue contains things that already happened, the sender probably doesn't care who receives it. From its perspective, the event is in the past and is already forgotten.

  - *The scope of the queue tends to be broader.* Event queues are often used to *broadcast* events to any and all interested parties. To allow maximum flexibility for which parties can be interested, these queues tend to be more globally visible.

- **If you queue messages:**

  A "message" or "request" describes an action that we *want* to happen *in the future*, like "play sound". You can think of this as an asynchronous API to a service.

  - *You are more likely to have a single listener.* In the example, the queued messages are requests specifically for *the audio API* to play a sound. If other random parts of the game engine started stealing messages off the queue, it wouldn't do much good.

Another word for "request" is "command", as in the Command pattern (p. 21), and queues can be used there too.

I say "more likely" here, because you can enqueue messages without caring which code processes it, as long as it gets processed *how* you expect. In that case, you're doing something akin to a service locator (p. 251).

### Who can read from the queue?

In our example, the queue is encapsulated and only the `Audio` class can read from it. In a user interface's event system, you can register listeners to your heart's content. You sometimes hear the terms "single-cast" and "broadcast" to distinguish these, and both styles are useful.

- **A single-cast queue:**

  This is the natural fit when a queue is part of a class's API. Like in our audio example, from the caller's perspective, they just see a `playSound()` method they can call.

  - *The queue becomes an implementation detail of the reader.* All the sender knows is that it sent a message.

  - *The queue is more encapsulated.* All other things being equal, more encapsulation is usually better.

- *You don't have to worry about contention between listeners.* With multiple listeners, you have to decide if they *all* get every item (broadcast) or if *each* item in the queue is parceled out to *one* listener (something more like a work queue).

  In either case, the listeners may end up doing redundant work or interfering with each other, and you have to think carefully about the behavior you want. With a single listener, that complexity disappears.

- **A broadcast queue:**

  This is how most "event" systems work. If you have ten listeners when an event comes in, all ten of them see the event.

  - *Events can get dropped on the floor.* A corollary to the previous point is that if you have *zero* listeners, all zero of them see the event. In most broadcast systems, if there are no listeners at the point in time that an event is processed, the event gets discarded.

  - *You may need to filter events.* Broadcast queues are often widely visible to much of the program, and you can end up with a bunch of listeners. Multiply lots of events times lots of listeners, and you end up with a ton of event handlers to invoke.

    To cut that down to size, most broadcast event systems let a listener winnow down the set of events they receive. For example, they may say they only want to receive mouse events or events within a certain region of the UI.

- **A work queue:**

  Like a broadcast queue, here you have multiple listeners too. The difference is that each item in the queue only goes to *one* of them. This is a common pattern for parceling out jobs to a pool of concurrently running threads.

  - *You have to schedule.* Since an item only goes to one listener, the queue needs logic to figure out the best one to choose. This may be as simple as round robin or random choice, or it could be some more complex prioritizing system.

### Who can write to the queue?

This is the flip side of the previous design choice. This pattern works with all of the possible read/write configurations: one-to-one, one-to-many, many-to-one, or many-to-many.

You sometimes hear "fan-in" used to describe many-to-one communication systems and "fan-out" for one-to-many.

- **With one writer:**

  This style is most similar to the synchronous Observer pattern (p. 43). You have one privileged object that generates events that others can then receive.

  - *You implicitly know where the event is coming from.* Since there's only one object that can add to the queue, any listener can safely assume that's the sender.

  - *You usually allow multiple readers.* You can have a one-sender-one-receiver queue, but that starts to feel less like the communication system this pattern is about and more like a vanilla queue data structure.

- **With multiple writers:**

  This is how our audio engine example works. Since `playSound()` is a public method, any part of the codebase can add a request to the queue. "Global" or "central" event buses work like this too.

  - *You have to be more careful of cycles.* Since anything can potentially put something onto the queue, it's easier to accidentally enqueue something in the middle of handling an event. If you aren't careful, that may trigger a feedback loop.

  - *You'll likely want some reference to the sender in the event itself.* When a listener gets an event, it doesn't know who sent it, since it could be anyone. If that's something they need to know, you'll want to pack that into the event object so that the listener can use it.

### What is the lifetime of the objects in the queue?

With a synchronous notification, execution doesn't return to the sender until all of the receivers have finished processing the message. That means the message itself can safely live in a local variable on the stack. With a queue, the message outlives the call that enqueues it.

If you're using a garbage collected language, you don't need to worry about this too much. Stuff the message in the queue, and it will stick around in memory as long as it's needed. In C or C++, it's up to you to ensure the object lives long enough.

- **Pass ownership:**

This is the traditional way to do things when managing memory manually. When a message gets queued, the queue claims it and the sender no longer owns it. When it gets processed, the receiver takes ownership and is responsible for deallocating it.

In C++, `unique_ptr<T>` gives you these exact semantics out of the box.

- **Share ownership:**

These days, now that even C++ programmers are more comfortable with garbage collection, shared ownership is more acceptable. With this, the message sticks around as long as anything has a reference to it and is automatically freed when forgotten.

Likewise, the C++ type for this is `shared_ptr<T>`.

- **The queue owns it:**

Another option is to have messages *always* live on the queue. Instead of allocating the message itself, the sender requests a "fresh" one from the queue. The queue returns a reference to a message already in memory inside the queue, and the sender fills it in. When the message gets processed, the receiver refers to the same message in the queue.

In other words, the backing store for the queue is an object pool (p. 305).

## See Also

- I've mentioned this a few times already, but in many ways, this pattern is the asynchronous cousin to the well-known Observer pattern (p. 43).

- Like many patterns, event queues go by a number of aliases. One established term is "message queue". It's usually referring to a higher-level manifestation. Where our event queues are *within* an application, message queues are usually used for communicating *between* them.

    Another term is "publish/subscribe", sometimes abbreviated to "pubsub". Like "message queue", it usually refers to larger distributed systems unlike the humble coding pattern we're focused on.

- A finite state machine, similar to the Gang of Four's State pattern (p. 87), requires a stream of inputs. If you want it to respond to those asynchronously, it makes sense to queue them.

    When you have a bunch of state machines sending messages to each other, each with a little queue of pending inputs (called a *mailbox*), then you've re-invented the *actor model* of computation.

- The Go programming language's built-in "channel" type is essentially an event or message queue.

# Service Locator

# 16

*Provide a global point of access to a service without coupling users to the concrete class that implements it.*

## Motivation

Some objects or systems in a game tend to get around, visiting almost every corner of the codebase. It's hard to find a part of the game that *won't* need a memory allocator, logging, or random numbers at some point. Systems like those can be thought of as *services* that need to be available to the entire game.

For our example, we'll consider audio. It doesn't have quite the reach of something lower-level like a memory allocator, but it still touches a bunch of game systems. A falling rock hits the ground with a crash (physics). A sniper NPC fires his rifle and a shot rings out (AI). The user selects a menu item with a beep of confirmation (user interface).

Each of these places will need to be able to call into the audio system with something like one of these:

```
// Use a static class?
AudioSystem::playSound(VERY_LOUD_BANG);

// Or maybe a singleton?
AudioSystem::instance()->playSound(VERY_LOUD_BANG);
```

Either gets us where we're trying to go, but we stumbled into some sticky coupling along the way. Every place in the game calling into our audio system directly references the concrete `AudioSystem` class and the mechanism for accessing it—either as a static class or a singleton (p. 73).

These call sites, of course, have to be coupled to *something* in order to make a sound play, but letting them poke at the concrete audio implementation directly is like giving a hundred strangers directions to your house just so they can drop a letter on your doorstep. Not only is it a little bit *too* personal, it's a real pain when you move and you have to tell each person the new directions.

There's a better solution: a phone book. People that need to get in touch with us can look us up by name and get our current address. When we move, we tell the phone company. They update the book, and everyone gets the new address. In fact, we don't even need to give out our real address at all. We can list a P.O. box or some other "representation" of ourselves instead. By having callers go through the book to find us, we have *a convenient single place where we control how we're found*.

This is the Service Locator pattern in a nutshell—it decouples code that needs a service from both *who* it is (the concrete implementation type) and *where* it is (how we get to the instance of it).

## The Pattern

A **service** class defines an abstract interface to a set of operations. A concrete **service provider** implements this interface. A separate **service locator** provides access to the service by finding an appropriate provider while hiding both the provider's concrete type and the process used to locate it.

## When to Use It

Anytime you make something accessible to every part of your program, you're asking for trouble. That's the main problem with the Singleton pattern (p. 73), and this pattern is no different. My simplest advice for when to use a service locator is: *sparingly*.

Instead of using a global mechanism to give some code access to an object it needs, first consider *passing the object to it instead*. That's dead simple, and it makes the coupling completely obvious. That will cover most of your needs.

*But...* there are some times when manually passing around an object is gratuitous or actively makes code harder to read. Some systems, like logging or memory management, shouldn't be part of a module's public API. The parameters to your rendering code should have to do with *rendering*, not stuff like logging.

Likewise, other systems represent facilities that are fundamentally singular in nature. Your game probably only has one audio device or display system that it can talk to. It is an ambient property of the environment, so plumbing it through ten layers of methods just so one deeply nested call can get to it is adding needless complexity to your code.

In those kinds of cases, this pattern can help. As we'll see, it functions as a more flexible, more configurable cousin of the Singleton pattern. When used well, it can make your codebase more flexible with little runtime cost.

Conversely, when used poorly, it carries with it all of the baggage of the Singleton pattern with worse runtime performance.

# Keep in Mind

The core difficulty with a service locator is that it takes a dependency—a bit of coupling between two pieces of code—and defers wiring it up until runtime. This gives you flexibility, but the price you pay is that it's harder to understand what your dependencies are by reading the code.

## The service actually has to be located

With a singleton or a static class, there's no chance for the instance we need to *not* be available. Calling code can take for granted that it's there. But since this pattern has to *locate* the service, we may need to handle cases where that fails. Fortunately, we'll cover a strategy later to address this and guarantee that we'll always get *some* service when you need it.

## The service doesn't know who is locating it

Since the locator is globally accessible, any code in the game could be requesting a service and then poking at it. This means that the service must be able to work correctly in any circumstance. For example, a class that expects to be used only during the simulation portion of the game loop and not during rendering may not work as a service—it wouldn't be able to ensure that it's being used at the right time. So, if a class expects to be used only in a certain context, it's safest to avoid exposing it to the entire world with this pattern.

# Sample Code

Getting back to our audio system problem, let's address it by exposing the system to the rest of the codebase through a service locator.

### The service

We'll start off with the audio API. This is the interface that our service will be exposing:

```
class Audio
{
public:
  virtual ~Audio() {}
  virtual void playSound(int soundID) = 0;
  virtual void stopSound(int soundID) = 0;
  virtual void stopAllSounds() = 0;
};
```

A real audio engine would be much more complex than this, of course, but this shows the basic idea. What's important is that it's an abstract interface class with no implementation bound to it.

### The service provider

By itself, our audio interface isn't very useful. We need a concrete implementation. This book isn't about how to write audio code for a game console, so you'll have to imagine there's some actual code in the bodies of these functions, but you get the idea:

```
class ConsoleAudio : public Audio
{
public:
  virtual void playSound(int soundID)
  {
    // Play sound using console audio api...
  }

  virtual void stopSound(int soundID)
  {
    // Stop sound using console audio api...
  }

  virtual void stopAllSounds()
  {
    // Stop all sounds using console audio api...
  }
};
```

Now we have an interface and an implementation. The remaining piece is the service locator—the class that ties the two together.

## A simple locator

The implementation here is about the simplest kind of service locator you can define:

```
class Locator
{
public:
  static Audio* getAudio() { return service_; }

  static void provide(Audio* service)
  {
    service_ = service;
  }

private:
  static Audio* service_;
};
```

The static `getAudio()` function does the locating. We can call it from anywhere in the codebase, and it will give us back an instance of our `Audio` service to use:

```
Audio *audio = Locator::getAudio();
audio->playSound(VERY_LOUD_BANG);
```

The way it "locates" is very simple—it relies on some outside code to register a service provider before anything tries to use the service. When the game is starting up, it calls some code like this:

```
ConsoleAudio *audio = new ConsoleAudio();
Locator::provide(audio);
```

The key part to notice here is that the code that calls `playSound()` isn't aware of the concrete `ConsoleAudio` class; it only knows the abstract `Audio` interface. Equally important, not even the *locator* class is coupled to the concrete service provider. The *only* place in code that knows about the actual concrete class is the initialization code that provides the service.

There's one more level of decoupling here: the `Audio` interface isn't aware of the fact that it's being accessed in most places through a service locator. As far as it knows, it's just a regular abstract base class. This is useful because it means we can apply this pattern to *existing* classes that weren't necessarily designed around it. This is in contrast with Singleton (p. 73), which affects the design of the "service" class itself.

The technique this uses is called *dependency injection*, an awkward bit of jargon for a very simple idea. Say you have one class that depends on another. In our case, our `Locator` class needs an instance of the `Audio` service. Normally, the locator would be responsible for constructing that instance itself. Dependency injection instead says that outside code is responsible for *injecting* that dependency into the object that needs it.

## A null service

Our implementation so far is certainly simple, and it's pretty flexible too. But it has one big shortcoming: if we try to use the service before a provider has been registered, it returns NULL. If the calling code doesn't check that, we're going to crash the game.

I sometimes hear this called "temporal coupling"—two separate pieces of code that must be called in the right order for the program to work correctly. All stateful software has some degree of this, but as with other kinds of coupling, reducing temporal coupling makes the codebase easier to manage.

Fortunately, there's another design pattern called "Null Object" that we can use to address this. The basic idea is that in places where we would return NULL when we fail to find or create an object, we instead return a special object that implements the same interface as the desired object. Its implementation basically does nothing, but it allows code that receives the object to safely continue on as if it had received a "real" one.

To use this, we'll define another "null" service provider:

```
class NullAudio: public Audio
{
public:
  virtual void playSound(int soundID)
  virtual void stopSound(int soundID)
  virtual void stopAllSounds()
};
```

As you can see, it implements the service interface, but doesn't actually do anything. Now, we change our locator to this:

```
class Locator
{
public:
  static void initialize()
  {
    service_ = &nullService_;
  }

  static Audio& getAudio() { return *service_; }

  static void provide(Audio* service)
  {
    // Revert to null service.
    if (service == NULL) service = &nullService_;

    service_ = service;
  }

private:
  static Audio* service_;
  static NullAudio nullService_;
};
```

You may notice we're returning the service by reference instead of by pointer now. Since references in C++ are (in theory!) never NULL, returning a reference is a hint to users of the code that they can expect to always get a valid object back.

The other thing to notice is that we're checking for NULL in the `provide()` function instead of checking for the accessor. That requires us to call `initialize()` early on to make sure that the locator initially correctly defaults to the null provider. In return, it moves the branch out of `getAudio()`, which will save us a couple of cycles every time the service is accessed.

Calling code will never know that a "real" service wasn't found, nor does it have to worry about handling NULL. It's guaranteed to always get back a valid object.

This is also useful for *intentionally* failing to find services. If we want to disable a system temporarily, we now have an easy way to do so: simply don't register a provider for the service, and the locator will default to a null provider.

## Logging decorator

Now that our system is pretty robust, let's discuss another refinement this pattern lets us do—decorated services. I'll explain with an example.

During development, a little logging when interesting events occur can help you figure out what's going on under the hood of your game engine. If you're working on AI, you'd like to know when an entity changes AI states. If you're the sound programmer, you may want a record of every sound as it plays so you can check that they trigger in the right order.

The typical solution is to litter the code with calls to some log() function. Unfortunately, that replaces one problem with another—now we have *too much* logging. The AI coder doesn't care when sounds are playing, and the sound person doesn't care about AI state transitions, but now they both have to wade through each other's messages.

Ideally, we would be able to selectively enable logging for just the stuff we care about, and in the final game build, there'd be no logging at all. If the different systems we want to conditionally log are exposed as services, then we can solve this using the Decorator pattern. Let's define another audio service provider implementation like this:

Turning off audio is handy during development. It frees up some memory and CPU cycles. More importantly, when you break into a debugger just as a loud sound starts playing, it saves you from having your eardrums shredded. There's nothing like twenty milliseconds of a scream sound effect looping at full volume to get your blood flowing in the morning.

```
class LoggedAudio : public Audio
{
public:
  LoggedAudio(Audio &wrapped) : wrapped_(wrapped) {}

  virtual void playSound(int soundID)
  {
    log("play sound");
    wrapped_.playSound(soundID);
  }

  virtual void stopSound(int soundID)
  {
    log("stop sound");
    wrapped_.stopSound(soundID);
  }

  virtual void stopAllSounds()
  {
    log("stop all sounds");
    wrapped_.stopAllSounds();
  }

private:
  void log(const char* message)
  {
    // Code to log message...
  }

  Audio &wrapped_;
};
```

As you can see, it wraps another audio provider and exposes the same interface. It forwards the actual audio behavior to the inner provider, but it also logs each sound call. If a programmer wants to enable audio logging, they call this:

```
void enableAudioLogging()
{
  // Decorate the existing service.
  Audio *service = new LoggedAudio(
      Locator::getAudio());

  // Swap it in.
  Locator::provide(service);
}
```

Now, any calls to the audio service will be logged before continuing as before. And, of course, this plays nicely with our null service, so you can both *disable* audio and yet still log the sounds that it *would* play if sound were enabled.

# Design Decisions

We've covered a typical implementation, but there are a couple of ways that it can vary based on differing answers to a few core questions:

## How is the service located?

- **Outside code registers it:**

  This is the mechanism our sample code uses to locate the service, and it's the most common design I see in games:

  - *It's fast and simple.* The `getAudio()` function simply returns a pointer. It will often get inlined by the compiler, so we get a nice abstraction layer at almost no performance cost.

  - *We control how the provider is constructed.* Consider a service for accessing the game's controllers. We have two concrete providers: one for regular games and one for playing online. The online provider passes controller input over the network so that, to the rest of the game, remote players appear to be using local controllers.

    To make this work, the online concrete provider needs to know the IP address of the other remote player. If the locator itself was constructing the object, how would it know what to pass in? The `Locator` class doesn't know anything about online at all, much less some other user's IP address.

    Externally registered providers dodge the problem. Instead of the locator constructing the class, the game's networking code instantiates the online-specific service provider, passing in the IP address it needs. Then it gives that to the locator, who knows only about the service's abstract interface.

  - *We can change the service while the game is running.* We may not use this in the final game, but it's a neat trick during development. While testing, we can swap out, for example, the audio service with the null service we talked about earlier to temporarily disable sound while the game is still running.

  - *The locator depends on outside code.* This is the downside. Any code accessing the service presumes that some code somewhere has already registered it. If that initialization doesn't happen, we'll either crash or have a service mysteriously not working.

- **Bind to it at compile time:**

The idea here is that the "location" process actually occurs at compile time using preprocessor macros. Like so:

```
class Locator
{
public:
  static Audio& getAudio() { return service_; }

private:
  #if DEBUG
    static DebugAudio service_;
  #else
    static ReleaseAudio service_;
  #endif
};
```

Locating the service like this implies a few things:

- *It's fast.* Since all of the real work is done at compile time, there's nothing left to do at runtime. The compiler will likely inline the `getAudio()` call, giving us a solution that's as fast as we could hope for.

- *You can guarantee the service is available.* Since the locator owns the service now and selects it at compile time, we can be assured that if the game compiles, we won't have to worry about the service being unavailable.

- *You can't change the service easily.* This is the major downside. Since the binding happens at build time, anytime you want to change the service, you've got to recompile and restart the game.

- **Configure it at runtime:**

Over in the khaki-clad land of enterprise business software, if you say "service locator", this is what they'll have in mind. When the service is requested, the locator does some magic at runtime to hunt down the actual implementation requested.

Typically, this means loading a configuration file that identifies the provider and then using reflection to instantiate that class at runtime. This does a few things for us:

- *We can swap out the service without recompiling.* This is a little more flexible than a compile-time-bound service, but not quite as flexible

*Reflection* is a capability of some programming languages to interact with the type system at runtime. For example, we could find a class with a given name, find its constructor, and then invoke it to create an instance.

Dynamically typed languages like Lisp, Smalltalk, and Python get this by their very nature, but newer static languages like C# and Java also support it.

as a registered one where you can actually change the service while the game is running.

- *Non-programmers can change the service.* This is nice for when the designers want to be able to turn certain game features on and off but aren't comfortable mucking through source code. (Or, more likely, the *coders* aren't comfortable with them mucking through it.)

- *The same codebase can support multiple configurations simultaneously.* Since the location process has been moved out of the codebase entirely, we can use the same code to support multiple service configurations simultaneously.

  This is one of the reasons this model is appealing over in enterprise web-land: you can deploy a single app that works on different server setups just by changing some configs. Historically, this was less useful in games since console hardware is pretty well-standardized, but as more games target a heaping hodgepodge of mobile devices, this is becoming more relevant.

- *It's complex.* Unlike the previous solutions, this one is pretty heavyweight. You have to create some configuration system, possibly write code to load and parse a file, and generally *do some stuff* to locate the service. Time spent writing this code is time not spent on other game features.

- *Locating the service takes time.* And now the smiles really turn to frowns. Going with runtime configuration means you're burning some CPU cycles locating the service. Caching can minimize this, but that still implies that the first time you use the service, the game's got to go off and spend some time hunting it down. Game developers *hate* burning CPU cycles on something that doesn't improve the player's game experience.

## What happens if the service can't be located?

- **Let the user handle it:**

The simplest solution is to pass the buck. If the locator can't find the service, it just returns NULL. This implies:

- *It lets users determine how to handle failure.* Some users may consider failing to find a service a critical error that should halt the game. Others may be able to safely ignore it and continue. If the locator can't define a blanket policy that's correct for all cases, then passing the failure down the line lets each call site decide for itself what the right response is.

- *Users of the service must handle the failure.* Of course, the corollary to this is that each call site *must* check for failure to find the service. If almost all of them handle failure the same way, that's a lot duplicate code spread throughout the codebase. If just one of the potentially hundreds of places that use the service fails to make that check, our game is going to crash.

- **Halt the game:**

I said that we can't *prove* that the service will always be available at compile-time, but that doesn't mean we can't *declare* that availability is part of the runtime contract of the locator. The simplest way to do this is with an assertion:

The Singleton chapter (p. 73) explains the `assert()` function if you've never seen it before.

```
class Locator
{
public:
  static Audio& getAudio()
  {
    Audio* service = NULL;
    // Code here to locate service...

    assert(service != NULL);
    return *service;
  }
};
```

If the service isn't located, the game stops before any subsequent code tries to use it. The `assert()` call there doesn't solve the problem of failing to locate the service, but it does make it clear whose problem it is. By asserting here, we say, "Failing to locate a service is a bug in the locator."

So what does this do for us?

- *Users don't need to handle a missing service.* Since a single service may be used in hundreds of places, this can be a significant code saving. By declaring it the locator's job to always provide a service, we spare the users of the service from having to pick up that slack.

- *The game is going to halt if the service can't be found.* On the off chance that a service really can't be found, the game is going to halt. This is good in that it forces us to address the bug that's preventing the service from being located (likely some initialization code isn't being called when it should), but it's a real drag for everyone else who's blocked until it's fixed. With a large dev team, you can incur some painful programmer downtime when something like this breaks.

- **Return a null service:**

  We showed this refinement in our sample implementation. Using this means:

  - *Users don't need to handle a missing service.* Just like the previous option, we ensure that a valid service object will always be returned, simplifying code that uses the service.

  - *The game will continue if the service isn't available.* This is both a boon and a curse. It's helpful in that it lets us keep running the game even when a service isn't there. This can be really helpful on a large team when a feature we're working on may be dependent on some other system that isn't in place yet.

    The downside is that it may be harder to debug an *unintentionally* missing service. Say the game uses a service to access some data and then make a decision based on it. If we've failed to register the real service and that code gets a null service instead, the game may not behave how we want. It will take some work to trace that issue back to the fact that a service wasn't there when we thought it would be.

We can alleviate this by having the null service print some debug output whenever it's used.

Among these options, the one I see used most frequently is simply asserting that the service will be found. By the time a game gets out the door, it's been very heavily tested, and it will likely be run on a reliable piece of hardware. The chances of a service failing to be found by then are pretty slim.

On a larger team, I encourage you to throw a null service in. It doesn't take much effort to implement, and can spare you from some downtime during development when a service isn't available. It also gives you an easy way to turn off a service if it's buggy or is just distracting you from what you're working on.

## What is the scope of the service?

Up to this point, we've assumed that the locator will provide access to the service to *anyone* who wants it. While this is the typical way the pattern is used, another option is to limit access to a single class and its descendants, like so:

```
class Base
{
  // Methods to locate service and set service_...

protected:
  // Derived classes can use service
  static Audio& getAudio() { return *service_; }

private:
  static Audio* service_;
};
```

With this, access to the service is restricted to classes that inherit `Base`. There are advantages either way:

- **If access is global:**

  - *It encourages the entire codebase to all use the same service.* Most services are intended to be singular. By allowing the entire codebase to have access to the same service, we can avoid random places in code instantiating their own providers because they can't get to the "real" one.

  - *We lose control over where and when the service is used.* This is the obvious cost of making something global—anything can get to it. The Singleton chapter (p. 73) has a full cast of characters for the horror show that global scope can spawn.

- **If access is restricted to a class:**

  - *We control coupling.* This is the main advantage. By limiting a service to a branch of the inheritance tree, we can make sure systems that should be decoupled stay decoupled.

  - *It can lead to duplicate effort.* The potential downside is that if a couple of unrelated classes *do* need access to the service, they'll each need to have their own reference to it. Whatever process is used to locate or register the service will have to be duplicated between those classes.

    (The other option is to change the class hierarchy around to give those classes a common base class, but that's probably more trouble than it's worth.)

My general guideline is that if the service is restricted to a single domain in the game, then limit its scope to a class. For example, a service for getting access to the network can probably be limited to online classes. Services that get used more widely like logging should be global.

## See Also

- The Service Locator pattern is a sibling to Singleton (p. 73) in many ways, so it's worth looking at both to see which is most appropriate for your needs.

- The Unity framework uses this pattern in concert with the Component pattern (p. 213) in its `GetComponent()` method.

- Microsoft's XNA framework for game development has this pattern built into its core `Game` class. Each instance has a `GameServices` object that can be used to register and locate services of any type.

# Optimization
# Patterns

# VI.

While the rising tide of faster and faster hardware has lifted most software above worrying about performance, games are one of the few remaining exceptions. Players always want richer, more realistic and exciting experiences. Screens are crowded with games vying for a player's attention—and cash!—and the game that pushes the hardware the furthest often wins.

Optimizing for performance is a deep art that touches all aspects of software. Low-level coders master the myriad idiosyncrasies of hardware architectures. Meanwhile, algorithms researchers compete to prove mathematically whose procedure is the most efficient.

Here, I touch on a few mid-level patterns that are often used to speed up a game. Data Locality (p. 269) introduces you to the modern computer's memory hierarchy and how you can use it to your advantage. The Dirty Flag pattern (p. 291) helps you avoid unnecessary computation while Object Pools (p. 305) help you avoid unnecessary allocation. Spatial Partitioning (p. 321) speeds up the virtual world and its inhabitants' arrangement in space.

# Data Locality

# 17

*Accelerate memory access by arranging data to take advantage of CPU caching.*

## Motivation

We've been lied to. They keep showing us charts where CPU speed goes up and up every year as if Moore's Law isn't just a historical observation but some kind of divine right. Without lifting a finger, we software folks watch our programs magically accelerate just by virtue of new hardware.

Chips *have* been getting faster (though even that's plateauing now), but the hardware heads failed to mention something. Sure, we can *process* data faster than ever, but we can't *get* that data faster.

For your super-fast CPU to blow through a ream of calculations, it actually has to get the data out of main memory and into registers. As you can see on the next page, RAM hasn't been keeping up with increasing CPU speeds. Not even close.

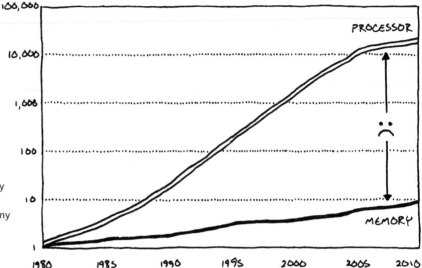

*Figure 17.1 – Processor and RAM speed relative to their respective speeds in 1980*

As you can see, CPUs have grown in leaps and bounds, but RAM access is lagging far behind.

Data for this is from *Computer Architecture: A Quantitative Approach* by John L. Hennessy, David A. Patterson, Andrea C. Arpaci-Dusseau by way of Tony Albrecht's "Pitfalls of Object-Oriented Programming".

It's called "random access memory" because, unlike disc drives, you can theoretically access any piece of it as quick as any other. You don't have to worry about reading things consecutively like you do a disc.

Or, at least, you *didn't*. As we'll see, RAM isn't so random access anymore.

I probably shouldn't have used a job I know absolutely nothing about in this analogy.

With today's hardware, it can take *hundreds* of cycles to fetch a byte of data from RAM. If most instructions need data, and it takes hundreds of cycles to get it, how is it that our CPUs aren't sitting idle 99% of the time waiting for data?

Actually, they *are* stuck waiting on memory an astonishingly large fraction of time these days, but it's not as bad as it could be. To explain how, let's take a trip to the Land of Overly Long Analogies...

### A data warehouse

Imagine you're an accountant in a tiny little office. Your job is to request a box of papers and then do some accountant-y stuff with them—add up a bunch of numbers or something. You must do this for specific labeled boxes according to some arcane logic that only makes sense to other accountants.

Thanks to a mixture of hard work, natural aptitude, and stimulants, you can finish an entire box in, say, a minute. There's a little problem, though. All of those boxes are stored in a warehouse in a separate building. To get a box, you have to ask the warehouse guy to bring it to you. He goes and gets a forklift and drives around the aisles until he finds the box you want.

It takes him, seriously, an entire day to do this. Unlike you, he's not getting employee of the month any time soon. This means that no matter how fast you are, you only get one box a day. The rest of the time, you just sit there and question the life decisions that led to this soul-sucking job.

One day, a group of industrial designers shows up. Their job is to improve the efficiency of operations—things like making assembly lines go faster. After watching you work for a few days, they notice a few things:

- Pretty often, when you're done with one box, the next box you request is right next to it on the same shelf in the warehouse.

- Using a forklift to carry a single box of papers is pretty dumb.

- There's actually a little bit of spare room in the corner of your office.

The technical term for using something near the thing you just used is *locality of reference*.

They come up with a clever fix. Whenever you request a box from the warehouse guy, he'll grab an entire pallet of them. He gets the box you want and then some more boxes that are next to it. He doesn't know if you want those (and, given his work ethic, clearly doesn't care); he simply takes as many as he can fit on the pallet.

He loads the whole pallet and brings it to you. Disregarding concerns for workplace safety, he drives the forklift right in and drops the pallet in the corner of your office.

When you need a new box, now, the first thing you do is see if it's already on the pallet in your office. If it is, great! It only takes you a second to grab it and get back to crunching numbers. If a pallet holds fifty boxes and you got lucky and *all* of the boxes you need happen to be on it, you can churn through fifty times more work than you could before.

But if you need a box that's *not* on the pallet, you're back to square one. Since you can only fit one pallet in your office, your warehouse friend will have to take that one back and then bring you an entirely new one.

## A pallet for your CPU

Strangely enough, this is similar to how CPUs in modern computers work. In case it isn't obvious, you play the role of the CPU. Your desk is the CPU's registers, and the box of papers is the data you can fit in them. The warehouse is your machine's RAM, and that annoying warehouse guy is the bus that pulls data from main memory into registers.

If I were writing this chapter thirty years ago, the analogy would stop there. But as chips got faster and RAM, well, *didn't*, hardware engineers started looking for solutions. What they came up with was *CPU caching*.

Modern computers have a little chunk of memory right inside the chip. The CPU can pull data from this much faster than it can from main memory. It's small because it has to fit in the chip and because the faster type of memory it uses (static RAM or "SRAM") is way more expensive.

This little chunk of memory is called a *cache* (in particular, the chunk on the chip is your *L1 cache*), and in my belabored analogy, its part was played by the pallet of boxes. Whenever your chip needs a byte of data from RAM, it automatically grabs a whole chunk of contiguous memory—usually around 64 to 128 bytes—and puts it in the cache. This dollop of memory is called a *cache line*.

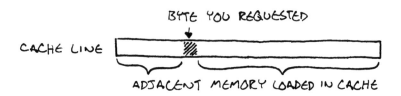

*Figure 17.2 – A byte of data and the cache line it lives on*

If the next byte of data you need happens to be in that chunk, the CPU reads it straight from the cache, which is *much* faster than hitting RAM. Successfully finding a piece of data in the cache is called a *cache hit*. If it can't find it in there and has to go to main memory, that's a *cache miss*.

When a cache miss occurs, the CPU *stalls*—it can't process the next instruction because it needs data. It sits there, bored out of its mind for a few hundred cycles until the fetch completes. Our mission is to avoid that. Imagine you're trying to optimize some performance-critical piece of game code and it looks like this:

```
for (int i = 0; i < NUM_THINGS; i++)
{
  sleepFor500Cycles();
  things[i].doStuff();
}
```

What's the first change you're going to make to that code? Right. Take out that pointless, expensive function call. That call is equivalent to the performance cost of a cache miss. Every time you bounce to main memory, it's like you put a delay in your code.

### Wait, data is performance?

When I started working on this chapter, I spent some time putting together little game-like programs that would trigger best case and worst case cache usage. I wanted benchmarks that would thrash the cache so I could see first-hand how much bloodshed it causes.

When I got some stuff working, I was surprised. I knew it was a big deal, but there's nothing quite like seeing it with your own eyes. I wrote two programs that did the *exact same* computation. The only difference was how many cache misses they caused. The slow one was *fifty times* slower than the other.

This was a real eye-opener to me. I'm used to thinking of performance being an aspect of *code*, not *data*. A byte isn't slow or fast, it's just some static thing sitting there. But because of caching, *the way you organize data directly impacts performance.*

The challenge now is to wrap that up into something that fits into a chapter here. Optimization for cache usage is a huge topic. I haven't even touched on *instruction caching*. Remember, code is in memory too and has to be loaded onto the CPU before it can be executed. Someone more versed on the subject could write an entire book on it.

Since you're already reading *this* book right now, though, I have a few basic techniques that will get you started along the path of thinking about how data structures impact your performance.

It all boils down to something pretty simple: whenever the chip reads some memory, it gets a whole cache line. The more you can use stuff in that cache line, the faster you go. So the goal then is to *organize your data structures so that the things you're processing are next to each other in memory*.

In other words, if your code is crunching on `Thing`, then `Another`, then `Also`, you want them laid out in memory like this:

*Figure 17.3 – Three objects snuggled up next to each other in memory*

Note, these aren't *pointers* to `Thing`, `Another`, and `Also`. This is the actual data for them, in place, lined up one after the other. As soon as the CPU reads in `Thing`, it will start to get `Another` and `Also` too (depending on how big they are and how big a cache line is). When you start working on them next, they'll already be cached. Your chip is happy, and you're happy.

There are a lot of caveats here. In particular, different computers have different cache setups, so my machine may be different from yours, and dedicated game consoles are very different from PCs, which are quite different from mobile devices.

Your mileage will vary.

In fact, someone *did* write a book on it: *Data-Oriented Design*, by Richard Fabian.

There's a key assumption here, though: one thread. If you are modifying nearby data on multiple threads, it's faster to have it on *different* cache lines. If two threads try to tweak data on the same cache line, both cores have to do some costly synchronization of their caches.

## The Pattern

Modern CPUs have **caches to speed up memory access**. These can access memory **adjacent to recently accessed memory much quicker**. Take advantage of that to improve performance by **increasing data locality**—keeping data in **contiguous memory in the order that you process it**.

## When to Use It

Like most optimizations, the first guideline for using the Data Locality pattern is *when you have a performance problem*. Don't waste time applying this to some infrequently executed corner of your codebase. Optimizing code that doesn't need it just makes your life harder since the result is almost always more complex and less flexible.

With this pattern specifically, you'll also want to be sure your performance problems *are caused by cache misses*. If your code is slow for other reasons, this won't help. The cheap way to profile is to manually add a bit of instrumentation that checks how much time has elapsed between two points in the code, hopefully using a precise timer. To catch cache misses, you'll want something a little more sophisticated. You really want to see how many cache misses are occurring and where.

Fortunately, there are profilers out there that report this. It's worth spending the time to get one of these working and make sure you understand the (surprisingly complex) numbers it throws at you before you do major surgery on your data structures.

That being said, cache misses *will* affect the performance of your game. While you shouldn't spend a ton of time pre-emptively optimizing for cache usage, do think about how cache-friendly your data structures are throughout the design process.

Unfortunately, most of those tools aren't cheap. If you're on a console dev team, you probably already have licenses for them.

If not, an excellent free option is Cachegrind. It runs your program on top of a simulated CPU and cache hierarchy and then reports all of the cache interactions.

## Keep in Mind

One of the hallmarks of software architecture is *abstraction*. A large chunk of this book is about patterns to decouple pieces of code from each other so that they can be changed more easily. In object-oriented languages, this almost always means interfaces.

In C++, using interfaces implies accessing objects through pointers or references. But going through a pointer means hopping across memory, which leads to the cache misses this pattern works to avoid.

In order to please this pattern, you will have to sacrifice some of your precious abstractions. The more you design your program around data locality, the more you will have to give up inheritance, interfaces, and the benefits those tools can provide. There's no silver bullet here, only challenging trade-offs. That's what makes it fun!

The other half of interfaces is *virtual method calls*. Those require the CPU to look up an object's vtable and then find the pointer to the actual method to call there. So, again, you're chasing pointers, which can cause cache misses.

## Sample Code

If you really go down the rathole of optimizing for data locality, you'll discover countless ways to slice and dice your data structures into pieces your CPU can most easily digest. To get you started, I'll show an example for each of a few of the most common ways to organize your data. We'll cover them in the context of some specific part of a game engine, but (as with other patterns), keep in mind that the general technique can be applied anywhere it fits.

### Contiguous arrays

Let's start with a game loop (p. 123) that processes a bunch of game entities. Those entities are decomposed into different domains—AI, physics, and rendering—using the Component pattern (p. 213). Here's the `GameEntity` class:

```
class GameEntity
{
public:
  GameEntity(AIComponent* ai,
             PhysicsComponent* physics,
             RenderComponent* render)
  : ai_(ai), physics_(physics), render_(render)
  {}

  AIComponent* ai() { return ai_; }
  PhysicsComponent* physics() { return physics_; }
  RenderComponent* render() { return render_; }

private:
  AIComponent* ai_;
  PhysicsComponent* physics_;
  RenderComponent* render_;
};
```

Each component has a relatively small amount of state, maybe little more than a few vectors or a matrix, and then a method to update it. The details aren't important here, but imagine something roughly along the lines of:

As the name implies, these are examples of the Update Method pattern (p. 139). Even `render()` is this pattern, just by another name.

```
class AIComponent
{
public:
  void update()
  {
    // Work with and modify state...
  }

private:
  // Goals, mood, etc. ...
};

class PhysicsComponent
{
public:
  void update()
  {
    // Work with and modify state...
  }

private:
  // Rigid body, velocity, mass, etc. ...
};

class RenderComponent
{
public:
  void render()
  {
    // Work with and modify state...
  }

private:
  // Mesh, textures, shaders, etc. ...
};
```

The game maintains a big array of pointers to all of the entities in the world. Each spin of the game loop, we need to run the following:

1. Update the AI components for all of the entities.

2. Update the physics components for them.

3. Render them using their render components.

Lots of game engines implement that like so:

```
while (!gameOver)
{
  for (int i = 0; i < numEntities; i++)
  {
    entities[i]->ai()->update();
  }

  for (int i = 0; i < numEntities; i++)
  {
    entities[i]->physics()->update();
  }

  for (int i = 0; i < numEntities; i++)
  {
    entities[i]->render()->render();
  }

  // Other game loop machinery for timing...
}
```

Before you ever heard of a CPU cache, this looked totally innocuous. But by now, you've got an inkling that something isn't right here. This code isn't just thrashing the cache, it's taking it around back and beating it to a pulp. Watch what it's doing:

- The array of game entities is storing *pointers* to them, so for each element in the array, we have to traverse that pointer. That's a cache miss.

- Then the game entity has a pointer to the component. Another cache miss.

- Then we update the component.

- Now we go back to step one for *every component of every entity in the game.*

The scary part is that we have no idea how these objects are laid out in memory. We're completely at the mercy of the memory manager. As entities get allocated and freed over time, the heap is likely to become increasingly randomly organized.

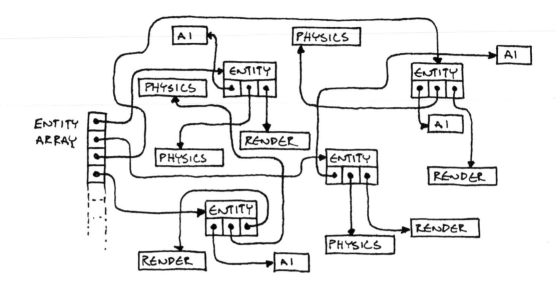

*Figure 17.4 – Every frame, the game loop follows those arrows to get the data it needs*

The term for wasting a bunch of time traversing pointers is "pointer chasing", which it turns out is nowhere near as fun as it sounds.

If our goal was to take a whirlwind tour around the game's address space like some "256MB of RAM in Four Nights!" cheap vacation package, this would be a fantastic deal. But our goal is to run the game quickly, and traipsing all over main memory is *not* the way to do that. Remember that `sleepFor500Cycles()` function? Well this code is effectively calling that *all the time.*

Let's do something better. Our first observation is that the only reason we follow a pointer to get to the game entity is so we can immediately follow *another* pointer to get to a component. `GameEntity` itself has no interesting state and no useful methods. The *components* are what the game loop cares about.

Instead of a giant constellation of game entities and components scattered across the inky darkness of address space, we're going to get back down to Earth. We'll have a big array for each type of component: a flat array of AI components, another for physics, and another for rendering. Like this:

My least favorite part about using components is how long the word "component" is.

```
AIComponent* aiComponents =
    new AIComponent[MAX_ENTITIES];
PhysicsComponent* physicsComponents =
    new PhysicsComponent[MAX_ENTITIES];
RenderComponent* renderComponents =
    new RenderComponent[MAX_ENTITIES];
```

Let me stress that these are arrays of *components* and not *pointers to components*. The data is all there, one byte after the other. The game loop can then walk these directly:

```
while (!gameOver)
{
  for (int i = 0; i < numEntities; i++)
  {
    aiComponents[i].update();
  }

  for (int i = 0; i < numEntities; i++)
  {
    physicsComponents[i].update();
  }

  for (int i = 0; i < numEntities; i++)
  {
    renderComponents[i].render();
  }

  // Other game loop machinery for timing...
}
```

One hint that we're doing better here is how few -> operators there are in the new code. If you want to improve data locality, look for indirection operators you can get rid of.

We've ditched all of that pointer chasing. Instead of skipping around in memory, we're doing a straight crawl through three contiguous arrays.

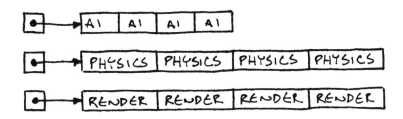

*Figure 17.5 – Nice homogenous rows of components*

This pumps a solid stream of bytes right into the hungry maw of the CPU. In my testing, this change made the update loop *fifty times* faster than the previous version.

Interestingly, we haven't lost much encapsulation here. Sure, the game loop is updating the components directly instead of going through the game entities, but it was doing that before to ensure they were processed in the right order. Even so, each component itself is still nicely encapsulated. It owns its own data and methods. We simply changed the way it's used.

This doesn't mean we need to get rid of GameEntity either. We can leave it as it is with pointers to its components. They'll just point into those arrays. This is still useful for other parts of the game where you want to pass around a conceptual "game entity" and everything that goes with it. The important part is that the performance-critical game loop sidesteps that and goes straight to the data.

### Packed data

Say we're doing a particle system. Following the advice of the previous section, we've got all of our particles in a nice big contiguous array. Let's wrap it in a little manager class too:

```
class Particle
{
public:
  void update() { /* Gravity, etc. ... */ }
  // Position, velocity, etc. ...
};
```

The ParticleSystem class is an example of an object pool (p. 305) custom built for a single type of object.

```
class ParticleSystem
{
public:
  ParticleSystem()
  : numParticles_(0)
  {}

  void update();

private:
  static const int MAX_PARTICLES = 100000;

  int numParticles_;
  Particle particles_[MAX_PARTICLES];
};
```

A rudimentary update method for the system just looks like this:

```
void ParticleSystem::update()
{
  for (int i = 0; i < numParticles_; i++)
  {
    particles_[i].update();
  }
}
```

But it turns out that we don't actually need to process *all* of the particles all the time. The particle system has a fixed-size pool of objects, but they aren't usually all actively twinkling across the screen. The easy answer is something like this:

```
for (int i = 0; i < numParticles_; i++)
{
  if (particles_[i].isActive())
  {
    particles_[i].update();
  }
}
```

We give `Particle` a flag to track whether its in use or not. In the update loop, we check that for each particle. That loads the flag into the cache along with all of that particle's other data. If the particle *isn't* active, then we skip over it to the next one. The rest of the particle's data that we loaded into the cache is a waste.

The fewer active particles there are, the more we're skipping across memory. The more we do that, the more cache misses there are between actually doing useful work updating active particles. If the array is large and has *lots* of inactive particles in it, we're back to thrashing the cache again.

Having objects in a contiguous array doesn't solve much if the objects we're actually processing aren't contiguous in it. If it's littered with inactive objects we have to dance around, we're right back to the original problem.

Given the title of this section, you can probably guess the answer. Instead of *checking* the active flag, we'll *sort* by it. We'll keep all of the active particles in the front of the list. If we know all of those particles are active, we don't have to check the flag at all.

We can also easily keep track of how many active particles there are. With this, our update loop turns into this thing of beauty:

```
for (int i = 0; i < numActive_; i++)
{
  particles[i].update();
}
```

Now we aren't skipping over *any* data. Every byte that gets sucked into the cache is a piece of an active particle that we actually need to process.

Of course, I'm not saying you should quicksort the entire collection of particles every frame. That would more than eliminate the gains here. What we want to do is *keep* the array sorted.

Assuming the array is already sorted—and it is at first when all particles are inactive—the only time it can become *un*sorted is when a particle has been activated or deactivated. We can handle those two cases pretty easily. When a particle gets activated, we move it up to the end of the active particles by swapping it with the first *in*active one:

Savvy low-level coders can see another problem here. Doing an `if` check for every particle can cause a *branch misprediction* and a *pipeline stall*. In modern CPUs, a single "instruction" actually takes several clock cycles. To keep the CPU busy, instructions are *pipelined* so that the subsequent instructions start processing before the first one finishes.

To do that, the CPU has to guess which instructions it will be executing next. In straight line code, that's easy, but with control flow, it's harder. While it's executing the instructions for that `if`, does it guess that the particle is active and start executing the code for the `update()` call, or does it guess that it isn't?

To answer that, the chip does *branch prediction*—it sees which branches your code previously took and guesses that it will do that again. But when the loop is constantly toggling between particles that are and aren't active, that prediction fails.

When it does, the CPU has to ditch the instructions it had started speculatively processing (a *pipeline flush*) and start over. The performance impact of this varies widely by machine, but this is why you sometimes see developers avoid flow control in hot code.

```
void ParticleSystem::activateParticle(int index)
{
    // Shouldn't already be active!
    assert(index >= numActive_);

    // Swap it with the first inactive particle right
    // after the active ones.
    Particle temp = particles_[numActive_];
    particles_[numActive_] = particles_[index];
    particles_[index] = temp;

    numActive_++;
}
```

To deactivate a particle, we just do the opposite:

```
void ParticleSystem::deactivateParticle(int index)
{
    // Shouldn't already be inactive!
    assert(index < numActive_);

    numActive_--;

    // Swap it with the last active particle right
    // before the inactive ones.
    Particle temp = particles_[numActive_];
    particles_[numActive_] = particles_[index];
    particles_[index] = temp;
}
```

Lots of programmers (myself included) have developed allergies to moving things around in memory. Schlepping a bunch of bytes around *feels* heavyweight compared to assigning a pointer. But when you add in the cost of *traversing* that pointer, it turns out that our intuition is sometimes wrong. In some cases, it's cheaper to push things around in memory if it helps you keep the cache full.

There's a neat consequence of keeping the particles *sorted* by their active state—we don't need to store an active flag in each particle at all. It can be inferred by its position in the array and the numActive_ counter. This makes our particle objects smaller, which means we can pack more in our cache lines, and that makes them even faster.

It's not all rosy, though. As you can see from the API, we've lost a bit of object orientation here. The Particle class no longer controls its own active state. You can't call some activate() method on it since it doesn't know its index. Instead, any code that wants to activate particles needs access to the particle *system*.

In this case, I'm OK with ParticleSystem and Particle being tightly tied like this. I think of them as a single *concept* spread across two

This is your friendly reminder to *profile* when making these kinds of decisions.

physical *classes*. It just means accepting the idea that particles are *only* meaningful in the context of some particle system. Also, in this case it's likely to be the particle system that will be spawning and killing particles anyway.

## Hot/cold splitting

OK, this is the last example of a simple technique for making your cache happier. Say we've got an AI component for some game entity. It has some state in it—the animation it's currently playing, a goal position its heading towards, energy level, etc.—stuff it checks and tweaks every single frame. Something like:

```
class AIComponent
{
public:
  void update() { /* ... */ }

private:
  Animation* animation_;
  double energy_;
  Vector goalPos_;
};
```

But it also has some state for rarer eventualities. It stores some data describing what loot it drops when it has an unfortunate encounter with the noisy end of a shotgun. That drop data is only used once in the entity's lifetime, right at its bitter end:

```
class AIComponent
{
public:
  void update() { /* ... */ }

private:
  // Previous fields...
  LootType drop_;
  int minDrops_;
  int maxDrops_;
  double chanceOfDrop_;
};
```

Assuming we followed the earlier patterns, when we update these AI components, we walk through a nice packed, contiguous array of data. But that data includes all of the loot drop information. That makes each component bigger, which reduces the number of components we can fit in a cache line. We get more cache misses because the total memory we walk over is larger. The loot data gets pulled into the cache for every component in every frame, even though we aren't even touching it.

The solution for this is called "hot/cold splitting". The idea is to break our data structure into two separate pieces. The first holds the "hot" data, the state we need to touch every frame. The other piece is the "cold" data, everything else that gets used less frequently.

The hot piece is the *main* AI component. It's the one we need to use the most, so we don't want to chase a pointer to find it. The cold component can be off to the side, but we still need to get to it, so we give the hot component a pointer to it, like so:

```cpp
class AIComponent
{
public:
  // Methods...
private:
  Animation* animation_;
  double energy_;
  Vector goalPos_;

  LootDrop* loot_;
};

class LootDrop
{
  friend class AIComponent;
  LootType drop_;
  int minDrops_;
  int maxDrops_;
  double chanceOfDrop_;
};
```

Now when we're walking the AI components every frame, the only data that gets loaded into the cache is stuff we are actually processing (with the exception of that one little pointer to the cold data).

You can see how this starts to get fuzzy, though. In my example here, it's pretty obvious which data should be hot and cold, but in a real game it's rarely so clear-cut. What if you have fields that are used when an entity is in a certain mode but not in others? What if entities use a certain chunk of data only when they're in certain parts of the level?

Doing this kind of optimization is somewhere between a black art and a rathole. It's easy to get sucked in and spend endless time pushing data around to see what speed difference it makes. It will take practice to get a handle on where to spend your effort.

We could conceivably ditch the pointer too by having parallel arrays for the hot and cold components. Then we can find the cold AI data for a component since both pieces will be at the same index in their respective arrays.

# Design Decisions

This pattern is really about a mindset—it's getting you to think about your data's arrangement in memory as a key part of your game's performance story. The actual concrete design space is wide open. You can let data locality affect your whole architecture, or maybe it's just a localized pattern you apply to a few core data structures.

The biggest questions you'll need to answer are when and where you apply this pattern, but here are a couple of others that may come up.

Noel Llopis' famous article that got a lot more people thinking about designing games around cache usage calls this "data-oriented design".

### How do you handle polymorphism?

Up to this point, we've avoided subclassing and virtual methods. We have assumed we have nice packed arrays of *homogenous* objects. That way, we know they're all the exact same size. But polymorphism and dynamic dispatch are useful tools too. How do we reconcile this?

- **Don't:**

    The simplest answer is to avoid subclassing, or at least avoid it in places where you're optimizing for cache usage. Software engineer culture is drifting away from heavy use of inheritance anyway.

    One way to keep much of the flexibility of polymorphism without using subclassing is through the Type Object pattern (p. 193).

    - *It's safe and easy.* You know exactly what class you're dealing with, and all objects are obviously the same size.

    - *It's faster.* Dynamic dispatch means looking up the method in the vtable and then traversing that pointer to get to the actual code. While the cost of this varies widely across different hardware, there is *some* cost to dynamic dispatch.

    As usual, the only absolute is that there are no absolutes. In most cases, a C++ compiler will require an indirection for a virtual method call. But in *some* cases, the compiler may be able to do *devirtualization* and statically call the right method if it knows what concrete type the receiver is. Devirtualization is more common in just-in-time compilers for languages like Java and JavaScript.

    - *It's inflexible.* Of course, the reason we use dynamic dispatch is because it gives us a powerful way to vary behavior between objects. If you want different entities in your game to have their own rendering styles or their own special moves and attacks, virtual methods are a proven way to model that. Having to instead stuff all of that code into a single non-virtual method that does something like a big `switch` gets messy quickly.

- **Use separate arrays for each type:**

    We use polymorphism so that we can invoke behavior on an object whose type we don't know. In other words, we have a mixed bag of stuff, and we want each object in there to do its own thing when we tell it to go.

But that raises the question of why mix the bag to begin with? Instead, why not maintain separate, homogenous collections for each type?

- *It keeps objects tightly packed.* Since each array only contains objects of one class, there's no padding or other weirdness.

- *You can statically dispatch.* Once you've got objects partitioned by type, you don't need polymorphism at all any more. You can use regular, non-virtual method calls.

- *You have to keep track of a bunch of collections.* If you have a lot of different object types, the overhead and complexity of maintaining separate arrays for each can be a chore.

- *You have to be aware of every type.* Since you have to maintain separate collections for each type, you can't be decoupled from the *set* of classes. Part of the magic of polymorphism is that it's *open-ended*—code that works with an interface can be completely decoupled from the potentially large set of types that implement that interface.

- **Use a collection of pointers:**

  If you weren't worried about caching, this is the natural solution. Just have an array of pointers to some base class or interface type. You get all the polymorphism you could want, and objects can be whatever size they want.

  - *It's flexible.* The code that consumes the collection can work with objects of any type as long as it supports the interface you care about. It's completely open-ended.

  - *It's less cache-friendly.* Of course, the whole reason we're discussing other options here is because this means cache-unfriendly pointer indirection. But, remember, if this code isn't performance-critical, that's probably OK.

### How are game entities defined?

If you use this pattern in tandem with the Component pattern (p. 213), you'll have nice contiguous arrays for all of the components that make up your game entities. The game loop will be iterating over those directly, so the object for the game entity itself is less important, but it's still useful in other parts of the codebase where you want to work with a single conceptual "entity".

The question then is how should it be represented? How does it keep track of its components?

- **If game entities are classes with pointers to their components:**

This is what our first example looked like. It's sort of the vanilla OOP solution. You've got a class for `GameEntity`, and it has pointers to the components it owns. Since they're just pointers, it's agnostic about where and how those components are organized in memory.

  - *You can store components in contiguous arrays.* Since the game entity doesn't care where its components are, you can organize them in a nice packed array to optimize iterating over them.

  - *Given an entity, you can easily get to its components.* They're just a pointer indirection away.

  - *Moving components in memory is hard.* When components get enabled or disabled, you may want to move them around in the array to keep the active ones up front and contiguous. If you move a component while the entity has a raw pointer to it, though, that pointer gets broken if you aren't careful. You'll have to make sure to update the entity's pointer at the same time.

- **If game entities are classes with IDs for their components:**

The challenge with raw pointers to components is that it makes it harder to move them around in memory. You can address that by using something more abstract: an ID or index that can be used to *look up* a component.

The actual semantics of the ID and lookup process are up to you. It could be as simple as storing a unique ID in each component and walking the array, or more complex like a hash table that maps IDs to their current index in the component array.

  - *It's more complex.* Your ID system doesn't have to be rocket science, but it's still more work than a basic pointer. You'll have to implement and debug it, and there will be memory overhead for bookkeeping.

  - *It's slower.* It's hard to beat traversing a raw pointer. There may be some searching or hashing involved to get from an entity to one of its components.

  - *You'll need access to the component "manager".* The basic idea is that you have some abstract ID that identifies a component. You can use it to get a reference to the actual component object. But to do that, you need to hand that ID to something that can actually find the component. That will be the class that wraps your raw contiguous array of component objects.

With raw pointers, if you have a game entity, you can find its components. With this, you need the game entity *and the component registry too.*

You may be thinking, "I'll just make it a singleton! Problem solved!" Well, sort of. You might want to check out the chapter on those first (p. 73).

- **If the game entity is itself just an ID:**

This is a newer style that some game engines use. Once you've moved all of your entity's behavior and state out of the main class and into components, what's left? It turns out, not much. The only thing an entity does is bind a set of components together. It exists just to say *this* AI component and *this* physics component and *this* render component define one living entity in the world.

That's important because components interact. The render component needs to know where the entity is, which may be a property of the physics component. The AI component wants to move the entity, so it needs to apply a force to the physics component. Each component needs a way to get the other sibling components of the entity it's a part of.

Some smart people realized all you need for that is an ID. Instead of the entity knowing its components, the components know their entity. Each component knows the ID of the entity that owns it. When the AI component needs the physics component for its entity, it simply asks for the physics component with the same entity ID that it holds.

Your entity *classes* disappear entirely, replaced by a glorified wrapper around a number.

- *Entities are tiny.* When you want to pass around a reference to a game entity, it's just a single value.

- *Entities are empty.* Of course, the downside of moving everything out of entities is that you *have* to move everything out of entities. You no longer have a place to put non-component-specific state or behavior. This style doubles down on the Component pattern (p. 213).

- *You don't have to manage their lifetime.* Since entities are just dumb value types, they don't need to be explicitly allocated and freed. An entity implicitly "dies" when all of its components are destroyed.

- *Looking up a component for an entity may be slow.* This is the same problem as the previous answer, but in the opposite direction. To find a component for some entity, you have to map an ID to an object. That process may be costly.

  This time, though, it *is* performance-critical. Components often interact with their siblings during update, so you will need to find components frequently. One solution is to make the "ID" of an entity the index of the component in its array.

  If every entity has the same set of components, then your component arrays are completely parallel. The component in slot three of the AI component array will be for the same entity that the physics component in slot three of *its* array is associated with.

  Keep in mind, though, that this *forces* you to keep those arrays in parallel. That's hard if you want to start sorting or packing them by different criteria. You may have some entities with disabled physics and others that are invisible. There's no way to sort the physics and render component arrays optimally for both cases if they have to stay in sync with each other.

# See Also

- Much of this chapter revolves around the Component pattern (p. 213), and that pattern is definitely one of the most common data structures that gets optimized for cache usage. In fact, using the Component pattern makes this optimization easier. Since entities are updated one "domain" (AI, physics, etc.) at a time, splitting them out into components lets you slice a bunch of entities into the right pieces to be cache-friendly.

  But that doesn't mean you can *only* use this pattern with components! Any time you have performance-critical code that touches a lot of data, it's important to think about locality.

- Tony Albrecht's "Pitfalls of Object-Oriented Programming" is probably the most widely-read introduction to designing your game's data structures for cache-friendliness. It made a lot more people (including me!) aware of how big of a deal this is for performance.

- Around the same time, Noel Llopis wrote a very influential blog post on the same topic called "Data-Oriented Design (Or Why You Might Be Shooting Yourself in The Foot With OOP)".

- This pattern almost invariably takes advantage of a contiguous array of homogenous objects. Over time, you'll very likely be adding and removing objects from that array. The Object Pool pattern (p. 305) is about exactly that.

- The Artemis game engine is one of the first and better-known frameworks that uses simple IDs for game entities.

# Dirty Flag

# 18

*Avoid unnecessary work by deferring it until the result is needed.*

## Motivation

Many games have something called a *scene graph*. This is a big data structure that contains all of the objects in the world. The rendering engine uses this to determine where to draw stuff on the screen.

At its simplest, a scene graph is just a flat list of objects. Each object has a model, or some other graphic primitive, and a *transform*. The transform describes the object's position, rotation, and scale in the world. To move or turn an object, we simply change its transform.

When the renderer draws an object, it takes the object's model, applies the transform to it, and then renders it there in the world. If we had a scene *bag* and not a scene *graph*, that would be it, and life would be simple.

However, most scene graphs are *hierarchical*. An object in the graph may have a parent object that it is anchored to. In that case, its transform is relative to the *parent's* position and isn't an absolute position in the world.

For example, imagine our game world has a pirate ship at sea. Atop the ship's mast is a crow's nest. Hunched in that crow's nest is a pirate. Clutching the pirate's shoulder is a parrot. The ship's local transform

The mechanics of *how* this transform is stored and manipulated are unfortunately out of scope here. The comically abbreviated summary is that it's a 4x4 matrix. You can make a single transform that combines two transforms—for example, translating and then rotating an object—by multiplying the two matrices.

How and why that works is left as an exercise for the reader.

positions the ship in the sea. The crow's nest's transform positions the nest on the ship, and so on.

*Figure 18.1 – Yarrr!*

This way, when a parent object moves, its children move with it automatically. If we change the local transform of the ship, the crow's nest, pirate, and parrot go along for the ride. It would be a total headache if, when the ship moved, we had to manually adjust the transforms of all the objects on it to keep them from sliding off.

To be honest, when you are at sea you *do* have to keep manually adjusting your position to keep from sliding off. Maybe I should have chosen a drier example.

But to actually draw the parrot on screen, we need to know its absolute position in the world. I'll call the parent-relative transform the object's *local transform*. To render an object, we need to know its *world transform*.

### Local and world transforms

Calculating an object's world transform is pretty straightforward—you just walk its parent chain starting at the root all the way down to the object, combining transforms as you go. In other words, the parrot's world transform is:

In the degenerate case where the object has no parent, its local and world transforms are equivalent.

*Figure 18.2 – Calculating the parrot's world transform from its parents' local transforms*

We need the world transform for every object in the world every frame, so even though there are only a handful of matrix multiplications per model, it's on the hot code path where performance is critical. Keeping them up to date is tricky because when a parent object moves, that affects the world transform of itself and all of its children, recursively.

The simplest approach is to calculate transforms on the fly while rendering. Each frame, we recursively traverse the scene graph starting at the top of the hierarchy. For each object, we calculate its world transform right then and draw it.

But this is terribly wasteful of our precious CPU juice! Many objects in the world are *not* moving every frame. Think of all of the static geometry that makes up the level. Recalculating their world transforms each frame even though they haven't changed is a waste.

## Cached world transforms

The obvious answer is to *cache* it. In each object, we store its local transform and its derived world transform. When we render, we only use the precalculated world transform. If the object never moves, the cached transform is always up to date and everything's happy.

When an object *does* move, the simple approach is to refresh its world transform right then. But don't forget the hierarchy! When a parent moves, we have to recalculate its world transform *and all of its children's, recursively.*

Imagine some busy gameplay. In a single frame, the ship gets tossed on the ocean, the crow's nest rocks in the wind, the pirate leans to the edge, and the parrot hops onto his head. We changed four local transforms. If we recalculate world transforms eagerly whenever a local transform changes, what ends up happening?

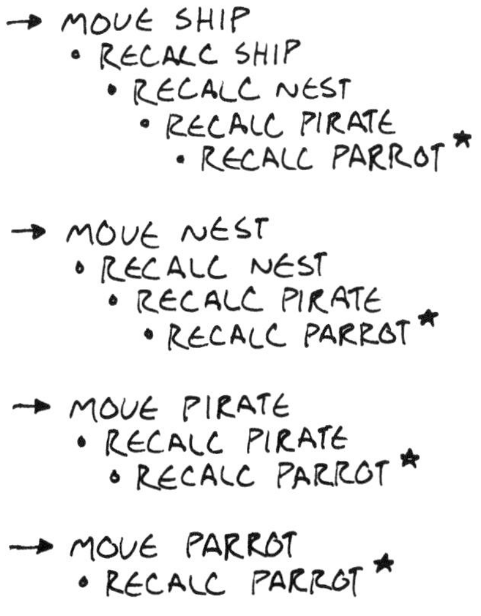

You can see on the lines marked ★ that we're recalculating the parrot's world transform *four* times when we only need the result of the final one.

*Figure 18.3 – Lots of redundant calculation*

We only moved four objects, but we did *ten* world transform calculations. That's six pointless calculations that get thrown out before they are ever used by the renderer. We calculated the parrot's world transform *four* times, but it is only rendered once.

The problem is that a world transform may depend on several local transforms. Since we recalculate immediately each time *one* of the transforms changes, we end up recalculating the same transform multiple times when more than one of the local transforms it depends on changes in the same frame.

## Deferred recalculation

We'll solve this by decoupling changing local transforms from updating the world transforms. This lets us change a bunch of local transforms in a single batch and *then* recalculate the affected world transform just once after all of those modifications are done, right before we need it to render.

To do this, we add a *flag* to each object in the graph. "Flag" and "bit" are synonymous in programming—they both mean a single micron of data that can be in one of two states. We call those "true" and "false", or sometimes "set" and "cleared". I'll use all of these interchangeably.

When the local transform changes, we set it. When we need the object's world transform, we check the flag. If it's set, we calculate the world transform and then clear the flag. The flag represents, "Is the world transform out of date?" For reasons that aren't entirely clear, the traditional name for this "out-of-date-ness" is "dirty". Hence: *a dirty flag*. "Dirty bit" is an equally common name for this pattern, but I figured I'd stick with the name that didn't seem as prurient.

If we apply this pattern and then move all of the objects in our previous example, the game ends up doing:

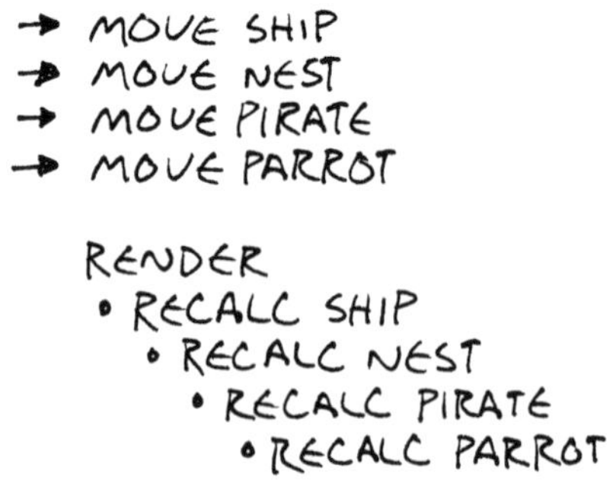

*Figure 18.4 – No more redundant calculation*

It's interesting how much of software architecture is intentionally engineering a little slippage.

Wikipedia's editors don't have my level of self-control—their article is "Dirty bit".

That's the best you could hope to do—the world transform for each affected object is calculated exactly once. With only a single bit of data, this pattern does a few things for us:

- It collapses modifications to multiple local transforms along an object's parent chain into a single recalculation on the object.

- It avoids recalculation on objects that didn't move.

- And a minor bonus: if an object gets removed before it's rendered, it doesn't calculate its world transform at all.

## The Pattern

A set of **primary data** changes over time. A set of **derived data** is determined from this using some **expensive process**. A **"dirty" flag** tracks when the derived data is out of sync with the primary data. It is **set when the primary data changes**. If the flag is set when the derived data is needed, then **it is reprocessed and the flag is cleared.** Otherwise, the previous **cached derived data** is used.

## When to Use It

Compared to some other patterns in this book, this one solves a pretty specific problem. Also, like most optimizations, you should only reach for it when you have a performance problem big enough to justify the added code complexity.

Dirty flags are applied to two kinds of work: *calculation* and *synchronization*. In both cases, the process of going from the primary data to the derived data is time-consuming or otherwise costly.

In our scene graph example, the process is slow because of the amount of math to perform. When using this pattern for synchronization, on the other hand, it's more often that the derived data is *somewhere else*—either on disk or over the network on another machine—and simply getting it from point A to point B is what's expensive.

There are a couple of other requirements too:

- **The primary data has to change more often than the derived data is used.** This pattern works by avoiding processing derived data when a subsequent primary data change would invalidate it before it gets used. If you find yourself always needing that derived data after every single modification to the primary data, this pattern can't help.

- **It should be hard to update incrementally.** Let's say the pirate ship in our game can only carry so much booty. We need to know the total weight of everything in the hold. We *could* use this pattern and have a dirty flag for the total weight. Every time we add or remove some loot, we set the flag. When we need the total, we add up all of the booty and clear the flag.

  But a simpler solution is to *keep a running total*. When we add or remove an item, just add or remove its weight from the current total. If we can "pay as we go" like this and keep the derived data updated, then that's often a better choice than using this pattern and calculating the derived data from scratch when needed.

This makes it sound like dirty flags are rarely appropriate, but you'll find a place here or there where they help. Searching your average game codebase for the word "dirty" will often turn up uses of this pattern.

# Keep in Mind

Even after you've convinced yourself this pattern is a good fit, there are a few wrinkles that can cause you some discomfort.

### There is a cost to deferring for too long

This pattern defers some slow work until the result is actually needed, but when it is, it's often needed *right now*. But the reason we're using this pattern to begin with is because calculating that result is slow!

This isn't a problem in our example because we can still calculate world coordinates fast enough to fit within a frame, but you can imagine other cases where the work you're doing is a big chunk that takes noticeable time to chew through. If the game doesn't *start* chewing until right when the player expects to see the result, that can cause an unpleasant visible pause.

Another problem with deferring is that if something goes wrong, you may fail to do the work at all. This can be particularly problematic when you're using this pattern to save some state to a more persistent form.

For example, text editors know if your document has "unsaved changes". That little bullet or star in your file's title bar is literally the dirty flag visualized. The primary data is the open document in memory, and the derived data is the file on disk.

From my research, it also turns up a lot of comments apologizing for "dirty" hacks.

This mirrors the different garbage collection strategies in systems that automatically manage memory. Reference counting frees memory the second it's no longer needed, but it burns CPU time updating ref counts eagerly every time references are changed.

Simple garbage collectors defer reclaiming memory until it's really needed, but the cost is the dreaded "GC pause" that can freeze your entire game until the collector is done scouring the heap.

In between the two are more complex systems like deferred ref-counting and incremental GC that reclaim memory less eagerly than pure ref-counting but more eagerly than stop-the-world collectors.

*Figure 18.5 - A graphical user interface for a dirty flag*

Many programs don't save to disk until either the document is closed or the application is exited. That's fine most of the time, but if you accidentally kick the power cable out, there goes your masterpiece.

Editors that auto-save a backup in the background are compensating specifically for this shortcoming. The auto-save frequency is a point on the continuum between not losing too much work when a crash occurs and not thrashing the file system too much by saving all the time.

### You have to be sure to set the flag *every* time the state changes

Since the derived data is calculated from the primary data, it's essentially a cache. Whenever you have cached data, the trickiest aspect of it is *cache invalidation*—correctly noting when the cache is out of sync with its source data. In this pattern, that means setting the dirty flag when *any* primary data changes.

Miss it in one place, and your program will incorrectly use stale derived data. This leads to confused players and bugs that are very hard to track down. When you use this pattern, you'll have to take care that any code that modifies the primary state also sets the dirty flag.

One way to mitigate this is by encapsulating modifications to the primary data behind some interface. If anything that can change the state goes through a single narrow API, you can set the dirty flag there and rest assured that it won't be missed.

Phil Karlton famously said, "There are only two hard things in Computer Science: cache invalidation and naming things."

### You have to keep the previous derived data in memory

When the derived data is needed and the dirty flag *isn't* set, it uses the previously calculated data. This is obvious, but that does imply that you have to keep that derived data around in memory in case you end up needing it later.

If you weren't using this pattern, you could calculate the derived data on the fly whenever you needed it, then discard it when you were done. That avoids the expense of keeping it cached in memory at the cost of having to do that calculation every time you need the result.

Like many optimizations, then, this pattern trades memory for speed. In return for keeping the previously calculated data in memory, you avoid

This isn't much of an issue when you're using this pattern to synchronize the primary state to some other place. In that case, the derived data isn't usually in memory at all.

having to recalculate it when it hasn't changed. This trade-off makes sense when the calculation is slow and memory is cheap. When you've got more time than memory on your hands, it's better to calculate it as needed.

## Sample Code

Let's assume we've met the surprisingly long list of requirements and see how the pattern looks in code. As I mentioned before, the actual math behind transform matrices is beyond the humble aims of this book, so I'll just encapsulate that in a class whose implementation you can presume exists somewhere out in the æther:

```
class Transform
{
public:
  static Transform origin();

  Transform combine(Transform& other);
};
```

The only operation we need here is `combine()` so that we can get an object's world transform by combining all of the local transforms along its parent chain. It also has a method to get an "origin" transform—basically an identity matrix that means no translation, rotation, or scaling at all.

Next, we'll sketch out the class for an object in the scene graph. This is the bare minimum we need *before* applying this pattern:

```
class GraphNode
{
public:
  GraphNode(Mesh* mesh)
  : mesh_(mesh),
    local_(Transform::origin()) {}

private:
  Transform local_;
  Mesh* mesh_;

  GraphNode* children_[MAX_CHILDREN];
  int numChildren_;
};
```

Each node has a local transform which describes where it is relative to its parent. It has a mesh which is the actual graphic for the object. (We'll allow `mesh_` to be `NULL` too to handle non-visual nodes that are used just to group their children.) Finally, each node has a possibly empty collection of child nodes.

With this, a "scene graph" is really only a single root `GraphNode` whose children (and grandchildren, etc.) are all of the objects in the world:

```
GraphNode* graph_ = new GraphNode(NULL);
// Add children to root graph node...
```

In order to render a scene graph, all we need to do is traverse that tree of nodes, starting at the root, and call the following function for each node's mesh with the right world transform:

```
void renderMesh(Mesh* mesh, Transform transform);
```

We won't implement this here, but if we did, it would do whatever magic the renderer needs to draw that mesh at the given location in the world. If we can call that correctly and efficiently on every node in the scene graph, we're happy.

## An unoptimized traversal

To get our hands dirty, let's throw together a basic traversal for rendering the scene graph that calculates the world positions on the fly. It won't be optimal, but it will be simple. We'll add a new method to `GraphNode`:

```
void GraphNode::render(Transform parentWorld)
{
  Transform world = local_.combine(parentWorld);
  if (mesh_) renderMesh(mesh_, world);

  for (int i = 0; i < numChildren_; i++)
  {
    children_[i]->render(world);
  }
}
```

We pass the world transform of the node's parent into this using `parentWorld`. With that, all that's left to get the correct world transform of *this* node is to combine that with its own local transform. We don't have to walk *up* the parent chain to calculate world transforms because we calculate as we go while walking *down* the chain.

We calculate the node's world transform and store it in `world`, then we render the mesh, if we have one. Finally, we recurse into the child nodes, passing in *this* node's world transform. All in all, it's a tight, simple recursive method.

To draw an entire scene graph, we kick off the process at the root node:

```
graph_->render(Transform::origin());
```

### Let's get dirty

So this code does the right thing—it renders all the meshes in the right place — but it doesn't do it efficiently. It's calling `local_.combine(parentWorld)` on every node in the graph, every frame. Let's see how this pattern fixes that. First, we need to add two fields to `GraphNode`:

```
class GraphNode
{
public:
  GraphNode(Mesh* mesh)
  : mesh_(mesh),
    local_(Transform::origin()),
    dirty_(true)
  {}

  // Other methods...

private:
  Transform world_;
  bool dirty_;

  // Other fields...
};
```

The `world_` field caches the previously calculated world transform, and `dirty_`, of course, is the dirty flag. Note that the flag starts out `true`. When we create a new node, we haven't calculated its world transform yet. At birth, it's already out of sync with the local transform.

The only reason we need this pattern is because objects can *move*, so let's add support for that:

```
void GraphNode::setTransform(Transform local)
{
  local_ = local;
  dirty_ = true;
}
```

The important part here is that it sets the dirty flag too. Are we forgetting anything? Right—the child nodes!

When a parent node moves, all of its children's world coordinates are invalidated too. But here, we aren't setting their dirty flags. We *could* do that, but that's recursive and slow. Instead, we'll do something clever when we go to render. Let's see:

```
void GraphNode::render(Transform parentWorld,
                       bool dirty)
{
  dirty |= dirty_;
  if (dirty)
  {
    world_ = local_.combine(parentWorld);
    dirty_ = false;
  }

  if (mesh_) renderMesh(mesh_, world_);

  for (int i = 0; i < numChildren_; i++)
  {
    children_[i]->render(world_, dirty);
  }
}
```

This is similar to the original naïve implementation. The key changes are that we check to see if the node is dirty before calculating the world transform and we store the result in a field instead of a local variable. When the node is clean, we skip `combine()` completely and use the old-but-still-correct `world_` value.

The clever bit is that `dirty` parameter. That will be `true` if any node above this node in the parent chain was dirty. In much the same way that `parentWorld` updates the world transform incrementally as we traverse down the hierarchy, `dirty` tracks the dirtiness of the parent chain.

This lets us avoid having to recursively mark each child's `dirty_` flag in `setTransform()`. Instead, we pass the parent's dirty flag down to its children when we render and look at that too to see if we need to recalculate the world transform.

The end result here is exactly what we want: changing a node's local transform is just a couple of assignments, and rendering the world calculates the exact minimum number of world transforms that have changed since the last frame.

## Design Decisions

This pattern is fairly specific, so there are only a couple of knobs to twiddle:

There's a subtle assumption here that the `if` check is faster than a matrix multiply. Intuitively, you would think it is; surely testing a single bit is faster than a bunch of floating point arithmetic.

However, modern CPUs are fantastically complex. They rely heavily on *pipelining*—queueing up a series of sequential instructions. A branch like our `if` here can cause a *branch misprediction* and force the CPU to lose cycles refilling the pipeline.

The Data Locality chapter (p. 269) has more about how modern CPUs try to go faster and how you can avoid tripping them up like this.

Note that this clever trick only works because `render()` is the *only* thing in `GraphNode` that needs an up-to-date world transform. If other things accessed it, we'd have to do something different.

### When is the dirty flag cleaned?

- **When the result is needed:**

  - *It avoids doing calculation entirely if the result is never used.* For primary data that changes much more frequently than the derived data is accessed, this can be a big win.

  - *If the calculation is time-consuming, it can cause a noticeable pause.* Postponing the work until the player is expecting to see the result can affect their gameplay experience. It's often fast enough that this isn't a problem, but if it is, you'll have to do the work earlier.

- **At well-defined checkpoints:**

  Sometimes, there is a point in time or in the progression of the game where it's natural to do the deferred processing. For example, we may want to save the game only when the pirate sails into port. Or the sync point may not be part of the game mechanics. We may just want to hide the work behind a loading screen or a cut scene.

  - *Doing the work doesn't impact the user experience.* Unlike the previous option, you can often give something to distract the player while the game is busy processing.

  - *You lose control over when the work happens.* This is sort of the opposite of the earlier point. You have micro-scale control over when you process, and can make sure the game handles it gracefully.

    What you *can't* do is ensure the player actually makes it to the checkpoint or meets whatever criteria you've defined. If they get lost or the game gets in a weird state, you can end up deferring longer than you expect.

- **In the background:**

  Usually, you start a fixed timer on the first modification and then process all of the changes that happen between then and when the timer fires.

  - *You can tune how often the work is performed.* By adjusting the timer interval, you can ensure it happens as frequently (or infrequently) as you want.

  - *You can do more redundant work.* If the primary state only changes a tiny amount during the timer's run, you can end up processing a large chunk of mostly unchanged data.

The term in human-computer interaction for an intentional delay between when a program receives user input and when it responds is *hysteresis*.

- *You need support for doing work asynchronously.* Processing the data "in the background" implies that the player can keep doing whatever it is that they're doing at the same time. That means you'll likely need threading or some other kind of concurrency support so that the game can work on the data while it's still being played.

   Since the player is likely interacting with the same primary state that you're processing, you'll need to think about making that safe for concurrent modification too.

## How fine-grained is your dirty tracking?

Imagine our pirate game lets players build and customize their pirate ship. Ships are automatically saved online so the player can resume where they left off. We're using dirty flags to determine which decks of the ship have been fitted and need to be sent to the server. Each chunk of data we send to the server contains some modified ship data and a bit of metadata describing where on the ship this modification occurred.

- **If it's more fine-grained:**

   Say you slap a dirty flag on each tiny plank of each deck.

   - *You only process data that actually changed.* You'll send exactly the facets of the ship that were modified to the server.

- **If it's more coarse-grained:**

   Alternatively, we could associate a dirty bit with each deck. Changing anything on it marks the entire deck dirty.

   - *You end up processing unchanged data.* Add a single barrel to a deck and you'll have to send the whole thing to the server.

   - *Less memory is used for storing dirty flags.* Add ten barrels to a deck and you only need a single bit to track them all.

   - *Less time is spent on fixed overhead.* When processing some changed data, there's often a bit of fixed work you have to do on top of handling the data itself. In the example here, that's the metadata required to identify where on the ship the changed data is. The bigger your processing chunks, the fewer of them there are, which means the less overhead you have.

I could make some terrible joke about it needing to be swabbed here, but I'll refrain.

## See Also

- This pattern is common outside of games in browser-side web frameworks like Angular. They use dirty flags to track which data has been changed in the browser and needs to be pushed up to the server.

- Physics engines track which objects are in motion and which are resting. Since a resting body won't move until an impulse is applied to it, they don't need processing until they get touched. This "is moving" bit is a dirty flag to note which objects have had forces applied and need to have their physics resolved.

# Object Pool

# 19

*Improve performance and memory use by reusing objects from a fixed pool instead of allocating and freeing them individually.*

## Motivation

We're working on the visual effects for our game. When the hero casts a spell, we want a shimmer of sparkles to burst across the screen. This calls for a *particle system*, an engine that spawns little sparkly graphics and animates them until they wink out of existence.

Since a single wave of the wand could cause hundreds of particles to be spawned, our system needs to be able to create them very quickly. More importantly, we need to make sure that creating and destroying these particles doesn't cause *memory fragmentation*.

### The curse of fragmentation

Programming for a game console or mobile device is closer to embedded programming than PC programming in many ways. Memory is scarce, users expect games to be rock solid, and efficient compacting memory managers are rarely available. In this environment, memory fragmentation is deadly.

It's like trying to parallel park on a busy street where the already parked cars are spread out a bit too far. If they'd bunch up, there would be room, but the free space is *fragmented* into bits of open curb between half a dozen cars.

Fragmentation means the free space in our heap is broken into smaller pieces of memory instead of one large open block. The *total* memory available may be large, but the largest *contiguous* region might be painfully small. Say we've got fourteen bytes free, but it's fragmented into two seven-byte pieces with a chunk of in-use memory between them. If we try to allocate a twelve-byte object, we'll fail. No more sparklies on screen.

Here's how a heap becomes fragmented and how it can cause an allocation to fail even where there's theoretically enough memory available:

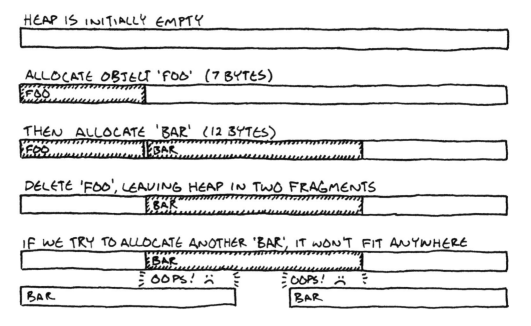

*Figure 19.1 – Enough total memory, but not enough contiguous memory*

Most console makers require games to pass "soak tests" where they leave the game running in demo mode for several days. If the game crashes, they don't allow it to ship. While soak tests sometimes fail because of a rarely occurring bug, it's usually creeping fragmentation or memory leakage that brings the game down.

Even if fragmentation is infrequent, it can still gradually reduce the heap to an unusable foam of open holes and filled-in crevices, ultimately hosing the game completely.

## The best of both worlds

Because of fragmentation and because allocation may be slow, games are very careful about when and how they manage memory. A simple solution is often best — grab a big chunk of memory when the game starts, and don't free it until the game ends. But this is a pain for systems where we need to create and destroy things while the game is running.

An object pool gives us the best of both worlds. To the memory manager, we're just allocating one big hunk of memory up front and not freeing it while the game is playing. To the users of the pool, we can freely allocate and deallocate objects to our heart's content.

# The Pattern

Define a **pool** class that maintains a collection of **reusable objects**. Each object supports an **"in use" query** to tell if it is currently "alive". When the pool is initialized, it creates the entire collection of objects up front (usually in a single contiguous allocation) and initializes them all to the "not in use" state.

When you want a new object, ask the pool for one. It finds an available object, initializes it to "in use", and returns it. When the object is no longer needed, it is set back to the "not in use" state. This way, objects can be freely created and destroyed without needing to allocate memory or other resources.

# When to Use It

This pattern is used widely in games for obvious things like game entities and visual effects, but it is also used for less visible data structures such as currently playing sounds. Use Object Pool when:

- You need to frequently create and destroy objects.

- Objects are similar in size.

- Allocating objects on the heap is slow or could lead to memory fragmentation.

- Each object encapsulates a resource such as a database or network connection that is expensive to acquire and could be reused.

# Keep in Mind

You normally rely on a garbage collector or `new` and `delete` to handle memory management for you. By using an object pool, you're saying, "I know better how these bytes should be handled." That means the onus is on you to deal with this pattern's limitations.

### The pool may waste memory on unneeded objects

The size of an object pool needs to be tuned for the game's needs. When tuning, it's usually obvious when the pool is too *small* (there's nothing like a crash to get your attention). But also take care that the pool isn't too *big*. A smaller pool frees up memory that could be used for other fun stuff.

### Only a fixed number of objects can be active at any one time

In some ways, this is a good thing. Partitioning memory into separate pools for different types of objects ensures that, for example, a huge sequence of explosions won't cause your particle system to eat *all* of the available memory, preventing something more critical like a new enemy from being created.

Nonetheless, this also means being prepared for the possibility that your attempt to reuse an object from the pool will fail because they are all in use. There are a few common strategies to handle this:

- *Prevent it outright.* This is the most common "fix": tune the pool sizes so that they never overflow regardless of what the user does. For pools of important objects like enemies or gameplay items, this is often the right answer. There may be no "right" way to handle the lack of a free slot to create the big boss when the player reaches the end of the level, so the smart thing to do is make sure that never happens.

  The downside is that this can force you to sit on a lot of memory for object slots that are needed only for a couple of rare edge cases. Because of this, a single fixed pool size may not be the best fit for all game states. For instance, some levels may feature effects prominently while others focus on sound. In such cases, consider having pool sizes tuned differently for each scenario.

- *Just don't create the object.* This sounds harsh, but it makes sense for cases like our particle system. If all particles are in use, the screen is probably full of flashing graphics. The user won't notice if the next explosion isn't quite as impressive as the ones currently going off.

- *Forcibly kill an existing object.* Consider a pool for currently playing sounds, and assume you want to start a new sound but the pool is full. You do *not* want to simply ignore the new sound—the user will notice if their magical wand swishes dramatically *sometimes* and stays stubbornly silent other times. A better solution is to find the quietest sound already playing and replace that with our new sound. The new sound will mask the audible cutoff of the previous sound.

In general, if the *disappearance* of an existing object would be less noticeable than the *absence* of a new one, this may be the right choice.

- *Increase the size of the pool.* If your game lets you be a bit more flexible with memory, you may be able to increase the size of the pool at runtime or create a second overflow pool. If you do grab more memory in either of these ways, consider whether or not the pool should contract to its previous size when the additional capacity is no longer needed.

## Memory size for each object is fixed

Most pool implementations store the objects in an array of in-place objects. If all of your objects are of the same type, this is fine. However, if you want to store objects of different types in the pool, or instances of subclasses that may add fields, you need to ensure that each slot in the pool has enough memory for the *largest* possible object. Otherwise, an unexpectedly large object will stomp over the next one and trash memory.

At the same time, when your objects vary in size, you waste memory. Each slot needs to be big enough to accommodate the largest object. If objects are rarely that big, you're throwing away memory every time you put a smaller one in that slot. It's like going through airport security and using a huge carry-on-sized luggage tray just for your keys and wallet.

When you find yourself burning a lot of memory this way, consider splitting the pool into separate pools for different sizes of object—big trays for luggage, little trays for pocket stuff.

This is a common pattern for implementing speed-efficient memory managers. The manager has a number of pools of different block sizes. When you ask it to allocate a block, it finds in an open slot in the pool of the appropriate size and allocates from that pool.

## Reused objects aren't automatically cleared

Most memory managers have a debug feature that will clear freshly allocated or freed memory to some obvious magic value like `0xdeadbeef`. This helps you find painful bugs caused by uninitialized variables or using memory after it's freed.

Since our object pool isn't going through the memory manager any more when it reuses an object, we lose that safety net. Worse, the memory used for a "new" object previously held an object of the exact same type. This makes it nearly impossible to tell if you forgot to initialize something when you created the new object: the memory where the object is stored may already contain *almost* correct data from its past life.

Because of this, pay special care that the code that initializes new objects in the pool *fully* initializes the object. It may even be worth spending a bit of time adding a debug feature that clears the memory for an object slot when the object is reclaimed.

I'd be honored if you clear it to `0x1deadb0b`.

### Unused objects will remain in memory

Object pools are less common in systems that support garbage collection because the memory manager will usually deal with fragmentation for you. But pools are still useful there to avoid the cost of allocation and deallocation, especially on mobile devices with slower CPUs and simpler garbage collectors.

If you do use an object pool in concert with a garbage collector, beware of a potential conflict. Since the pool doesn't actually deallocate objects when they're no longer in use, they remain in memory. If they contain references to *other* objects, it will prevent the collector from reclaiming those too. To avoid this, when a pooled object is no longer in use, clear any references it has to other objects.

# Sample Code

Real-world particle systems will often apply gravity, wind, friction, and other physical effects. Our much simpler sample will only move particles in a straight line for a certain number of frames and then kill the particle. Not exactly film caliber, but it should illustrate how to use an object pool.

We'll start with the simplest possible implementation. First up is the little particle class:

```cpp
class Particle
{
public:
  Particle()
  : framesLeft_(0)
  {}

  void init(double x, double y,
            double xVel, double yVel, int lifetime);

  void animate();

  bool inUse() const { return framesLeft_ > 0; }

private:
  int framesLeft_;
  double x_, y_;
  double xVel_, yVel_;
};
```

The default constructor initializes the particle to "not in use". A later call to init() initializes the particle to a live state:

```
void Particle::init(double x, double y,
    double xVel, double yVel, int lifetime)
{
  x_ = x;
  y_ = y;
  xVel_ = xVel;
  yVel_ = yVel;
  framesLeft_ = lifetime;
}
```

Particles are animated over time using the unsurprisingly named `animate()` function, which should be called once per frame:

```
void Particle::animate()
{
  if (!inUse()) return;

  framesLeft_--;
  x_ += xVel_;
  y_ += yVel_;
}
```

This `animate()` method is an example of the Update Method pattern (p. 139).

The pool needs to know which particles are available for reuse. It gets this from the particle's `inUse()` function. This function takes advantage of the fact that particles have a limited lifetime and uses the `_framesLeft` variable to discover which particles are in use without having to store a separate flag.

The pool class is also simple:

```
class ParticlePool
{
public:
  void create(double x, double y,
              double xVel, double yVel,
              int lifetime);

  void animate();

private:
  static const int POOL_SIZE = 100;
  Particle particles_[POOL_SIZE];
};
```

The `create()` function lets external code create new particles. The game calls `animate()` once per frame, which in turn animates each particle in the pool:

```
void ParticlePool::animate()
{
  for (int i = 0; i < POOL_SIZE; i++)
  {
    particles_[i].animate();
  }
}
```

The particles themselves are simply stored in a fixed-size array in the class. In this sample implementation, the pool size is hardcoded in the class declaration, but this could be defined externally by using a dynamic array of a given size or by using a value template parameter.

Creating a new particle is straightforward:

```
void ParticlePool::create(double x, double y,
                          double xVel, double yVel,
                          int lifetime)
{
  for (int i = 0; i < POOL_SIZE; i++)
  {
    if (!particles_[i].inUse())
    {
      particles_[i].init(x, y, xVel, yVel, lifetime);
      return;
    }
  }
}
```

We iterate through the pool looking for the first available particle. When we find it, we initialize it and we're done. Note that in this implementation, if there aren't any available particles, we simply don't create a new one.

That's all there is to a simple particle system, aside from rendering the particles, of course. We can now create a pool and create some particles using it. The particles will automatically deactivate themselves when their lifetime has expired.

This is good enough to ship a game, but keen eyes may have noticed that creating a new particle requires iterating through (potentially) the entire collection until we find an open slot. If the pool is very large and mostly full, that can get slow. Let's see how we can improve that.

Creating a particle has *O(n)* complexity, for those of us who remember our algorithms class.

### A free list

If we don't want to waste time *finding* free particles, the obvious answer is to not lose track of them. We could store a separate list of pointers to each unused particle. Then, when we need to create a particle, we remove the first pointer from the list and reuse the particle it points to.

Unfortunately, this would require us to maintain an entire separate array with as many pointers as there are objects in the pool. After all, when we first create the pool, *all* particles are unused, so the list would initially have a pointer to every object in the pool.

It would be nice to fix our performance problems *without* sacrificing any memory. Conveniently, there is some memory already lying around that we can borrow — the data for the unused particles themselves.

When a particle isn't in use, most of its state is irrelevant. Its position and velocity aren't being used. The only state it needs is the stuff required to tell if it's dead. In our example, that's the _framesLeft member. All those other bits can be reused. Here's a revised particle:

```
class Particle
{
public:
  // Previous stuff...
  Particle* getNext() const { return state_.next; }
  void setNext(Particle* next)
  {
    state_.next = next;
  }

private:
  int framesLeft_;

  union
  {
    // State when it's in use.
    struct
    {
      double x, y, xVel, yVel;
    } live;

    // State when it's available.
    Particle* next;
  } state_;
};
```

We've moved all of the member variables except for framesLeft_ into a live struct inside a state_union. This struct holds the particle's state when it's being animated. When the particle is unused, the other case of the union, the next member, is used. It holds a pointer to the next available particle after this one.

We can use these pointers to build a linked list that chains together every unused particle in the pool. We have the list of available particles we need, but we didn't need to use any additional memory. Instead, we cannibalize the memory of the dead particles themselves to store the list.

Unions don't seem to be used that often these days, so the syntax may be unfamiliar to you. If you're on a game team, you've probably got a "memory guru", that beleaguered compatriot whose job it is to come up with a solution when the game has inevitably blown its memory budget. Ask them about unions. They'll know all about them and other fun bit-packing tricks.

This clever technique is called a *free list*. For it to work, we need to make sure the pointers are initialized correctly and are maintained when particles are created and destroyed. And, of course, we need to keep track of the list's head:

```
class ParticlePool
{
  // Previous stuff...
private:
  Particle* firstAvailable_;
};
```

When a pool is first created, *all* of the particles are available, so our free list should thread through the entire pool. The pool constructor sets that up:

```
ParticlePool::ParticlePool()
{
  // The first one is available.
  firstAvailable_ = &particles_[0];

  // Each particle points to the next.
  for (int i = 0; i < POOL_SIZE - 1; i++)
  {
    particles_[i].setNext(&particles_[i + 1]);
  }

  // The last one terminates the list.
  particles_[POOL_SIZE - 1].setNext(NULL);
}
```

*O(1) complexity, baby! Now we're cooking!*

Now to create a new particle, we jump directly to the first available one:

```
void ParticlePool::create(double x, double y,
                          double xVel, double yVel,
                          int lifetime)
{
  // Make sure the pool isn't full.
  assert(firstAvailable_ != NULL);

  // Remove it from the available list.
  Particle* newParticle = firstAvailable_;
  firstAvailable_ = newParticle->getNext();

  newParticle->init(x, y, xVel, yVel, lifetime);
}
```

We need to know when a particle dies so we can add it back to the free list, so we'll change animate() to return true if the previously live particle gave up the ghost in that frame:

```
bool Particle::animate()
{
  if (!inUse()) return false;

  framesLeft_--;
  x_ += xVel_;
  y_ += yVel_;

  return framesLeft_ == 0;
}
```

When that happens, we simply thread it back onto the list:

```
void ParticlePool::animate()
{
  for (int i = 0; i < POOL_SIZE; i++)
  {
    if (particles_[i].animate())
    {
      // Add this particle to the front of the list.
      particles_[i].setNext(firstAvailable_);
      firstAvailable_ = &particles_[i];
    }
  }
}
```

There you go, a nice little object pool with constant-time creation and deletion.

## Design Decisions

As you've seen, the simplest object pool implementation is almost trivial: create an array of objects and reinitialize them as needed. Production code is rarely that minimal. There are several ways to expand on that to make the pool more generic, safer to use, or easier to maintain. As you implement pools in your games, you'll need to answer these questions:

### Are objects coupled to the pool?

The first question you'll run into when writing an object pool is whether the objects themselves know they are in a pool. Most of the time they will, but you won't have that luxury when writing a generic pool class that can hold arbitrary objects.

- **If objects are coupled to the pool:**

  - *The implementation is simpler.* You can simply put an "in use" flag or function in your pooled object and be done with it.

- *You can ensure that the objects can only be created by the pool.* In C++, a simple way to do this is to make the pool class a friend of the object class and then make the object's constructor private.

```cpp
class Particle
{
  friend class ParticlePool;

private:
  Particle() : inUse_(false) {}

  bool inUse_;
};

class ParticlePool
{
  Particle pool_[100];
};
```

  This relationship documents the intended way to use the class and ensures your users don't create objects that aren't tracked by the pool.

- *You may be able to avoid storing an explicit "in use" flag.* Many objects already retain some state that could be used to tell whether it is alive or not. For example, a particle may be available for reuse if its current position is offscreen. If the object class knows it may be used in a pool, it can provide an `inUse()` method to query that state. This saves the pool from having to burn some extra memory storing a bunch of "in use" flags.

- **If objects are not coupled to the pool:**

  - *Objects of any type can be pooled.* This is the big advantage. By decoupling objects from the pool, you may be able to implement a generic reusable pool class.

  - *The "in use" state must be tracked outside the objects.* The simplest way to do this is by creating a separate bit field:

```cpp
template <class TObject>
class GenericPool
{
private:
  static const int POOL_SIZE = 100;

  TObject pool_[POOL_SIZE];
  bool    inUse_[POOL_SIZE];
};
```

## What is responsible for initializing the reused objects?

In order to reuse an existing object, it must be reinitialized with new state. A key question here is whether to reinitialize the object inside the pool class or outside.

- **If the pool reinitializes internally:**

  - *The pool can completely encapsulate its objects.* Depending on the other capabilities your objects need, you may be able to keep them completely internal to the pool. This makes sure that other code doesn't maintain references to objects that could be unexpectedly reused.

  - *The pool is tied to how objects are initialized.* A pooled object may offer multiple functions that initialize it:

```
class Particle
{
  // Multiple ways to initialize.
  void init(double x, double y);
  void init(double x, double y, double angle);
  void init(double x, double y,
            double xVel, double yVel);
};
```

  If the pool manages initialization, its interface needs to support all of those and forward them to the object:

```
class ParticlePool
{
public:
  void create(double x, double y)
  {
    // Forward to Particle...
  }

  void create(double x, double y, double angle)
  {
    // Forward to Particle...
  }

  void create(double x, double y,
              double xVel, double yVel)
  {
    // Forward to Particle...
  }
};
```

- **If outside code initializes the object:**

  - *The pool's interface can be simpler.* Instead of offering multiple functions to cover each way an object can be initialized, the pool can simply return a reference to the new object:

```
class Particle
{
public:
  // Multiple ways to initialize.
  void init(double x, double y);
  void init(double x, double y, double angle);
  void init(double x, double y, double xVel,
double yVel);
};

class ParticlePool
{
public:
  Particle* create()
  {
     // Return reference to available particle...
  }
private:
  Particle pool_[100];
};
```

  The caller can then initialize the object by calling any method the object exposes:

```
ParticlePool pool;

pool.create()->init(1, 2);
pool.create()->init(1, 2, 0.3);
pool.create()->init(1, 2, 3.3, 4.4);
```

  - *Outside code may need to handle the failure to create a new object.* The previous example assumes that **create()** will always successfully return a pointer to an object. If the pool is full, though, it may return **NULL** instead. To be safe, you'll need to check for that before you try to initialize the object:

```
Particle* particle = pool.create();
if (particle != NULL) particle->init(1, 2);
```

# See Also

- This looks a lot like the Flyweight pattern (p. 33). Both maintain a collection of reusable objects. The difference is what "reuse" means. Flyweight objects are reused by sharing the same instance between multiple owners *simultaneously*. The Flyweight pattern avoids *duplicate* memory usage by using the same object in multiple contexts.

  The objects in a pool get reused too, but only over time. "Reuse" in the context of an object pool means reclaiming the memory for an object *after* the original owner is done with it. With an object pool, there isn't any expectation that an object will be shared within its lifetime.

- Packing a bunch of objects of the same type together in memory helps keep your CPU cache full as the game iterates over those objects. The Data Locality pattern (p. 269) is all about that.

# Spatial Partition    **20**

*Efficiently locate objects by storing them in a data structure organized by their positions.*

## Motivation

Games let us visit other worlds, but those worlds typically aren't so different from our own. They often share the same basic physics and tangibility of our universe. This is why they can feel real despite being crafted of mere bits and pixels.

One bit of fake reality that we'll focus on here is *location*. Game worlds have a sense of *space*, and objects are somewhere in that space. This manifests itself in a bunch of ways. The obvious one is physics—objects move, collide, and interact—but there are other examples. The audio engine may take into account where sound sources are relative to the player so that distant sounds are quieter. Online chat may be restricted to nearby players.

This means your game engine often needs to answer to the question, "What objects are near this location?" If it has to answer this enough times each frame, it can start to be a performance bottleneck.

### Units on the field of battle

Say we're making a real-time strategy game. Opposing armies with hundreds of units will clash together on the field of battle. Warriors need to know which nearby enemy to swing their blades at. The naïve way to handle this is by looking at every pair of units and seeing how close they are to each other:

```
void handleMelee(Unit* units[], int numUnits)
{
  for (int a = 0; a < numUnits - 1; a++)
  {
    for (int b = a + 1; b < numUnits; b++)
    {
      if (units[a]->position() ==
          units[b]->position())
      {
        handleAttack(units[a], units[b]);
      }
    }
  }
}
```

The inner loop doesn't actually walk all of the units. It only walks the ones the outer loop hasn't already visited. This avoids comparing each pair of units *twice*, once in each order. If we've already handled a collision between A and B, we don't need to check it again for B and A.

In Big-O terms, though, this is still $O(n^2)$.

Here we have a doubly nested loop where each loop is walking all of the units on the battlefield. That means the number of pairwise tests we have to perform each frame increases with the *square* of the number of units. Each additional unit we add has to be compared to *all* of the previous ones. With a large number of units, that can spiral out of control.

### Drawing battle lines

The problem we're running into is that there's no underlying order to the array of units. To find a unit near some location, we have to walk the entire array. Now, imagine we simplify our game a bit. Instead of a 2D battle*field*, imagine it's a 1D battle*line*.

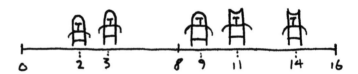

*Figure 20.1 – A number line of battle*

A binary search has $O(log\ n)$ complexity, which means find all battling units goes from $O(n^2)$ to $O(n\ log\ n)$. Something like a *pigeonhole sort* could get that down to $O(n)$.

In that case, we could make things easier on ourselves by *sorting* the array of units by their positions on the battleline. Once we do that, we can use something like a binary search to find nearby units without having to scan the entire array.

The lesson is pretty obvious: if we store our objects in a data structure organized by their locations, we can find them much more quickly. This pattern is about applying that idea to spaces that have more than one dimension.

## The Pattern

For a set of **objects**, each has a **position in space**. Store them in a **spatial data structure** that organizes the objects by their positions. This data structure lets you **efficiently query for objects at or near a location**. When an object's position changes, **update the spatial data structure** so that it can continue to find the object.

## When to Use It

This is a common pattern for storing both live, moving game objects and also the static art and geometry of the game world. Sophisticated games often have multiple spatial partitions for different kinds of content.

The basic requirements for this pattern are that you have a set of objects that each have some kind of position and that you are doing enough queries to find objects by location that your performance is suffering.

## Keep in Mind

Spatial partitions exist to knock an $O(n)$ or $O(n^2)$ operation down to something more manageable. The *more* objects you have, the more valuable that becomes. Conversely, if your $n$ is small enough, it may not be worth the bother.

Since this pattern involves organizing objects by their positions, objects that *change* position are harder to deal with. You'll have to reorganize the data structure to keep track of an object at a new location, and that adds code complexity *and* spends CPU cycles. Make sure the trade-off is worth it.

Imagine a hash table where the keys of the hashed objects can change spontaneously, and you'll have a good feel for why it's tricky.

A spatial partition also uses additional memory for its bookkeeping data structures. Like many optimizations, it trades memory for speed. If you're shorter on memory than you are on clock cycles, that may be a losing proposition.

# Sample Code

The nature of patterns is that they *vary*—each implementation will be a bit different, and spatial partitions are no exception. Unlike other patterns, though, many of these variations are well-documented. Academia likes publishing papers that prove performance gains. Since I only care about the concept behind the pattern, I'm going to show you the simplest spatial partition: a *fixed grid*.

See the last section of this chapter for a list of some of the most common spatial partitions used in games.

### A sheet of graph paper

Imagine the entire field of battle. Now, superimpose a grid of fixed-size squares onto it like a sheet of graph paper. Instead of storing our units in a single array, we put them in the cells of this grid. Each cell stores the list of units whose positions are within that cell's boundary.

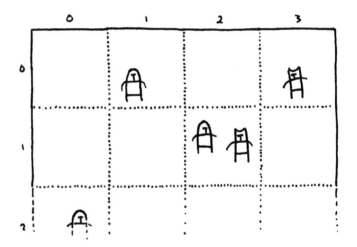

*Figure 20.2 – The field of battle, sliced into squares*

When we handle combat, we only consider units within the same cell. Instead of comparing each unit in the game with every other unit, we've *partitioned* the battlefield into a bunch of smaller mini-battlefields, each with many fewer units.

## A grid of linked units

OK, let's get coding. First, some prep work. Here's our basic `Unit` class:

```
class Unit
{
  friend class Grid;

public:
  Unit(Grid* grid, double x, double y)
  : grid_(grid),
    x_(x),
    y_(y)
  {}

  void move(double x, double y);

private:
  double x_, y_;
  Grid* grid_;
};
```

Each unit has a position (in 2D) and a pointer to the `Grid` that it lives on. We make `Grid` a `friend` class because, as we'll see, when a unit's position changes, it has to do an intricate dance with the grid to make sure everything is updated correctly.

Here's a sketch of the grid:

```
class Grid
{
public:
  Grid()
  {
    // Clear the grid.
    for (int x = 0; x < NUM_CELLS; x++)
    {
      for (int y = 0; y < NUM_CELLS; y++)
      {
        cells_[x][y] = NULL;
      }
    }
  }

  static const int NUM_CELLS = 10;
  static const int CELL_SIZE = 20;

private:
  Unit* cells_[NUM_CELLS][NUM_CELLS];
};
```

Note that each cell is just a pointer to a unit. Next, we'll extend Unit with next and prev pointers:

```
class Unit
{
  // Previous code...

private:
  Unit* prev_;
  Unit* next_;
};
```

This lets us organize units into a doubly linked list instead of an array.

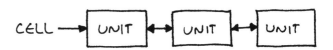

*Figure 20.3 – A cell is a pointer to the head of a linked list of units*

Each cell in the grid points to the first unit in the list of units within that cell, and each unit has pointers to the units before it and after it in the list. We'll see why soon.

### Entering the field of battle

The first thing we need to do is make sure new units are actually placed into the grid when they are created. We'll make Unit handle this in its constructor:

```
Unit::Unit(Grid* grid, double x, double y)
: grid_(grid),
  x_(x),
  y_(y),
  prev_(NULL),
  next_(NULL)
{
  grid_->add(this);
}
```

This add() method is defined like so:

```
void Grid::add(Unit* unit)
{
  // Determine which grid cell it's in.
  int cellX = (int)(unit->x_ / Grid::CELL_SIZE);
  int cellY = (int)(unit->y_ / Grid::CELL_SIZE);

  // Add to the front of list for the cell it's in.
  unit->prev_ = NULL;
  unit->next_ = cells_[cellX][cellY];
  cells_[cellX][cellY] = unit;

  if (unit->next_ != NULL)
  {
    unit->next_->prev_ = unit;
  }
}
```

Dividing by the cell size converts world coordinates to cell space. Then, casting to an `int` truncates the fractional part so we get the cell index.

It's a little finicky like linked list code always is, but the basic idea is pretty simple. We find the cell that the unit is sitting in and then add it to the front of that list. If there is already a list of units there, we link it in after the new unit.

## A clash of swords

Once all of the units are nestled in their cells, we can let them start hacking at each other. With this new grid, the main method for handling combat looks like this:

```
void Grid::handleMelee()
{
  for (int x = 0; x < NUM_CELLS; x++)
  {
    for (int y = 0; y < NUM_CELLS; y++)
    {
      handleCell(cells_[x][y]);
    }
  }
}
```

It walks each cell and then calls `handleCell()` on it. As you can see, we really have partitioned the battlefield into little isolated skirmishes. Each cell then handles its combat like so:

```
void Grid::handleCell(Unit* unit)
{
  while (unit != NULL)
  {
    Unit* other = unit->next_;
    while (other != NULL)
    {
      if (unit->x_ == other->x_ &&
          unit->y_ == other->y_)
      {
        handleAttack(unit, other);
      }
      other = other->next_;
    }

    unit = unit->next_;
  }
}
```

Aside from the pointer shenanigans to deal with walking a linked list, note that this is exactly like our original naïve method for handling combat. It compares each pair of units to see if they're in the same position.

The only difference is that we no longer have to compare *all* of the units in the battle to each other—just the ones close enough to be in the same cell. That's the heart of the optimization.

From a simple analysis, it looks like we've actually made the performance *worse*. We've gone from a doubly nested loop over the units to a *triply* nested loop over the cells and then the units. The trick here is that the two inner loops are now over a smaller number of units, which is enough to cancel out the cost of the outer loop over the cells.

However, that does depend a bit on the granularity of our cells. Make them too small and that outer loop can start to matter.

### Charging forward

We've solved our performance problem, but we've created a new problem in its stead. Units are now stuck in their cells. If we move a unit past the boundary of the cell that contains it, units in the cell won't see it anymore, but neither will anyone else. Our battlefield is a little *too* partitioned.

To fix that, we'll need to do a little work each time a unit moves. If it crosses a cell's boundary lines, we need to remove it from that cell and add it to the new one. First, we'll give Unit a method for changing its position:

```
void Unit::move(double x, double y)
{
  grid_->move(this, x, y);
}
```

Presumably, this gets called by the AI code for computer-controlled units and by the user input code for the player's units. All it does is hand off control to the grid, which then does:

```
void Grid::move(Unit* unit, double x, double y)
{
  // See which cell it was in.
  int oldCellX = (int)(unit->x_ / Grid::CELL_SIZE);
  int oldCellY = (int)(unit->y_ / Grid::CELL_SIZE);

  // See which cell it's moving to.
  int cellX = (int)(x / Grid::CELL_SIZE);
  int cellY = (int)(y / Grid::CELL_SIZE);

  unit->x_ = x;
  unit->y_ = y;

  // If it didn't change cells, we're done.
  if (oldCellX == cellX && oldCellY == cellY) return;

  // Unlink it from the list of its old cell.
  if (unit->prev_ != NULL)
  {
    unit->prev_->next_ = unit->next_;
  }

  if (unit->next_ != NULL)
  {
    unit->next_->prev_ = unit->prev_;
  }

  // If it's the head of a list, remove it.
  if (cells_[oldCellX][oldCellY] == unit)
  {
    cells_[oldCellX][oldCellY] = unit->next_;
  }

  // Add it back to the grid at its new cell.
  add(unit);
}
```

That's a mouthful of code, but it's pretty straightforward. The first bit checks to see if we've crossed a cell boundary at all. If not, all we need to do is update the unit's position and we're done.

If the unit *has* left its current cell, we remove it from that cell's linked list and then add it back to the grid. Like with adding a new unit, that will insert the unit in the linked list for its new cell.

This is why we're using a doubly linked list—we can very quickly add and remove units from lists by setting a few pointers. With lots of units moving around each frame, that can be important.

### At arm's length

This seems pretty simple, but I have cheated in one way. In the example I've been showing, units only interact when they have the *exact same* position. That's true for checkers and chess, but less true for more realistic games. Those usually have attack *distances* to take into account.

This pattern still works fine. Instead of just checking for an exact location match, we'll do something more like:

```
if (distance(unit, other) < ATTACK_DISTANCE)
{
  handleAttack(unit, other);
}
```

When range gets involved, there's a corner case we need to consider: units in different cells may still be close enough to interact.

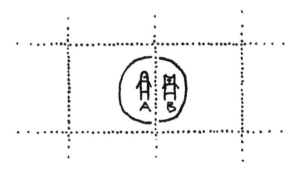

*Figure 20.4 – So close, yet so far away*

Here, B is within A's attack radius even through their centerpoints are in different cells. To handle this, we will need to compare units not only in the same cell, but in neighboring cells too. To do this, first we'll split the inner loop out of **handleCell()**:

```
void Grid::handleUnit(Unit* unit, Unit* other)
{
  while (other != NULL)
  {
    if (distance(unit, other) < ATTACK_DISTANCE)
    {
      handleAttack(unit, other);
    }

    other = other->next_;
  }
}
```

Now we have a function that will take a single unit and a list of other units and see if there are any hits. Then we'll make `handleCell()` use that:

```
void Grid::handleCell(int x, int y)
{
  Unit* unit = cells_[x][y];
  while (unit != NULL)
  {
    // Handle other units in this cell.
    handleUnit(unit, unit->next_);
    unit = unit->next_;
  }
}
```

Note that we now also pass in the coordinates of the cell, not just its unit list. Right now, this doesn't do anything differently from the previous example, but we'll expand it slightly:

```
void Grid::handleCell(int x, int y)
{
  Unit* unit = cells_[x][y];
  while (unit != NULL)
  {
    // Handle other units in this cell.
    handleUnit(unit, unit->next_);

    // Also try the neighboring cells.
    if (x > 0) handleUnit(unit, cells_[x - 1][y]);
    if (y > 0) handleUnit(unit, cells_[x][y - 1]);
    if (x > 0 && y > 0)
        handleUnit(unit, cells_[x - 1][y - 1]);
    if (x > 0 && y < NUM_CELLS - 1)
        handleUnit(unit, cells_[x - 1][y + 1]);

    unit = unit->next_;
  }
}
```

Those additional `handleUnit()` calls look for hits between the current unit and units in four of the eight neighboring cells. If any unit in those neighboring cells is close enough to the edge to be within the unit's attack radius, it will find the hit.

We only look at *half* of the neighbors for the same reason that the inner loop starts *after* the current unit— to avoid comparing each pair of units twice. Consider what would happen if we did check all eight neighboring cells.

Let's say we have two units in adjacent cells close enough to hit each other, like the previous example. Here's what would happen if we looked at all eight cells surrounding each unit:

The cell with the unit is U, and the neighboring cells it looks at are X.

*Figure 20.5 – Half of the adjacent cells*

1. When finding hits for A, we would look at its neighbor on the right and find B. So we'd register an attack between A and B.

2. Then, when finding hits for B, we would look at its neighbor on the *left* and find A. So we'd register a *second* attack between A and B.

Only looking at half of the neighboring cells fixes that. *Which* half we look at doesn't matter at all.

There's another corner case we may need to consider too. Here, we're assuming the maximum attack distance is smaller than a cell. If we have small cells and large attack distances, we may need to scan a bunch of neighboring cells several rows out.

## Design Decisions

There's a relatively short list of well-defined spatial partitioning data structures, and one option would be to go through them one at a time here. Instead, I tried to organize this by their essential characteristics. My hope is that once you do learn about quadtrees and binary space partitions (BSPs) and the like, this will help you understand *how* and *why* they work and why you might choose one over the other.

### Is the partition hierarchical or flat?

They usually split it in two, four, or eight—nice round numbers to a programmer.

Our grid example partitioned space into a single flat set of cells. In contrast, hierarchical spatial partitions divide the space into just a couple of regions. Then, if one of these regions still contains many objects, it's subdivided. This process continues recursively until every region has fewer than some maximum number of objects in it.

- **If it's a flat partition:**

  - *It's simpler.* Flat data structures are easier to reason about and simpler to implement.

This is a design point I mention in almost every chapter, and for good reason. Whenever you can, take the simpler option. Much of software engineering is fighting against complexity.

  - *Memory usage is constant.* Since adding new objects doesn't require creating new partitions, the memory used by the spatial partition can often be fixed ahead of time.

  - *It can be faster to update when objects change their positions.* When an object moves, the data structure needs to be updated to find the object in its new location. With a hierarchical spatial partition, this can mean adjusting several layers of the hierarchy.

- **If it's hierarchical:**

  - *It handles empty space more efficiently.* Imagine in our earlier example if one whole side of the battlefield was empty. We'd have a large number of empty cells that we'd still have to allocate memory for and walk each frame.

    Since hierarchical space partitions don't subdivide sparse regions, a large empty space will remain a single partition. Instead of lots of little partitions to walk, there is a single big one.

  - *It handles densely populated areas more efficiently.* This is the other side of the coin: if you have a bunch of objects all clumped together, a non-hierarchical partition can be ineffective. You'll end up with one partition that has so many objects in it that you may as well not be partitioning at all. A hierarchical partition will adaptively subdivide that into smaller partitions and get you back to having only a few objects to consider at a time.

## Does the partitioning depend on the set of objects?

In our sample code, the grid spacing was fixed beforehand, and we slotted units into cells. Other partitioning schemes are adaptable—they pick partition boundaries based on the actual set of objects and where they are in the world.

The goal is have a *balanced* partitioning where each region has roughly the same number of objects in order to get the best performance. Consider in our grid example if all of the units were clustered in one corner of the battlefield. They'd all be in the same cell, and our code for finding attacks would regress right back to the original $O(n^2)$ problem that we're trying to solve.

- **If the partitioning is object-independent:**

  - *Objects can be added incrementally.* Adding an object means finding the right partition and dropping it in, so you can do this one at a time without any performance issues.

  - *Objects can be moved quickly.* With fixed partitions, moving a unit means removing it from one and adding it to another. If the partition boundaries themselves change based on the set of objects, then moving one can cause a boundary to move, which can in turn cause lots of other objects to need to be moved to different partitions.

> This is directly analogous to sorted binary search trees like red-black trees or AVL trees: when you add a single item, you may end up needing to re-sort the tree and shuffle a bunch of nodes around.

- *The partitions can be imbalanced.* Of course, the downside of this rigidity is that you have less control over your partitions being evenly distributed. If objects clump together, you get worse performance there while wasting memory in the empty areas.

- **If the partitioning adapts to the set of objects:**

  Spatial partitions like BSPs and k-d trees split the world recursively so that each half contains about the same number of objects. To do this, you have to count how many objects are on each side when selecting the planes you partition along. Bounding volume hierarchies are another type of spatial partition that optimizes for the specific set of objects in the world.

  - *You can ensure the partitions are balanced.* This gives not just good performance, but *consistent* performance: if each partition has the same number of objects, you ensure that all queries in the world will take about the same amount of time. When you need to maintain a stable frame rate, this consistency may be more important than raw performance.

  - *It's more efficient to partition an entire set of objects at once.* When the *set* of objects affects where boundaries are, it's best to have all of the objects up front before you partition them. This is why these kinds of partitions are more frequently used for art and static geometry that stays fixed during the game.

- **If the partitioning is object-independent, but hierarchy is object-dependent:**

  A quadtree partitions 2D space. Its 3D analogue is the *octree*, which takes a *volume* and partitions it into eight *cubes*. Aside from the extra dimension, it works the same as its flatter sibling.

  One spatial partition deserves special mention because it has some of the best characteristics of both fixed partitions and adaptable ones: quadtrees. A quadtree starts with the entire space as a single partition. If the number of objects in the space exceeds some threshold, it is sliced into four smaller squares. The *boundaries* of these squares are fixed: they always slice space right in half.

  Then, for each of the four squares, we do the same process again, recursively, until every square has a small number of objects in it. Since we only recursively subdivide squares that have a high population, this partitioning adapts to the set of objects, but the partitions don't *move*.

  You can see the partitioning in action reading from left to right on the next page:

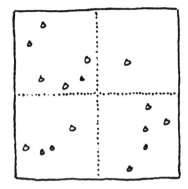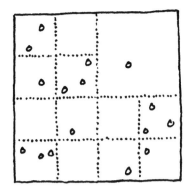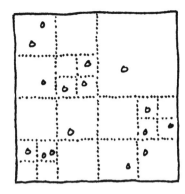

*Figure 20.6 – Each cell that has more than two units gets subdivided, recursively*

- *Objects can be added incrementally.* Adding a new object means finding the right square and adding it. If that bumps that square above the maximum count, it gets subdivided. The other objects in that square get pushed down into the new smaller squares. This requires a little work, but it's a *fixed* amount of effort: the number of objects you have to move will always be less than the maximum object count. Adding a single object can never trigger more than one subdivision.

  Removing objects is equally simple. You remove the object from its square and if the parent square's total count is now below the threshold, you can collapse those subdivisions.

- *Objects can be moved quickly.* This, of course, follows from the above. "Moving" an object is just an add and a remove, and both of those are pretty quick with quadtrees.

- *The partitions are balanced.* Since any given square will have less than some fixed maximum number of objects, even when objects are clustered together, you don't have single partitions with a huge pile of objects in them.

## Are objects only stored in the partition?

You can treat your spatial partition as *the* place where the objects in your game live, or you can consider it just a secondary cache to make look-up faster while also having another collection that directly holds the list of objects.

- **If it is the only place objects are stored:**

  - *It avoids the memory overhead and complexity of two collections.* Of course, it's always cheaper to store something once instead of twice.

Also, if you have two collections, you have to make sure to keep them in sync. Every time an object is created or destroyed, it has to be added or removed from both.

- **If there is another collection for the objects:**

  - *Traversing all objects is faster.* If the objects in question are "live" and have some processing they need to do, you may find yourself frequently needing to visit every object regardless of its location. Imagine if, in our earlier example, most of the cells were empty. Having to walk the full grid of cells to find the non-empty ones can be a waste of time.

    A second collection that just stores the objects gives you a way to walk all them directly. You have two data structures, one optimized for each use case.

## See Also

I've tried not to discuss specific spatial partitioning structures in detail here to keep the chapter high-level (and not too long!), but your next step from here should be to learn a few of the common structures. Despite their scary names, they are all surprisingly straightforward. The common ones are:

- Grid

- Quadtree

- BSP

- k-d tree

- Bounding volume hierarchy

Each of these spatial data structures basically extends an existing well-known data structure from 1D into more dimensions. Knowing their linear cousins will help you tell if they are a good fit for your problem:

- A grid is a persistent *bucket sort*.

- BSPs, k-d trees, and bounding volume hierarchies are *binary search trees*.

- Quadtrees and octrees are *tries*.

*This page intentionally left blank*
*as a playground for your imagination.*

# Index

## A

abstraction 274
abstract syntax tree 157
Ace of Base 56
`Achievements` class 45
`Actor` class 114
  buffered slap 118
  static buffer offset 121
actor model 250
Ada Lovelace 123
`AdditionExpression` class 158
aggregation 245
AI 26, 87, 104
`AIComponent` class 276
  hot and cold fields 283
  split out cold fields 284
algorithmic complexity , 312, 314

amortized. *See* amortized
  complexity
allocation 39, 201, 206
amortized complexity 244
Angular web framework 304
ANTLR 177
Antoine de Saint-Exupery 16
A Pattern Language 4
Artemis game engine 290
artificial intelligence. *See* AI
aspect-oriented programming 84
`assert()` function. *See* assertion
assertion 83
asynchronous processing 303
asynchronous-style programming
  246
`Audio` class 235, 240, 254
  head and tail pointers 242

`playSound()` method 235, 240
  aggregate requests 245
  append to list 242
  ring buffer 244
  `update()` method 241
  remove from list 243
  ring buffer 244
automata theory 91
AVL tree 333

## B

balanced partition 333
`Base` class 264
batch mode program 123
behavior 168
behavior tree 104
Big Electric Cat 218
Big-O 322

in Unity framework 231
Game Programming Gems 4
Gang of Four 4
garbage collection 296, 307–308, 310
generator 143
GenericPool class 316
Ghost class 61
Glenn Fiedler 137
global variables 78–79, 238
Go programming language 250
goto 174
GPU 33
Grace Hopper 123
GraphicsComponent class 221
    abstract base class 225
graphics, computer 108–110
GraphNode class 298
    render() method 299
        with dirty flag 301
    setTransform() method 300
    with dirty flag 300
grid 324–326
Grid class 325
    add() method 327
    handleCell() method 328
        test neighboring cells 331
    handleMelee() method 327
    handleUnit() method 330
    move() method 329

## H

handleMelee() function 322
hash table 245, 323
Haskell programming language 78, 228
head, of queue 241
heap 306–307
Henry Hatsworth in the Puzzling Adventure , 171

Heroine class 96
    concurrent states 101
    handleInput() method 88–90
        charge attack 94
        concurrent states 101
        state enum 92, 93
        state instances 97
        with enter action 99
    update() method 93
HeroineState class 95
    static instances 97
hierarchical state machine 101–103
hot/cold splitting 283
hysteresis 302

## I

immutability 38. See also mutability
inheritance 146, 183–184, 194–195, 201, 215, 285
    dynamic 66
    multiple. See multiple inheritance
    single. See single inheritance
InputComponent class 219
    abstract base class 222
InputHandler class 23
    handleInput() method
        button commands 25
        configurable buttons 24
        hardcoded buttons 22
instanced rendering 36
instruction caching 273
Instruction enum 163
instruction pipeline 301, 281
instruction set 160
interpreter 160
Interpreter pattern 156–159, 179
interrupt 234
intrinsic state 36

intrusive linked list 52
"is-a" relationship 194
iteration 156–157, 161
Ivan Sutherland 59

## J

Java programming language 260, 285
JavaScript programming language 67, 285
java.util.Observer 43
Java Virtual Machine 163
JIT. See just-in-time compiler
JSON 70, 204
JumpCommand class 23
just-in-time compiler 160
JVM. See Java Virtual Machine

## K

k-d tree 334, 336
Kismet scripting tool 179
Koen Witters 137

## L

L1, L2, L3 caches 272
lapsed listener problem 54
Law of Demeter 85
lazy initialization 76, 80–81
lex 171
linked list 326
linked list, intrusive 52
Lisp programming language 43, 260
literal 166
locality of reference 271
local transform 292
location 321
Locator class 255
    returning null object 256
    using assertion 262

20092684R00203

Made in the USA
Middletown, DE
14 May 2015